TIMPSON'S LEYLINES

TIMPSON'S LEYLINES

A LAYMAN TRACKING THE LEYS

JOHN TIMPSON

WITH PHOTOGRAPHY BY
DERRY BRABBS

CASSELL&CO

CONTENTS

For Pat, my navigator, companion and guide on this journey of discovery, as on so many others — including the most rewarding of them all, the one we set out on nearly fifty years ago.

What's it all about, Alfie?

A large, smooth stone sits outside the church porch in the tiny Norfolk village where I lived. It is more like a boulder, quite different from the stonework of the church itself or any other stone in the churchyard. It seems to serve no useful purpose, and as churchwarden I walked past it almost daily to check that all was well inside, without giving it a second thought. But it has turned out to be the foundation stone, one might say, on which this book is built.

It was a casual visitor who started it all. As we were chatting in the porch – I used to check the visitors too – she nodded casually at the stone. 'I see you have a leyline mark stone,' she said. 'There must be a leyline going through the church.' 'Oh yes,' I said knowledgeably. And then, after a pause – like so many of my friends when I have mentioned it to them since – 'Er, what actually is a leyline?'

The answer, or rather answers, have filled several books. It depends on which author you read, and sometimes which book you read by the same author, because they are inclined to change their minds over the years. And you can find almost as many books which dismiss the whole concept of leylines – 'the product of over-imaginative minds using inadequate evidence,' as one critic summed up.

It started in the 1920s with Alfred Watkins, who was a well-to-do and highly respected businessman in Hereford, though one sceptic described him as 'a brewery representative whose occupation may have contributed to the development of his ideas'. Actually, his family owned the brewery. He observed on his travels round the countryside that ancient pagan sites such as burial mounds and standing stones could often be linked by straight lines; and it is still accepted that this can be the case, though whether by intention or coincidence is again a matter for debate. Statisticians may argue that if you throw a bucketful of marbles in

the air, then let them roll in all directions, some of them are going to finish up in a straight line. Ley enthusiasts will reply that there are far too many straight leylines to be accounted for in that way; they may even mutter something about lies, damned lies and statistics. So should the statisticians discard their marbles – or have the leymen already lost theirs?

But, if these lines really exist – and a great many people believe they do – then why are they there, and what do they do? Or, as Alfred Watkins' friends might well have asked: 'What's it all about, Alfie?' Alfred reckoned they were prehistoric tracks, linking ancient meeting places and sacred sites. Our early ancestors, it seems, were a lot brighter than we generally assume. If the ancient Egyptians could build the Pyramids, why could the Ancient Britons not map out a network of straight tracks? Alfred believed that they used two sighting staves to align the sites they were linking. If he was right, it would provide a neat solution to the mystery of that famous chalk figure on the Sussex Downs, the Long Man of Wilmington, who holds a stick in each hand. He is not a prehistoric skier, just an ancient road surveyor.

Alfred coined the name 'ley' for his straight lines, from the Saxon word for a cleared glade; the glades were cleared, of course, to make the tracks. Spelt 'lea', it means a tract of open ground, which also fits nicely. And Alfred even devised a link with 'leye', an old word for fire: his straight tracks were sometimes marked by beacons. He soon found a name for his early surveyors too. 'Dod' crops up in place names on leylines, sometimes distorted into 'Dead' or 'Tot'; hence names like Deadman's Hill, and Totnes might have started as Dodnes. 'Dod' is an old name for a stalk or staff, such as those used by 'doddering' old men – and just like the ones carried by those road surveyors. So Alfred named them 'dod-men', and he reckoned he was finally proved correct when he found that in some rural areas (Norfolk is one of them) 'dodman' is the local name for a snail. On its head it carries two sighting staves, the implements of the dod-man.

It was hardly surprising, when he first published his theories, that the archaeological community either blew their tops or just fell about. 'Rot!' wrote one of them. 'How any man at any time can have made such a collection of damned nonsense I cannot imagine!' To some archaeologists today that still seems a very moderate assessment.

Even the most enthusiastic ley-man has to admit that leylines would make very impractical roads. They are inclined to go straight through swamps and lakes and over the top of very steep hills. Any dod-man who designed such a route would more likely be regarded as a dotty-man. So a theory developed that leylines were invisible energy currents passing through the earth, which our early ancestors could somehow detect and tap into by means of standing stones and other forms of sacred sites.

This got a considerable boost in the Swinging Sixties, when the idea of energy currents in leylines was adapted to fit almost any theory, from mystical happenings on Glastonbury Tor to landing sites for flying saucers. This 'New Age' approach was a lot more colourful than Alfred's prehistoric tracks, and many ley-hunters still favour it. I am rather taken by it myself, though some of its more extreme versions are too bizarre even for me. But as one fair-minded writer observed: 'The attraction of cranks to leylines is naturally no encouragement to take them seriously: but neither is it a reason for the subject to be rejected.'

In more recent years leylines have attracted some very serious thinking indeed. They have been linked with German ghost paths and Chinese feng shui, with fairy trails in Ireland and mysterious patterns in Peru. But most of these manifestations throughout the world have two common denominators: straight lines and the spirits of the dead.

Ghost paths are sometimes confused with the corpse trails of medieval times, when bodies in remote areas were often carried several miles to the nearest consecrated ground. I have followed corpse trails in the past, in the Lake District and the Yorkshire Dales, and they are anything but straight. The pall-bearers had the sense to take the easiest route, not necessarily the straightest. But with spirits, of course, it is a different matter. They can fly, in fact, 'dead straight'.

There is a strong argument that all versions of spirit paths go back to the ancient culture of shamanism, when the shaman – the village 'wise man' or witchdoctor, depending how you view them – was able to release his spirit from his body during a trance, so it could fly off – in a straight line, of course – to seek knowledge and inspiration, perhaps from other spirits. Leylines, it is suggested, are symbolic representations of these spirit paths.

This is one reason they can link medieval churches. It is not only because the churches stand on ancient pagan sites, as Alfred Watkins has it, but because of all the spirits that are based in their churchyards. This is encouraging news for the ley-hunter, of course. A churchyard is a much larger marker to aim at.

I could not attempt to tell the full story of shamanism. Paul Devereux, the leading author and lecturer on leylines, has written a whole book about it if you wish to delve more deeply: *Shamanism and the Mystery Lines*. He explains, for instance, why witches used to be depicted flying through the night on their broomsticks – in a straight line, no doubt. It was a symbolic portrayal of their spirits taking flight, and the broom handle had been used to apply a mind-affecting ointment on a certain part of the body...

And, of course, there is Father Christmas, up there with his reindeer. Another case of a symbolic spirit path? I can only quote Mr Devereux: 'The Arctic European and Siberian shamans all belonged to reindeer-herding tribes, and the colours of Santa's robes, red and white, are also the colour of the mind-altering mushroom which was used by them!' To his credit, the exclamation mark is his, not mine.

Before I was led too far up the spirit path, I felt I should try to get the whole leyline picture into perspective. So I read Alfred Watkins' book *The Old Straight Track*, and his follow-up, *The Ley Hunter's Manual*. Then I read the updated equivalents, *The Ley Hunter's Companion,* written by Paul Devereux and Ian Thomson in 1979, and *The New Ley Hunter's Guide*, written by Devereux on his own in 1994, in which he discarded some of the leylines they had described fifteen years earlier and switched his theories from earth currents to spirit paths. Among the other more serious books about leylines, both for and against, perhaps the most effective demolition job was carried out in 1983 by Tom Williamson and Liz Bellamy in *Ley Lines in Question*. They take Alfred's list of 'markers' and eliminate them one by one. On marker stones, for instance: 'There they lie, propping up sheds, hidden in hedges, occasionally bearing such mystical inscriptions as "Hereford 10 miles", unmoved and forgotten for millennia, until a ley hunter comes stumbling along and "discovers" them.' So much for the stone outside my village church; but it is not inscribed 'Norwich 30 miles' – and they could be wrong.

Through all the changing theories about leylines, and in spite of all the sceptics, one feature of Alfred's original discovery remains unaltered – and to me it remains quite fascinating. There are many ancient and unusual sites that for one reason or another – or none at all – can be connected by straight lines.

But to quote Paul Devereux's revised definition of the leylines in his *New Ley Hunter's Guide*: 'These lines all bear the name "ley" but they represent different groups of alignments, some prehistoric, others certainly medieval, some perhaps fragments of old church paths or corpse ways … Some of the cross-country church alignments might be indicative of invisible "ghost paths". Where there is a more equal mix of churches and pagan prehistoric sites we may be looking at a church path that was based on an earlier pagan line through the landscape.' In other words – who knows?

So I went ley-hunting. Not because I am convinced by any of these theories, nor because I want to disprove them, but just to discover where these lines might take me, and what I might find along their route that would interest not only the serious ley-man but also the curious layman who likes to look beyond the obvious for the unlikely, the unexpected and the definitely odd. With that in mind, I was rather selective about my lines. I kept away from urban areas, I kept the lines reasonably short (about twenty miles is the maximum), and I looked for five or more markers on each line which were reasonably accessible and had their own strange tale to tell. Alfred Watkins put mounds and stones at the top of his list, but to the untutored eye, one tumulus looks very like another, and a stone is just a stone – unless of course it is in a strange position, like the one outside my church.

Groups of standing stones, of course, are always good for a colourful legend, and they are high on my list as well as Alfred's. So too are medieval castles and churches that could well stand on ancient sites. We also share a liking for holy wells, ancient moats, which could have surrounded beacons or sacred sites, and mottes on which they might once have stood. He is very keen on groups of trees, particularly if they are on hilltops, and as they often look very striking I have included them occasionally too. He is even keener on fords, which are generally attractive, and crossroads, which are generally not; they can also be very busy or very boring. So fords are in and crossroads – unless I am desperate – are out.

The serious ley-man uses a compass to plot his lines, and Devereux for instance does this so accurately that a leyline of his will pass not just through a church, let us say, but through the west buttress of the south transept or two yards east of the chancel arch. I did it the easy way, with a pencil and ruler. If the line passed through a little black blob on the map with a cross on top, that was good enough for me. Not a very scientific approach, but this is not a very scientific book. These 'leylines' may be just lines, with no significance at all. But who knows for sure? There are more things, as they say, in heaven and earth …

Anyway, ley-hunting makes a great day out. I hope you enjoy it too.

NORFOLK

NORFOLK seems an appropriate place to start, not just because I happen to live there, but because for the layman ley-hunter it must be – quite literally – a happy hunting ground. Nearly 700 medieval churches and half-a-dozen Norman castles, any of which might arguably be on a prehistoric sacred site; a Neolithic henge; an assortment of Bronze Age barrows and Iron Age forts; the site of a Roman town with its pagan temple; and several places associated with the local Iceni tribe and their renowned Queen Boadicea – what more could an enterprising ley-hunter require? Put a ruler on any one of them on a large-scale map, jiggle it around a bit, and you can probably line it up with four or five more markers within twenty-odd miles.

One 'marker' was almost on my doorstep. The big, smooth stone outside Wellingham church, mentioned earlier, was the obvious starting point. But I felt I ought to get my eye in first, by following a leyline discovered by experts. It features in *The Ley Hunter's Companion*, though for no given reason it is rejected by one of the authors, Paul Devereux, in a later book. However, it is the only one mentioned in Norfolk, so I had a crack at it anyway. The *Companion* calls it the Quidenham Ley; I like to think of it, more romantically, as Queen Boadicea's Leyline.

Wymondham Abbey, a familiar Norfolk landmark –
but why is the porch out of alignment?

QUEEN BOADICEA'S LEYLINE (1)

It starts at Bunwell church and ends seventeen miles away at a barrow near Thetford, with three markers in between: a tumulus near New Buckenham, Viking's Mount at Quidenham (better known locally as Boadicea's burial mound) and West Harling church.

As a bonus, a group of children at New Buckenham told the *Companion*'s authors they had seen a whirlwind rise from the tumulus and move across the road, throwing hay and debris in the air, and strangely one of the authors (perhaps wisely the book does not say which) spotted 'a faint white circular shape' moving across the sky. In addition, the same children told them about a

mysterious 'black man' who appeared in the area at night. Alfred Watkins linked 'black' with the beacons on leylines. 'Could this be a folk memory of the "black" or beacon man,' the *Companion* speculates, 'who would have done this work at night?' A sceptic might have added, could the children have seen the authors coming?

In ley-hunting, obviously, there was no knowing what might lie round the next corner, or, since leys don't have corners, beyond the next marker. I crossed my fingers and set off.

The *Companion*'s only comment on St Michael's Church, Bunwell, is that it stands on raised ground on the site of a Norman church, 'if not older structures'. It is one of those vague links with pre-Norman times which critics would have great fun with, but I found another possible link which is rather more intriguing. Arthur Mee's *Norfolk* gave me the clue. 'The fine pulpit has panels of linenfold and tracery in which two leaves are cunningly contrived to show little faces with furrowed brows.' 'Cunningly contrived' indeed. Faces peering out of leaves are reminiscent of the Green Man, that survivor from pagan times. The faces, about the size of a two pence piece, are not easy to spot, but the brows are indeed furrowed, though one is grinning broadly and the other has a mischievous glint in his eye.

The tumulus at New Buckenham is hardly detectable, and unfortunately the children had long since gone, along with the whirlwind and the black man, but Viking's Mount, where Boadicea is reputed to be buried, is much more impressive. To the layman it is just a hillock with some fir trees on top, but to a ley-hunter it is an obvious marker.

St Andrew's at West Harling is impressive too. It is long since redundant, locked up and lonely in a remote field reached only by a potholed track. To add to the

Left *A grinning face on Bunwell's pulpit.* Right: *Viking's Mount – or Boadicea's grave.*

eeriness – and, ley-hunters would say, the authenticity – of this isolated marker there is an Iron Age fort close by, and even a moat on the site of the long-vanished hall.

The *Companion* mentions all this, but for good measure I discovered locally that a former rector wrote a poem about the 'Faery Wood' between the rectory and the church; did he know something as well? I was beginning to get the hang of this ley-hunting technique. From here the line passes through Shadwell Park, which contains St Chad's Well, described by Arthur Mee as 'once a shrine for pilgrims'. The *Companion* seemed to have missed it, and I congratulated myself on finding a new marker. Alas, I had fallen into the first of many traps that caught me out during the months to come. A friendly local archaeologist (and some archaeologists are still friendly about leylines) explained that the well was actually just an ornamental folly, installed by an earlier owner of Shadwell Park. The park was not named after St Chad's Well; he named the well after the park. So ley-hunters, beware!

The final barrow also proved to be an anti-climax. 'It is difficult to see', says the *Companion*, 'as it is screened by trees and heavily overgrown with thorn bushes.' That had been written nearly twenty years earlier, so my chances own of spotting it were pretty thin, and I never did.

But no matter. I had followed my first ley. I had found some curious carved heads, an eerily sited church, an ancient mound with a mysterious history, and some previously unexplored corners of the Norfolk countryside. True, I had not detected any unusual energy currents, and if a UFO was watching me, it kept well out of sight. But this was only the start.

I hastened back to my one-inch Ordnance Survey map and put one end of a ruler on Wellingham church. A few wiggles, and there were three more churches in alignment, and between them the line went over the encouragingly named Beacon Hill. I had my five markers and my first leyline. But to be on the safe side, let's just call it a line.

THE WELLINGHAM HERMIT'S LINE (2)

I walked past the mark stone by the porch, into the familiar surroundings of St Andrew's Church, and I looked around with a new eye. The most striking feature is the medieval rood-screen with its mystery saint – he is apparently trampling on a prostrate king, and the name beneath starts with 'Ma' before becoming illegible, but none of the St Maurices or even Margarets seems to be linked with a fallen monarch. However, even the most ingenious ley-hunter might have a problem devising a leyline connection, and I recalled something else in St Andrew's that might be more promising.

In the little vestry at the back of the church, almost

hidden by a table, is a very small brass in the floor. It is dated about 1450 and inscribed: *Hic jacet enim Thomas Leeke, Heremita*. A hermit called Thomas Leeke had lived either in the church or in a cell beside it. Hermits are often pictured as hairy fellows with scruffy robes and a wild expression, but by the 1450s they had gone more upmarket. Instead of dwelling in the wilderness, they sometimes lived along pilgrim routes, providing food and shelter and relying on the alms that the more prosperous pilgrims gave them in return.

These days Wellingham hardly seems to be on the way to anywhere and looks an unlikely place for a hermit to settle. It also seems odd that anyone should bother to install a brass in his memory. But Thomas Leeke may have known about leylines. He would certainly have known that Wellingham lay on the Pilgrims' Way from Palmers Green in London (where pilgrims picked up their symbolic palm leaves) to the shrine of Our Lady of Walsingham in Norfolk. The combination may have meant that Thomas did so well from the alms he received that he could even afford to leave enough money to pay for his brass.

I have already mentioned the significance of beacons on leylines, but there is no sign of one on Beacon Hill, the next marker. Indeed, it is not easy to identify the hill, which most people outside Norfolk would regard as just a modest undulation. I have never actually thought of it as a hill myself. But that is what it says on the map, and there is the circular eighty-metre contour line to prove it. So Beacon Hill it is.

The line continues across the River Wensum to Little Snoring church – a name that always delights visitors, especially when they find there is a local family called Gotobed. Like Wellingham, the church is dedicated to St Andrew, and some ley enthusiasts would think this very significant. They link St Andrew with Apollo, sun god and slayer of dragons – and dragons are mixed up with leylines too, as a symbol of earth forces.

Above: *Little Snoring church and its detached tower.*
Left: *The curious stone at Wellingham church.*

The link with Apollo is a little obscure, but I like the theory that the Romans identified him with the Celtic god Grannus, and when early Christians built churches on sites where Grannus had been worshipped, they dedicated them to St Andrew because the names sounded vaguely similar. Presumably they hoped the local pagans would not notice the difference.

Whatever the reason, there are a great many churches in Norfolk dedicated to Scotland's patron saint, even though Scotland is a long way away. It so happens that they include three of the four churches on this line. The one at Little Snoring is perhaps the most unusual; it is said to be one of only two churches in England with a detached round tower – nobody knows why.

There are remnants of the east side of the tower that show it was attached to the original Saxon church. Why that church was replaced by the Normans in about 1100, quite soon after it was built, and how the new one came to be sited separately and out of alignment with it remain a puzzle. It is assumed that it burned down or the Normans wanted a bigger church and pulled it down, leaving the tower. It is thought they rebuilt it a few yards away because the ground there did not slope so steeply. But could they have realized that the original church was slightly out of alignment with the Wellingham Hermit's Line?

Another unusual feature of the church – indeed it is claimed to be unique – is the splendid south doorway. Round the door is a plain Norman arch. Above it is a pointed Norman arch with a zigzag pattern and a lion's head at the apex, resting on capitals which confusingly date about 150 years later. And above that is a horse-shoe-shaped arch reminiscent of an Eastern mosque – perhaps inspired, the guidebook imaginatively suggests, by someone home from the Crusades.

It is thought the pointed arch was made up of stones from an earlier Norman archway, which was

originally round, the central stones being removed to
make it fit. But curiously, the leaf decorations on each
side are quite different, and the foliage decorations on
the outer arch are incomplete. Foliage was a popular
form of decoration, of course, but it is also associated
with pagan worship.

The next church on the line is St Martin's at
Hindringham, and here is another puzzle. The chancel
and the nave are not in line; the chancel is off-centre
and very slightly askew. 'This is termed a "weeping
chancel",' says the church guide. 'No satisfactory explanation is given.' In similar churches elsewhere it is
suggested that the slight angle represents Christ's head
hanging to one side on the Cross. Others say it was
angled to be directly in line with the rising sun on the
feast day of the church's patronal saint. I like to think
it was adjusted to line up, not with the sun, but with
the Wellingham Hermit's Line.

St Martin's also has an ancient parish chest dating
back to about 1175, one of the oldest oak chests in
England, and medieval stained glass featuring two

The ruined walls of Castle Acre's Norman castle.

angels, apparently wearing blue shorts. This seems
slightly bizarre, but only a football fan with an encyc-
lopedic knowledge of team colours could speculate on
their significance.

The final marker is St Andrew's at Field Dalling,
some seventeen miles from that first Andrew at
Wellingham. I found no hint of a leyline connection,
except perhaps for its name. But it obviously had some
special attraction for its incumbents; one of its vicars
remained in office for fifty years.

I extended the line south of Wellingham in the
hope of hitting Castle Acre's ruined priory and the
remains of its Norman castle, both of which would
make photogenic marks. Unfortunately, it missed completely, but I tried my luck again with the ruler, this
time linking Castle Acre with an Iron Age fort at
Narborough. The line continued eastwards through
two medieval churches and an ancient hermitage,
giving five markers for my next line.

THE FORT AND CASTLE LINE (3)

Experts say Narborough fort was built in the first century BC. Visitors to Narborough today may wonder why it needed one, but in prehistoric times the River Nar was navigable from the Wash, and this was one of the main crossing-places – a likely place for a ley, even without the fort. It was also one end of an earthwork named, like so many others, Devil's Dyke. Traces of it are still visible, but the site of the ancient settlement is better seen marked on a map than on the ground.

Castle Acre Castle, which overlooks the Nar some half-dozen winding miles upstream, is a very different matter. It is a vast earthwork with parts of the keep and the curtain wall still standing, protected by a moat and high grassy banks. Its eleventh-century gateway spans the road into the village.

The castle and subsequently the priory nearby were built by William de Warenne, who had shrewdly married the Conqueror's daughter. Castle Acre is known to be the site of a Roman camp, and the earthen ramparts may date back even earlier. Certainly the castle stands by the prehistoric Peddars Way, at its junction with a Roman road that probably ran from Peterborough to Caister-on-Sea on the coast. There is also a Saxon burial ground, where 100 urns were unearthed, and two stone coffins were found in the river. The Victorian parson at the time asked two men to carry the coffins up the hill to the church, but when he failed to pay them, they threw them back into the river and nobody cared to retrieve them.

The line misses the priory, but it does go through the parish church of St James, a fifteenth-century building with some quaint carved animals perched on the pew-ends; there are few clues to its earlier history. Perhaps if that parson had not been so mean and the stone coffins had been installed in the church, there might be a better excuse for linking it with earlier days.

The line from Castle Acre earthworks to Newton church.

The former hermit's chapel at Litcham, with its buttresses and niches for statues.

All Saints' at Newton-by-Castle-Acre, on the other hand, makes an excellent marker for the line, a mile from the castle on the other side of the river. It has an unmistakable Saxon tower, placed centrally over the church. As one gazetteer comments: 'All Saints' is one of the most attractive of the early churches of Norfolk, untouched by the great rebuilding of the fifteenth century, very simple and inspiring.' It is so simple, in fact, that there is little to seize upon in the way of leyline clues, but the Saxons constantly followed Pope Gregory's advice to build their early Christian churches on existing sacred sites, and All Saints' is a pretty safe bet.

Next in line is the former hermit's chapel at Litcham, further up the Nar. It is now called Priory Farm, but there is no direct link with a priory. The double buttresses that jut onto the pavement and the niche on each buttress for a statue are the most obvious indications of its origin. The hermits who manned this fourteenth-century chapel, like Thomas Leeke at nearby Wellingham, gave help and shelter to pilgrims on their way to Walsingham as they crossed the Nar. One of them, Thomas Canon, was a local man who owned two acres of land by the hermitage, but 'in compassion' he was not charged the full tax on it. However, there was no compassion shown by Henry VIII when he dissolved the monasteries, even though he is said to have stayed at the hermitage on his way to Walsingham. The shrine was destroyed, and the hermitage became a tannery. Today Priory Farm is a private house.

After Litcham the line leaves the Nar for its final marker, St Mary's at East Bilney, some seventeen miles from its starting point at Narborough. The church was almost entirely rebuilt by the Victorians, but there is a reminder of its earlier days and of East Bilney's most famous son. Thomas Bilney was ordained in 1519 but did not believe in worshipping relics or the mediation of saints, and he said so in his sermons. Eventually, the Bishop of Norwich, a Bishop Nix, had him burned at the stake for heresy, and a stained-glass window shows him preaching, then dying, with Norwich Cathedral in the background. Ironically, the bishop was then arrested for executing him without authority. All his property was confiscated, reducing him, one might say, to Nix. One might argue that, if a leyline does run through the church, it did little good for Thomas Bilney.

I did continue the line to North Elmham in the hope of including the site of the Saxon cathedral, but instead it goes through the crossroads at the entrance to the village. Alfred Watkins might accept that as a marker, and it does have a very good inn just beside it, so let us call it an optional extra – depending on your thirst.

Before leaving this area of Norfolk, there is one other site that merits a leyline. In 1998 the Norfolk Monuments Management Project literally unearthed more details about the Norman castle at Mileham. For many decades the castle ruins had been smothered by a wilderness of scrub and nettles, but the project uncovered not only the ruins but more of its history. I doubt the archaeologist had a leyline in mind, but a few wiggles with the ruler have produced another line, starting at Beetley and passing through the castle to Rougham and Grimston churches, with a couple of tumuli *en route*.

THE MILEHAM CASTLE LINE (4)

There was a church at Beetley, four or five miles from Mileham, before the castle was built. It is mentioned in the Domesday Book, and it is assumed that the present church of St Mary Magdalene is on the same site. The Saxon church, in its turn, could well have been on a pagan sacred site; and then there is the 'ley' in Beetley. The name comes from Bietel-lea, bietels being the wooden mallets that were used to drive in the stakes of a stockade or the supporting posts of an early church. The local trees came in handy again, 1000 years later, when the parapet was added to the tower in 1911. It was not made of wood, but it was paid for, regrettably one might think, by selling the oak trees in the churchyard.

One or two little mysteries survive from those early days. Two sundials are scratched on the porch, which may seem one too many, particularly as one seems to have an odd pattern of lines. Perhaps the mason just got it wrong the first time and tried again. And there is the piscina in the chancel, with something carved on it, which the church guide describes as 'traces of a strange little animal'. I could not identify it, but any suggestion of strange little animals is always welcomed, I imagine, by the ardent ley-hunter. Who knows what obscure connection it may have with earlier forms of worship?

Castle mottes or mounds are also a rich source of speculation. The one at Mileham was thirty feet high, surrounded by a moat and surmounted by a keep, though there is little to see of it now. I gather there is no evidence that the mound was there before the Normans – a sacred site protected by the moat – but who knows for certain?

From there the line heads for Weasenham Woods, where there is a Bronze Age cemetery dating from the second century BC. The line goes through two of the barrows, both about 150 feet across, but they are covered in vegetation and are not very dramatic. The woods are private anyway.

Rougham's faceless Apostles escorted by archangels.

At Rougham church, however, there is more to catch the eye, starting with a familiar-looking smooth boulder outside the lychgate. Could it be a marker, like the one at Wellingham – or is it just to deter car drivers from parking? Inside the tower is an ancient altar, which was in use until 1912. The church guide says it was in the original Saxon church, though one gazetteer calls it medieval, and Arthur Mee's *Norfolk* ignores it altogether. Instead, he goes for a venerable wood carving in the chancel, and says it shows six Apostles with archangels between them. Unfortunately, the Apostles' faces are flattened and impossible to identify, and the archangels look singularly unangelic spindly figures, with no wings and scaly legs. Now if those scaly legs had been on a dragon … Outside the church door there is the gravestone of Thomas Keppel North, whose family have been squires of Rougham for three or four centuries. Carved on the stone is the bi-plane he designed at Vickers for Alcock and Brown, and thus helped them to trace another kind of line on the map – all the way across the Atlantic.

The Mileham Castle Line – a mere twenty miles long – ends at St Botolph's Church, Grimston. Botolph was a seventh-century saint who is believed to have baptized people in the nearby springs. The church incorporated Roman bricks dating from much earlier. There is an encouraging carving of a dragon on one of the medieval choir stalls, and in case mermaids can be

Above: *The Grimston rocket.* Below: *One of the curious carved beast in Grimston church.*

linked with leylines, there is one of those too. After all, they do have scaly tails.

But I was particularly taken with an odd-shaped buttress outside, and even the church guide calls it 'very unusual'. Its base is a standard angled buttress, but then it becomes polygonal and culminates in a pointed cone on top. It is known as the Grimston rocket; I prefer to think of it as an appropriate finishing post for the Mileham Castle Line.

It also ends this set of mid-Norfolk lines, because there are other places in Norfolk that deserve a leyline or two, in particular the oldest sacred site in the country, the Neolithic woodhenge at Arminghall. A few miles south is the site of the Roman town of Venta Icenorum with its pagan connection, and in a straight line beyond this is the Iron Age fort at Tasburgh, plus a couple more likely markers.

THE ARMINGHALL WOODHENGE LINE (5)

The bad news about the woodhenge is that it was made of wood, so after more than 4000 years very little survives, unlike its famous counterpart at Stonehenge. The best way to discern the circular earthwork, about ninety feet across, that enclosed it is to hire a plane; in fact, that is how it was originally spotted. Experts say there was a horseshoe of eight timber posts, each one about three feet in diameter and sunk seven feet into the ground. They were either free-standing or supported a wooden building. It sounds fairly humdrum, but as one archaeologist has commented: 'This technical and symbolic achievement is as impressive for its time as the erection, 3000 years later and only two miles away, of Norwich Cathedral.' Ley-hunters give it an extra significance. One of them wrote: 'Interestingly enough, the site slightly to the east of Arminghall has been found suitable for a power station, and a network of overhead cables converge beside the remains of the henge.' The modern equivalent of those underground energy currents, I suppose.

Venta Icenorum, in what is now the parish of Caistor St Edmund, was built on a site which had also been a focus of activity since Neolithic times. Again, the only decent view of its grid-pattern of streets is from the air, but part of its surrounding wall still protects the medieval church of St Edmund, and stones from it were incorporated in the church itself. Roman relics found on the site include a head of the goddess Diana, presumably from a pagan temple here.

The line runs alongside the River Tas to Tasburgh, crossing it in the gardens of Rainthorpe Hall. The gardens are said to be haunted by Amy Robsart, who married Robert Dudley, Earl of Leicester, in Queen Elizabeth's time, and came to a violent end. A haunted garden is not a recognized ley marker, but any strange happening along the line is worth a mention.

The fort at Tasburgh, probably built by Boadicea's Iceni tribe, is a rather more recognized marker. One

The remains of the Roman wall at Caistor St Edmund.

leyline from it is said to go through Norwich Castle to the east coast, another through the hermit's chapel at Litcham (on my Castle Acre Line) and on to the Wash.

St Mary's Church was built in a corner of the earthwork in about 1050, though there was probably a wooden building before that. The fourteenth-century font looks promising – carved heads surrounded by leaves – but ley-hunters beware: it comes from a disused church in Norwich.

From Tasburgh the line ends at Wacton, which happens to have two ancient moats and both of them are on the line. Alfred Watkins, who rated moats highly as markers, would be impressed. But there is little to see of the first one, and the other is at Wacton Hall, which is privately owned.

One of the long-distance leylines from Tasburgh fort passes through Wymondham Abbey on its way to the Wash, forty miles away. The abbey ought to merit a shorter line than that, and indeed, by lining it up with Venta Icenorum instead of the fort, there were eight likely markers in twenty miles.

THE WYMONDHAM ABBEY LINE (6)

The line starts at Deopham church, west of Wymondham. It is dedicated to St Andrew, which gave it a head start. It has other heads, too, on the corbels supporting the roof. They include one with pointed ears and a whimsical expression, into which one can read almost anything. There is also a frieze of leaves over the west doorway, but these are vine leaves and may just illustrate one of the sayings of Jesus: 'I am the true vine ...'

Between Deopham and the abbey the line passes through a crossroads, which normally I would not consider, but this one is called Highoak, and the combination of a crossroads and a tall tree would certainly rate as a marker for Alfred, so this is one of my eight on the Wymondham Abbey line.

The abbey itself, as the guidebook says, is a building 'with a great capacity to surprise'. It refers primarily to the two great towers, one at each end. They are reminders of a long-running dispute between the monks and the townspeople, which was referred first to the Pope, then, 200 years later, to the Archbishop of Canterbury, and finally to Henry IV. It

was all because William D'Albini, when he founded the abbey (then a priory) on an earlier church site in 1107, decreed the priory church should also be used as the parish church – but failed to say which parts of it should be used by whom. After centuries of argument, which at times became violent, the townsfolk were at last allowed to build their own tower, and the Reformation gave them the final victory. The monks' tower has long been a ruin, and their end of the church has largely disappeared.

There are more surprises inside, such as the vast gilded altar-screen that covers the entire east wall, but for me the most fascinating discovery was in the roof. The lines of bosses that run the length of it are carved with foliage, and in some cases a face is peering out of the leaves. Is it just a coincidence that an ancient inn near the entrance to the abbey is called the Green Man?

There is one other strange feature. The north porch, added in the fifteenth century, is out of alignment with the main body of the building. When a chancel is askew like this, there are theories about catching the rising sun, or representing Christ's head hanging to one side on the Cross, but these can hardly apply to a porch. The guidebook says there have been various suggestions, 'but none seems wholly satisfactory'. Could it be something to do with the alignment of a leyline, perhaps?

The line then passes through Wymondham branch library, which normally would be unremarkable, but this library was originally the St Thomas à Becket Chapel, founded soon after his murder and still unmistakable in spite of all the bookshelves.

The next marker is Moot Hill, just outside the town. It is an oval-shaped earthwork, 500 feet long and 400 feet wide. It has a ditch and a low rampart surrounding a flat, open space, and how it originated is, one might say, a moot point. Theories range from a Norman fortification to a meeting place or moot, from

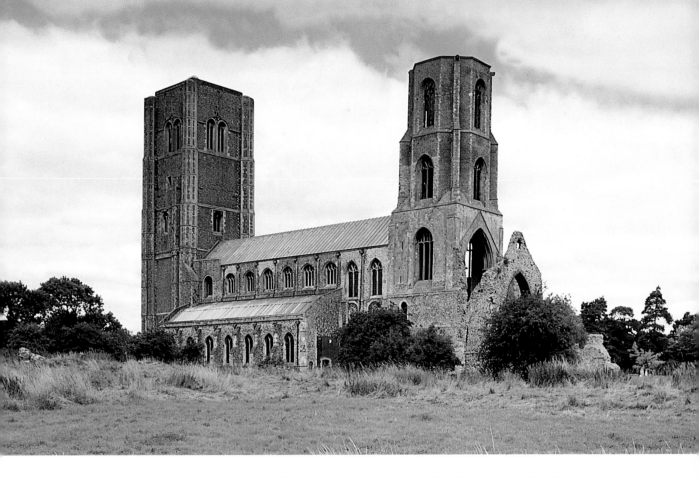

Above: *Wymondham Abbey, with its push-me-pull-you towers.*
Left: *An enigmatic head at Deopham church.*

a theatre for mystery plays to the site of a medieval manor.

That makes five markers. The line *could* end at Moot Hill, but it can be extended through Ketteringham church to Venta Icenorum, and on to St Peter's at Bramerton. At Ketteringham the church interior is largely Victorian, but it is on a Saxon church site. There is also what looks like a preaching cross on the approach to it, but take a closer look and you will see on its two arms the words 'Church' and 'Hall'. It is, in fact, a signpost, probably erected by a Victorian squire, Sir John Boileau, who is well remembered for his long-running battle with the rector, Mr Andrew. Perhaps he was determined that no friends of Mr Andrew, looking for the church, would arrive at the hall by mistake. They were directed, in fact, along the Wymondham Abbey Line.

Bramerton church, at the end of the line, also dates back to the Normans and before, but just one feature caught my eye. For no apparent reason there is a curious little carved face, all on its own at the foot of the rood stairway. It has large ears and a distinct twinkle in its eye, and I was reminded of that other face with distinctive ears in Deopham church, where the line began. Perhaps they knew all about leylines, long before I drew that line to link them, and they were sharing a joke at my expense.

Alfred Watkins mentions other churches in this part of Norfolk in *The Old Straight Track*, and they seemed worth a check. He quotes four on a leyline, but I needed a fifth to qualify, and anyway one of his seemed well off the line. So I extended it and found it passed through two churches in the same churchyard before ending, at Moot Hill. The other end of the line, seventeen miles away, is at Carleton St Peter, while the most westerly church, confusingly, is at East Carleton. So it is called the Two Carletons Line.

THE TWO CARLETONS LINE (7)

Starting from Moot Hill, East Carleton lies about six miles to the east, quite close, in fact, to Ketteringham. It used to be two parishes, and the two churches were built a stone's throw apart, with just a lane dividing them. The line passed through both – or it would have done until the sixteenth century, when St Peter's fell into decay. All that remains is part of the east wall, covered in ivy and surrounded by gravestones. Across the lane St Mary's fared rather better. It had a major restoration in the 1880s, when many earlier features were lost. Like a number of other churches on these lines it seems to have had a special attraction for its rectors. The Rev. Peter Coppin, for instance, arrived with his young bride in 1680 at the age of twenty-four and remained until his death forty-eight years later.

East Carleton is in line with three of Alfred's churches, but the old straight track would have to make quite a zigzag to hit his fourth marker, at Swardeston, which is a good half-mile to the north. Instead, it goes through Dunston Hall, now a hotel, which was built in the last century and I could find no earlier history.

It continues to St Mary's, Yelverton, with its cheerful yellow door-panels on one side, bright blue on the other. Another unexpected and much older piece of paintwork features on the screen. Below the usual panels of saints and angels there is a strange landscape, almost surreal, featuring sand dunes and palm trees. The church guide calls it 'quaint', but I would rate it rather higher. I have not seen another screen like it.

Above: Stained glass in Ashby church, but why the cockatrice?
Left: Carleton St Peter church. Below: *East Carleton church.*

The line then crosses Hellington – but with no devilish connection, I am sure – and just clips the corner of Ashby Hall, where there have been some unusual architectural discoveries, before reaching Alfred's next church, St Mary's where the best known curiosities are the 'his and hers' gravestones of George and Ann Basey,. surrounded by the geese and turkeys that they reared and drove to Smithfield Market, 100 miles away. But more interesting to the ley-hunter, are the grim-looking animals on the tower high above.

The splendid Norman doorway with its assortment of zigzags, stars and lozenges is a delight to the architectural eye, but mine was caught by a little roundel in the east window. It used to stand separately until the 1987 gales blew out some panes and it was used as a replacement, but I could not discover its origin. It shows a figure with its hands on two shields, one with the routine heraldic lions, the other with some kind of bird which has feathered legs and a long pointed tail curved over its head, like a dragon. It is, I believe, a cockatrice, sometimes called a basilisk, a thoroughly unpleasant mythical creature said to be hatched by a

serpent from a cock's egg, and with the power to kill with a glance. What can it be up to in Ashby church?

At Carleton St Peter the line ends, as it started, on a mound, but on this mound stands the church, and it would immediately appeal to Alfred Watkins. It is surrounded by flat fields and is accessible only by a grassy path across a meadow. On each side of the church there is a group of tall Scotch firs. The combination of this isolated mound, ancient church and tall trees provides a dramatic silhouette in the evening light. There is not a lot to catch the ley-hunter's eye inside, but I enjoyed the jolly musical angels painted on the little organ, and the modern clock on the wall of the nave, visible to most of the congregation but not to anyone in the pulpit, where it might do the most good. The lasting memory, though, is of that striking silhouette, almost unchanged over the centuries, providing an appropriate conclusion to the Two Carletons Line.

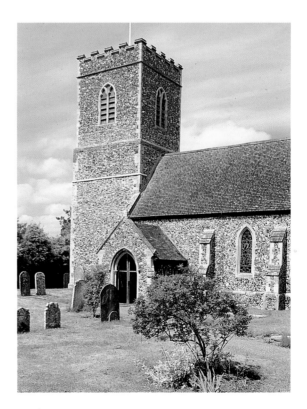

SUFFOLK

UFFOLK, like Norfolk, is about as far as you can get in an easterly direction from Alfred Watkins' Herefordshire, and one gathers from his books that he never actually got that far. He relied on local correspondents in these far-flung corners, and in Suffolk he had a distinguished historian, William Dutt, who wrote enthusiastically to Alfred: 'I have almost daily found evidence in support of the ley theory ... I found after tracing some leys on the Suffolk maps that I had ruled my lines through several earthworks not marked, and of which I had no knowledge until I read of them after aligning the leys.'

Unfortunately, he omits to say where any of these lines are, and that is the only mention of Suffolk in *The Old Straight Track*. In *The Ley Hunter's Companion* it gets no mention at all. Other writers, have treated it more kindly, and their main interest seems to be not in undiscovered earthworks, but in moats, in which Suffolk happens to be particularly rich, which would have pleased Alfred. He believed that moats originally encircled sacred mounds, and the water in them protected the mounds and reflected the light from the sky, or from a beacon at night, as a guide to travellers on the leylines. He could be right, but he may be pushing it a bit when he suggests it is no coincidence that 'mote' not only means a moat but 'a speck of light in the eye'. I thought it meant a speck, which hinders the eye rather than helps it. But let's not interrupt his argument, because it gets more interesting.

'Undoubtedly it was found that the early round moats formed desirable sites for defendable residences, not to mention castles.' It may have been tricky to erect a castle inside an existing moat, but never mind; they make very acceptable ley markers. Alas, most of Suffolk's moats surround 'defendable residences' which are either privately occupied or difficult to reach. So I looked for a more accessible marker to start with, and found a village, reconstructed on an original Saxon site. It lines up with an ancient abbey, two existing churches and the site of a third – plus, unavoidably, two of those moats.

A pre-Christian wodehouse in Wickham Skeith church.

THE WEST STOW SAXON VILLAGE LINE (8)

West Stow is where the prehistoric Icknield Way crosses the River Lark, and a crossing-place like that would rate high as a ley marker in itself. It was a major settlement from earliest times, long before the Romans and then the Anglo-Saxons took it over. The village was abandoned in the seventh century, and so much sand drifted over it that when it was excavated in the 1960s, much of it was still preserved. Some of the huts and other buildings were reconstructed, with walls of split tree-trunks and Saxon-style thatched roofs. They now form part of West Stow Country Park, and on certain days the 'villagers' have been known to return, to carry on where they left off, 1300 years ago.

Ixworth, six miles to the east, is also linked with the Icknield Way, if only by its name. The line passes through Ixworth Abbey, which was actually a priory and is now a private house. It was founded by the Blount family for the Augustinians in the twelfth century and prospered until Henry VIII dissolved it, along with all the others, 400 years later. Henry gave it to the Coddington family, as compensation for clearing them off their own estate in Surrey, which was a much handier site on which to build a grandiose palace for his new wife, Anne Boleyn.

The Coddingtons made the best of their compulsory rehabilitation and converted the priory into a handsome country house. The present owners open parts of the original building to the public at certain times. The priory has, in fact, fared rather better than Anne Boleyn's palace, which Henry called 'Nonsuch' because there was 'none such' like it. There is now, alas, No-such Palace; it was demolished in the 1680s. So perhaps Richard Coddington, in his splendid tomb in the parish church, has had the last laugh.

The site of the priory church was just in front of the house, and the line passes through that as well as the priory and St Mary's Church across the stream, where Richard Coddington lies. St Mary's was built a couple of hundred years later, and perhaps the architect knew about leylines when he chose the site. Certainly there are plenty of goggle-eyed gargoyles to scare off unwelcome spirits (as well as provide drainage, of course), and some knowing little faces around the porch.

The line then crosses the picturesque village street, now fortunately bypassed, where in 1930 the learned antiquarian Dr M.R. James spotted some ridge tiles

representing figures, 'of which I do not know the like'. I bet they were on the line too.

The next marker is a moat at Shrubbery Farm, then the line continues across country to the church at Wickham Skeith, behind the old manor house. There has been a church here since before the Normans, but the current one is mostly fourteenth century. One of the gargoyles on the tower is holding its mouth open with its hands, and there is another on the south porch doing the same thing. This seemed a bit unusual, but I did find a possible explanation. On the roof bosses inside the church there is the face of a pagan Green Man, with foliage coming out of his mouth; maybe those gargoyles had just got rid of theirs and were making sure there were no stray leaves left behind.

Round the font are more of the Green Man's friends, hairy 'wild men of the woods', who are generally thought to be associated with pre-Christian worship. And carved on the door between the nave and the tower there is more foliage with another human figure lurking in it, as well as assorted animals. Why, one wonders, did the wood-carvers and stonemasons

Above: *The reconstructed Saxon village at West Stow.*
Left above: *A carving at St Mary's Church, Ixworth.* Left below: *The Green Man at Wickham Skeith.*

install so many possible reminders of earlier gods? Maybe in those days no one was quite sure they wouldn't make a comeback – so these medieval crafts-men were just hedging their bets.

And all this in a church dedicated to St Andrew, the saint chosen by the early Christians, some ley enthusiasts say, because his name sounds similar to the Celtic god Grannus, who may have been worshipped on that site before. Yes, as a marker, St Andrew's at Wickham Skeith deserves full marks.

After all that excitement the line ends rather tamely at Colsey Wood moat, which is hardly surprising, because in this area of Suffolk moats are so numerous that some ley-hunters have been happy to devote entire leylines to them. I suppose it would be a pity to ignore the opportunity, so I found an example of a five-moat line, which is leavened by a fascinating church at the end of it.

THE FIVE MOAT LINE (9)

The first marker is at Maulkins Hall, which stands on its own near Pakenham. It is reached only by a private drive, and the moat is out of sight of the road. So are the next two, on private land south-east of Stowlangtoft – the fourth marker is more accessible, a tumulus on Mill Hill, close to the road south of Hunston Green. True, I did not spot the tumulus, but I did find a very dramatic oak tree where the tumulus should have been. It stands on what must have once been a crossways, where a footpath leads from the road to Hunston church at the foot of the hill. An ancient oak tree at a crossways on a hill would appeal to Alfred, and it looks sufficiently striking to appeal to me too.

The next moat, at Hall Farm, Great Ashfield, has a rather more impressive pedigree than the others, but again it is on private land. It is at Castle Hill, so named because the moat surrounded the castle of Robert le Blund at the time of the Norman Conquest. His family

were lords of the manor for 200 years, until Sir William le Blund died at the Battle of Lewes in 1264, leaving no heir. The castle mound and moat are still there, but I gather nothing remains of the castle.

The line misses what looks like an obvious marker at Great Ashfield, the carved Saxon cross in the garden of Ashfield House – surely an early preaching cross erected on a former pagan sacred site. I wondered how I had failed to include it, until I discovered it was neither a preaching cross nor on its original site.

According to local legend, the body of St Edmund, the Saxon king killed by the Danes, was brought into Great Ashfield's original Saxon church on the way to its final resting place at Bury St Edmunds. This is not the only church in Suffolk and Essex to make a similar claim, and if they are all correct, the pall-bearers must have taken a very circuitous route, but it is said that this Saxon cross was erected in the churchyard to commemorate the event, so they must have been reasonably sure that it was on the route.

After the Reformation some enterprising reformer took down the cross and laid it over the stream beside the church to act as a footbridge. Fortunately, it stayed in one piece, and in the nineteenth century it was retrieved by the rector's son, Lord Thurlow, who had just built Ashfield House. He put it in his garden, where it still enjoys a peaceful retirement.

The line continues eastward to Cotton church, which encouragingly is another St Andrew's, and it lives up to its ley-orientated dedication. The present fourteenth-century building stands on another ancient site, and its tower has an assortment of gargoyles. But, unlike similar towers of that period, it has no west door, just a massive archway which leaves the bell-ropes – and I assume the bell-ringers – 'open to wind and weather'. It would be nice to think this was a throw-back to the days of open-air worship – but I doubt the bell-ringers would recommend it. Perhaps the medieval

door-makers used up all their energy on the south doorway, which is claimed to be the finest of its kind in Suffolk. It is lavishly decorated with foliage – another reminder? – and it still has its original doors.

Inside the church you may find a few people lying prostrate on the pews, and ardent ley-hunters might hope they are re-creating some strange pagan ritual. Alas, they are just following the advice of the guide-book; this is the best way, it says, of appreciating the delights of the double hammer-beam roof. But they may also spot that the roof is slightly out of shape, and so is the west window in the south aisle, where the walls and arcades lean somewhat alarmingly. A last-minute attempt to re-align the church along a leyline, perhaps?

Above: *The moat at Great Ashfield*. Left: *Cotton church's curious curled-up creature, perched on the stair rail to the pulpit.*

The guidebook just puts it down to old age.But what fascinated me most in Cotton church was the curious carved animal perched on the stair-rail leading to the pulpit. What is it and why is it there? Alfred, I am sure, would have an interesting theory, but the guide, normally so helpful, merely says: 'Note the grotesque creature on the stair-rail.' So I have.

The final moat, in a field just outside the village, makes five on this line in less than twelve miles, which I think is quite remarkable in itself. But I was glad to find Cotton church planted on it too.

CAMBRIDGESHIRE AND HERTFORDSHIRE

Cambridge may have produced a wealth of academic experts on prehistoric Britain, but they have surprisingly few sites locally to work on. In fact, only one is mentioned in the whole of Cambridgeshire in a guide to prehistoric sites by Nicholas Thomas – admittedly an Oxford man. Fortunately for the academics, the site is quite near Cambridge; and fortunately for the ley-hunter, it not only has impeccable Iron Age credentials but also covers about fifteen acres, which allows quite a bit of leeway – one might call it leyway – when drawing leylines. And fortunately for us, it has acquired a colourful collection of contradictory legends.

Wandlebury Camp, as it is called, is in itself quite straightforward. It is an Iron Age hill-fort, first dug out in about the third century BC and refortified a couple of hundred years later. It had an outer bank reinforced with timbers and a ditch beyond that, but little of either survives. It is the location that makes it so fascinating. It lies on the Gogmagog Hills, a name rich in folklore and an ideal place to start looking for a leyline.

Certainly it has appealed to earlier ley-hunters, and it gets pride of place in *The Ley Hunter's Companion*. But the leyline in the *Companion* goes through the heart of Cambridge, and I prefer ones that avoid built-up areas as much as possible. This is not easy when Cambridge is so close and covers such a large area, but I found a line that just clips the southern outskirts.

The medieval glass at Trumpington church.

THE OUT-OF-TOWN GOGMAGOG LINE (10)

After moat-infested Suffolk, it may seem a little repetitive to start this line with two more, but there are quite a lot in Cambridgeshire as well. Are they all former burial mounds, one wonders, or is it something to do with the drainage in this part of East Anglia? Anyway, they are all recorded in Old English type on the maps, so they must have some historical significance. These two are a few miles south-west of Cambridge, and they line up nicely with St Mary and St Michael's Church, Trumpington, on the way to Wandlebury Camp.

Trumpington is in danger of being absorbed into Cambridge, but the church is in the old part of the village, not far from the helpfully named Green Man Inn. The present church dates back to 1200, but a Victorian architect gave it a new roof, and as the information leaflet politely observes: 'At the same time ... he generally tidied things up in the way that Victorian architects like to do.' In other words, many medieval oddities were probably swept away, just because they were old.

Happily, however, he did retain the original bosses in his new chancel roof, and there is the familiar foliage alternating with human faces, reminiscent of the Green Man down the road. Some ancient stained glass also survives, and indeed the window behind the vicar's stall has the oldest glass in the Cambridge area. It features a couple of rather jolly lions, apparently grinning to themselves at some private joke. Maybe they date back so far that they know something the vicar doesn't, and they are laughing at him behind his back.

There is another interesting animal on Trumpington's other ancient treasure, the 700-year-old brass to Sir Roger de Trumpington. It is one of the oldest in England, and possibly the only one to feature a hungry pet dog. It is trying to take a bite out of its master's sword.

Again, the information leaflet puts it rather more elegantly: 'a splendidly attentive dog crouches beneath his feet, gripping the end of the sword with his teeth'. Whatever it is up to, it may offer a clue to the knights identity, because there were two Sir Roger de Trumpingtons who died in the same period, and no one is quite sure which one this is. The answer would be to discover which one had a dog that liked chewing swords.

On now to Wandlebury Camp up on the Gogmagog Hills. The Camp, too, is uncomfortably close to Cambridge but is safely protected by the Cambridge Preservation Trust, It is a good place to recall the strange legends attached to these hills, with their various versions of a Gog and a Ma-Gog. By now you may be agog too.

Local folklore says that Gog was a giant who fell in love with a nymph called Granta. They must have made a bizarre couple, and not surprisingly it all ended in tears. Granta turned into a river, and Gog was metamorphosed into a hill. Another version has Gog as the sun god and Ma-Gog as the moon or earth goddess. But they have also been identified as two giants who

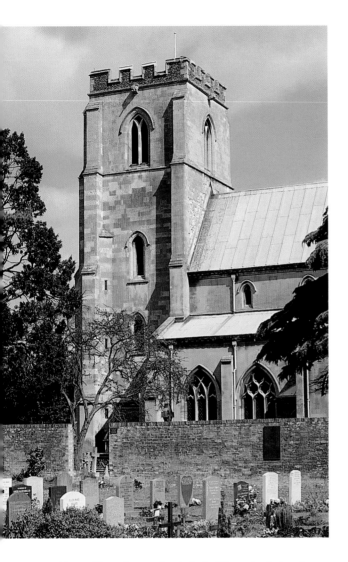

Above: *Trumpington church.* Left: *The stained-glass lions.*

were captured and taken to London to act as doormen at the royal palace. The site is now occupied by the present Guildhall – and effigies of the two Ancient British bouncers still stand guard outside it.

However, another effigy was discovered in the Gogmagog Hills, a figure carved in the turf near Wandlebury Camp. Some say it represents the goddess Ma-Gog, and indicates that Wandlebury was a sacred site. It is now overgrown again, but there is a photo-graph of it in the 1979 *Ley Hunter's Companion.* I have to say it looks to me more like a goggle-eyed elf than an earth goddess. Maybe the 'gog' in 'goggle-eyed' is the only real Gog connection.

From Wandlebury the line passes through a tumulus on Copley Hill, about a mile away, then climbs to the highest point in Cambridgeshire. Holy Trinity Church, Balsham, is 400 feet above sea level, which sounds fairly modest, but it is nearly twice as high as the Gogmagog Hills. The village lies on the prehistoric Icknield Way, and to prove it there is a milestone which says, remarkably clearly: 'Peddars Way 43 miles' in one direction and 'Ridgeway 63 miles' in the other. But I have to confess it was only put there in 1992.

Balsham also has a village sign illustrating the village's other claim to fame. During a Danish invasion in 1010, led by the dreaded Svend Forkbeard, the villagers put up such a gallant fight that he ordered them to be massacred to the last man. The last man, however, was not only brave but he was no fool. He took up a defensive position in the narrow doorway of the church tower. It was in fact so narrow – and still is – that only one Dane could fight him at a time. Finally, even the fearsome Forkbeard decided to waste no more time on him, and the church together with its gallant defender were left untouched.

Inside Holy Trinity is an Anglo-Saxon coffin lid which was dug up in the churchyard. It has never been identified, but I like to think it came from the grave of our heroic friend. Over the main church door, inciden-tally, there is an inscription: 'Ye shall keep My Sabbath and reverence My Sanctuary.' Perhaps His Sanctuary has not been reverenced enough, because these days, with no Saxon to keep out the vandals, the door is kept locked.

This is a pity, because there are many treasures inside. For the collector of unusual font covers, for instance, there is the massive one designed by a former rector which can be lifted without effort, thanks to its ingenious counter-balance, a First World War shell-case. For the brass-rubbing connoisseur there is the nine-foot brass of a fourteenth-century incumbent,

John de Sleford. For the antiquarian there is the original rood-loft as well as the more common rood-screen. And for the ley-hunter there is the fine assortment of strange beasts carved on the chancel stalls, possible links with earlier times.

Some churches on leylines generate a great loyalty in their rectors; some stay for half a century or more. Holy Trinity seems to generate great versatility. John de Sleford, for example, combined his parochial duties with those of Master of the Royal Wardrobe, Chaplain to the Queen, Canon of Ripon and Archdeacon of Wells. One of his successors, John Blodwell, was simultaneously Prebendary of Hereford, Prebendary of Lichfield and Canon of St David's – and in a spare moment he helped to prosecute Joan of Arc. Where, one wonders, did they get all their energy? Perhaps they plugged into the Gogmagog Line.

It seems, however, that the strange stories of

Wandlebury Camp.

Gogmagog had no appeal for Alfred Watkins. I found only one reference to Cambridgeshire in his books, by a correspondent called Leslie Keating, who ignored Wandlebury and based a leyline on two other ancient sites.

They were called Arbury Camp and the Chantry entrenchments, and apparently they both lay north of Cambridge, instead of south. Unfortunately, I could find no trace of them on the map or in the reference books; perhaps there is now an Arbury Avenue or a Chantry Close in their place. Other markers mentioned by Mr Keating seem to be out of alignment anyway. But I did trace what he called 'Ferry over Cam at Ditton', though the ferry has long since gone. And by using two of his markers and a couple of new ones, a revised line appeared.

THE CAM FERRY LINE (11)

All Saints' Church, Lolworth, stands exposed on a hill-side, as a good ley marker should, and it looks directly down on the A14, getting the full benefit of its steady roar. Inside, however, it is as quiet as Mr Keating would have remembered it, and it still has reminders of its early origins: a list of rectors going back to 1281, what looks like the base of a preaching cross brought in from the churchyard and a reproduction of a medieval wall-painting named as 'The Incredulity of St Thomas' – or more familiarly, Doubting Thomas.

The second church on the line is also quite near the A14, but rather quieter. Most people may only associate Girton with the former ladies' college – and indeed one guide to East Anglia comments, with a touch of male chauvinism: 'Except for the lovely grounds and many pretty girls, there is nothing to go and see.' But there is also a fine parish church with a history going back to early Saxon times, and it is dedicated to St Andrew, with his tenuous similarity in name to the Celtic god Grannus. Christianity came to Girton in the eighth century, when Gretton was 'a settlement on the gravel'. Early in the eleventh century it was acquired by the Abbey of Ramsey, and if any links with earlier religions remain I could not find them. But St Andrew's was a good enough marker for Mr Keating, and it is a useful one for me too.

From Girton the line crosses the A14, touches Cambridge's northern outskirts and reaches the River Cam opposite Fen Ditton, as Mr Keating's 'Ditton' is better known today. I was told that a ferry used to ply here between Fen Ditton and the Plough Inn on the opposite bank, laden with thirsty students. But it was inclined to get overloaded on the return journeys after closing time, and I gather that after it had tipped over a couple of times, the service was suspended.

Rowers with the wind always behind them on the church weathervane at Fen Ditton.

Fen Ditton High Street still runs down to a field by the Cam, and then a footpath leads to the river bank, but that is as far as you get. The path is still used, however, when the annual Oarsmen's Service is held at the church and everyone processes to the river. This is said to be the only church outside Henley with a weathervane representing a coxed eight, but I regret it didn't function too well when I was there, and no matter how energetically the oarsmen rowed, or how hard the wind blew, it would not budge.

The weathervane shares the tower with a demon-like gargoyle, and I was told a dowser had found traces of Saxon and Roman remains in the churchyard. For an oarsman who is also a ley-hunter, this must be the ideal marker.

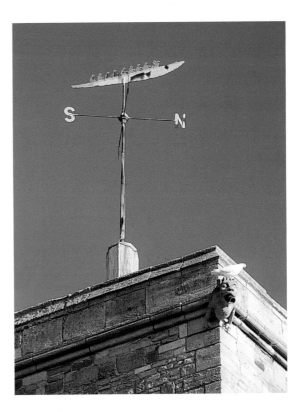

The line follows an uncommonly straight lane out of the village, parallel to the A14, then heads across country to Great Wilbraham – not to the parish church but to Wilbraham Temple. In the thirteenth century this was the local headquarters of the Knights Templar, who acquired the lordship of the manor and built the present church of St Nicholas. A century later Wilbraham Temple passed to their rivals, the Knights Hospitaller. The present Queen Anne house is still known as the Temple, but it is now privately owned and occupied. Maybe the Knights Templar took over the name, too?

Finally, the line reaches a more familiar marker, another of those moats, this time at Burrough Green. Like many of the others it is unremarkable, and perhaps it would be as well to leave moat country and

The real thing: rowing across the Cam – and along the line – to the local pub.

venture into markers new. How about an underground cavern?

The Ley Hunter's Companion does have another leyline in Cambridgeshire, starting at Westley Waterless and ending at Fowlmere, close to the Hertfordshire border. It was later rejected in Devereux's follow-up book, *The New Ley Hunter's Guide*, but if he had continued the line across the county boundary he would have come upon Royston Cavern. From there I found a line continuing into Hertfordshire that takes in a Bronze Age barrow cemetery, a tumulus on evocatively named Gallows Hill and a couple of ancient churches.

THE ROYSTON CAVERN LINE (12)

The cavern has always fascinated me, not only because of its uncertain history but also because of its bizarre position. You would normally look for mysterious underground caverns in fairly remote areas, but this one is right in the middle of Royston, under a busy crossroads. It is not a location I would normally want as a marker, but this is an ancient crossing of some significance. It is where the Roman Ermine Street crossed the prehistoric Icknield Way.

With a history linking periods so far apart, small wonder theories differ over the origin of the cavern underneath it. Some say it was the discreet retiring room of the Lady Roisia, who founded 'Roisia's-town'

in Norman times. Others maintain it was a secret headquarters of the Knights Templar. But it is also believed to date back much further, to the Iron Age and beyond.

It was discovered in 1742, when workmen were digging a hole for a post. It is bell- or bottle-shaped, with a narrow neck opening into a chamber some thirty feet high and seventeen feet across. These days you do not have to drop into it through the neck of the bottle; there is a winding passage which brings you in

Some of the strange carvings in Royston Cavern. Are they pagan or biblical?

lower down. Crude carvings were found on the walls, some pagan, some biblical. Was it a shrine to an earth god or a hermit's cell? But then, in 1852, an archaeologist dug out a depression in the floor and found fragments of iron, leather, bone and oak. That may sound like the remains of an early burial, but he said it meant the cavern originated as an ancient rubbish dump from a pre-Roman era. Sacred site or rubbish tip? I know which I prefer.

The line runs south-west from Royston alongside the Icknield Way, now the dual carriageway A505. It passes through a couple of barrows on Therfield Heath, the only Bronze Age cemetery in Hertfordshire. It shares the heath with a golf course, and it must sometimes be difficult to distinguish between barrows and bunkers, but these two are genuine enough.

The tumulus on Gallows Hill is some three miles further on. There is no sign of a gallows these days, but the clumps of trees on the skyline make a striking silhouette. The line continues to the secluded little village of Bygrave – so secluded that some 3-inch maps don't even show it. Its original name, Bygrafan, meant 'by the entrenchments', and the church stands in an area surrounded in pre-Roman times by banks and ditches. A fourteenth-century squire, converted them into moats, and the remains of one, still water-filled, adjoin the immaculate churchyard.

Nobody is quite sure of the church's original dedication, but it is called St Margaret's on the basis that a fair used to be held on St Margaret's Day, before Baldock became the main centre of population. Parts of it are twelfth century, but its most unusual feature was added about three hundred years later. Instead of a tower it has a narrow open-topped bell turret, like those minarets where mullahs call the faithful to prayer. I suppose the principle is much the same.

Parts of the outside walls have been cemented, which must have seemed a good idea at the time, but it does not enhance this otherwise picturesque little church. The interior, however, is unspoilt, from the remains of ancient wall paintings to the seventeenth-century hourglass on the pulpit. This was provided, either by wary churchwardens or by the rector himself, as a reminder of how long the sermon was lasting, so at least he kept it within the hour. In case he went on talking, the squire's pew used to be thoughtfully provided with a door leading to some steps to the road so that he could slip out discreetly when he had had enough.

The hourglass was functioning when Bygrave had a Huguenot rector, the Rev. Peter Fouillerade, who fled from France to escape persecution. A guidebook records that 'he preached his last sermon watching it while the sands of 1725 were running out'. It does not say if he finished on time, but I trust that even if he over-ran on that occasion, the squire stayed put. Like the pulpit and the hourglass, Peter Fouillerade's memorial stone still survives, not far away in the chancel.

This is a peaceful haven, but not all the incumbents kept it that way. According to the Assize Rolls, a fourteenth-century rector John Legat, with his chaplain and other supporters, went to the house of John de Walden, a member of the local aristocracy, and 'set about him, beat him furiously, and then killed him'. I hope it wasn't an argument over leylines.

From the backwater of Bygrave the line passes through the outskirts of Baldock to end at St Nicholas's Church, Norton. This was one of three parishes absorbed into Letchworth Garden City, but a new church was built in the 1960s to serve the built-up area of the parish, and the original old village around St Nicholas' has retained its rural flavour.

Norton's history goes back long before Saxon times; prehistoric remains have been found there. In 792 AD King Offa gave the manor of Norton to St Alban's Abbey, and they built the first church and the present one that succeeded it in the twelfth century. At that time it had two chapels, one dedicated to St Mary Magdalene, the other to St Andrew. If this was a vague gesture to the old gods, to keep away ill-fortune, it did not entirely work. In the fifteenth century one vicar was assaulted, another excommunicated (though later absolved), and of those who followed them one died, two resigned, two were deprived of their living and the seventh ran away – all within fifteen years.

Over the years St Nicholas's lost its two side chapels but gained a tower – in a rather unorthodox way. According to the guidebook, it was built separately from the church, then the nave was extended to join up with it. It would seem simpler to extend the nave first; was there some other reason, one wonders? Fortunately, the tower was correctly sited, and the nave was a perfect fit.

Above *A tranquil corner of Bygrave church*. Left: *Bygrave's bell tower looks rather like a minaret. Its purpose, after all is much the same.*

A memorial in the church also seems out of sequence. It records that a baby girl calledAnne Cole was born in September 1652 and died in February 1652 – apparently seven months earlier. And there are in fact a number of memorials around the country with a similar combination of dates. It used to occur before the calendar was altered in 1752. Until then each year started not on 1 January, but on Lady Day, 25 March, so February did indeed follow September. Perhaps it is just as well that not every strange puzzle from the past has such a logical explanation.

ESSEX

THERE is a delightful piece of leyline folklore – indeed, it may be true – that where leylines converge, deer will rut. I suppose the theory is that the combined energy currents in the earth generate activity in that part of the stag's body that is nearest to the ground. And presumably the longer the leylines, the stronger the currents and the livelier the deer.

In which case there is a site in Essex where they ought to enjoy themselves enormously. It is the junction of two lines, each of which is over sixty miles long. One runs west to east, from Luton to Clacton, the other north to south, from Thetford to the Thames estuary.

The snag is – and it is one of many snags about these leylines – they cross, as near as one can tell, at Rivenhall End crossroads. At the time these lines were reported to Alfred Watkins and published in *The Ley Hunter's Manual*, Rivenhall End was doubtless a quiet little village, where deer might safely relax. Today it lies by the A12 trunk road, one of the busiest in East Anglia, and instead of a country crossroads there is now a flyover to take the minor road across the dual carriageway. If a deer can feel romantic on a flyover, the leyline currents must be very strong indeed.

As I mentioned, there are *other* snags. These leylines, like the curate's egg, are only good in parts. After seventy years, some of the markers are unidentifiable, and those that can be located are not always in line. I gave up the struggle with the north–south line, but I did find enough existing markers on the Essex section of the Luton–Clacton line to form the basis for two much shorter ones. The first starts by Wallbury Camp, west of the M11 motorway, and ends some twenty miles away, at the renowned Rivenhall End crossroads – where deer may one day feel the urge to shed their inhibitions and live up to their legend. To encourage them, let us call it the Rutting Deer Line.

Great Braxted church.

42

THE RUTTING DEER LINE (13)

The original leyline in the *Manual*, contributed by a Miss E.M. Slader, went through Wallbury Camp itself, an Iron Age hill-fort set on a spur overlooking what is now the River Stort Navigation. 'The fort on the Stort' had banks and ditches enclosing an area of over thirty acres, which makes it a nice big target for a leyline. Even so, a straight line drawn through some of Miss Slader's other markers manages to miss it altogether.

That is the bad news. The good news is that, having passed the fort, the line continues down to the river, where a bridge and a lock could well have been a prehistoric crossing point. As it happens, the fort is on private land anyway, totally surrounded by trees, and I gather only a few of the earthworks survive. The river crossing is easily accessible, rather attractive on a

summer's day, and with a good view of the spur on which the hill-fort stands. As a leyline marker it is altogether more satisfying.

Miss Slader's line then goes through 'Little Hallingbury Camp', which I could not locate – it is not in the reference books – but the revised line passes through the south of Little Hallingbury parish, where three Celtic burial urns were discovered when gravel was being excavated. There were three Roman villas on the same site, and the present church of St Mary's contains a lot of Roman bricks and tiles.

Perhaps the village's greatest claim to fame is that it nearly got Charterhouse School. Thomas Sutton bought the Manor of Little Hallingbury in 1588 and intended to found a school and hospital there. His wife shared his interest in the project but died before if got off the drawing-board, and Sutton decided to found the school in London instead. However, he gave the Manor to the governors of Charterhouse, who are still patrons of the living, and any Brother of the Charterhouse has the right to be buried in a special section of the churchyard.

The revised line then crosses the M11 – no hint of any deer rutting here – and clips the corner of Monks' Wood, an evocative name but probably nothing more. Miss Slader's original line is about half a mile to the north, and her next marker is a place called Wollard's Ash. She does not explain if it commemorates a tree – or a cremation? Meanwhile the revised version passes through a moat at Broomshawbury, which may be more significant but is not a lot more exciting.

The two lines converge on the village of Ford End, but while Miss Slader's goes through the church and the ford, mine just goes through the ford, or where the ford used to be; a footpath still runs down to the river at this point. From here, my line joins Miss Slader's through three churches to Rivenhall End.

The first church is at Little Leighs, and she finds

Above: *An unexplained wall-painting in Fairstead church.*
Left: *The River Stort, which flows beneath Wallbury Camp.*

the name significant. 'Note the Little Leys Church,' she says, discreetly adjusting the spelling. But she may have a point. It was originally spelt Lees and Leez, so Leys could be another early alternative.

St John's Church was one of the first to be built after the Conquest, and in spite of an extensive restoration by the Victorians it still has some of its original Norman archways and windows. There is also an unusual effigy of a priest, carved from a block of oak, but it is the canopied arch in which it stands that would have been of more interest to Miss Slader, if she ever spotted it. There is no way of knowing, because Alfred Watkins' correspondents rarely gave any information about their leyline markers. The arch is carved with oak leaves and acorns, and two heads surrounded by foliage. The church guide points out that in the Decorated period 'the faithful representation of natural foliage prevailed' – but how about those heads? And what a pity that 'one of the most interesting monu-

ments in Essex', as the guide fairly describes it, should be tucked away behind the organ. The Victorians again, perhaps?

From here the line passes through Bishop's Hall Farm – which may be no more significant than Monks' Wood, but Miss Slader duly noted it – and on to St Mary's Church, Fairstead. This also has a feature that would have intrigued her. Among the medieval wall-paintings of biblical scenes and characters there is an incongruous human head with two horns. No one seems to have explained it – the church leaflet calls it 'a curious grotesque head' and leaves it at that. But a member of the local Earth Mysteries group told me that when she tried to photograph it, the camera would not function. She thought the battery had run down, but when she tested it outside it had recovered. In pagan folklore, can there be a camera-shy demon?

Miss Slader describes the next marker on the line as the 'un-named church', which sounds mysterious too, but she must have meant Faulkbourne church, dedicated to St Germanus. It is a pity she didn't discover this, because Germanus, before he was converted and became a bishop, was a great hunter, who had the unsavoury habit of hanging the heads of the animals he killed in the nearest tree. It is unlikely that the early Christians of Faulkbourne had this in mind when they dedicated their church, but Miss Slader would doubtless have noted this link with earlier offerings to the gods.

And so to Rivenhall End and the end of the Deer Rutting Line. Miss Slader's line does, in fact, continue, making a leap through marker-less countryside, to what she calls Mersey Island Beacons (again she has adjusted the spelling, but this time only a Liverpudlian ley-hunter could explain why), then Brightlingsea Ferry and St Osyth's Priory on the far mainland. Unfortunately, nobody at Mersea Island Museum has heard of any beacons, and the likely site of the now defunct ferry does not line up with the priory and the rest of her leyline. However, the island does have an ancient barrow and a moated church, which line up with a couple of other churches and some ancient salt workings on the mainland, to form a revised version.

THE MERSEA ISLAND LINE (14)

The line starts at Great Braxted church, a couple of miles south-east of the now familiar Rivenhall End. It is not easy to find, tucked away in a far corner of Braxted Park and a mile or so from the village itself. But it was not ever thus. There are traces of a Roman settlement where All Saints' stands, and that area continued to be the centre of the village until the 1820s. Then the church was isolated from its parishioners by Peter du Cane, the lord of the manor, when he built a high brick wall nearly five miles long to enclose 500 acres of parkland for his personal enjoyment. The villagers moved, leaving a 'ghost village', of which there is now little trace.

The church is generally kept locked, but one interesting feature is visible from outside, the carved head of a strange beast in a corner of the porch. The church leaflet ignores it, but I am sure Miss Slader would not.

St Nicholas's Church, Little Wigborough, is also about a mile from the village it serves, this time at the end of a long cul-de-sac through open country. You then walk through the front garden of Copt Hall. The two buildings stand isolated above the meadows and marshes that slope down to the channel between the mainland and Mersea Island. It is a noted area for bird-watchers.

The church is obviously old but there are few hints of its early history. Instead, on the wall of the tower, there is a bizarre relic of the First World War, a strut from a German Zeppelin, which was shot down not far away. The crew of twenty-one were able to walk away from it to neighbouring Peldon, where they were met by Special Constable Edgar Nicholas on his bicycle. Constable Nicholas, it seems, was unshaken by this encounter with a large party of airmen – and they took things pretty calmly, too. 'They asked the way to Colchester,' says a contemporary report, 'and he took them in charge.'

There is a postscript to this very British episode. Apparently a quarter of a million people came to see the wreckage of the Zeppelin, and the shrewd villagers went round with collecting boxes and raised a handsome £74 4s 10d for the Red Cross and other charities.

The Copt Hall estate is now owned by the National Trust, and it is possible to follow the Mersea Island Line down to the site of the ancient salt workings, opposite the island. But to get to the island itself you have to return to the main road and use the causeway, known as the Strood – making sure, incidentally, that you do not coincide with any of the higher high tides that make it impassable. It was thought the Strood was built by the Romans – it is, after all, very straight – but oak piles were discovered underneath it which date it about AD 700, so the Saxons should get the credit. It was probably built for the religious establishments that had already been on the island for many years.

Above: *The burial mound on Mersea Island.* Left: *This disconcerting stare greets visitors to Great Braxted church.*

A burial mound stands beside the road from the Strood to the village of East Mersea. It is about thirty feet high and 120 feet across, and when it was excavated in 1912 they found the centre was lined with tiles and contained a glass bowl holding the remains of a human body. Experts assume it was probably the grave of a local ruler, about the time the Romans arrived. Other remains found on the island show that it was inhabited as far back as the Bronze Age.

Among the later arrivals were the Vikings, who are thought to have built a major camp where East Mersea church, the final marker on the line, now stands. It was surrounded by a moat which enclosed some five acres, including a well; parts of the moat still survive.

This was probably the base from which the Vikings sent an invading army across to the mainland in the days of King Alfred, and the moated church of St Edmund the Martyr – another warrior king – has been a centre of military activity on more than one occasion since. During the Civil War it was occupied by Roundhead troops, and in the Napoleonic Wars it was occupied by a garrison in case of invasion. The massive tower with its armoured door would have been an excellent defence position.

This martial background may have influenced one of St Edmund's Victorian rectors, the Rev. Sabine Baring-Gould, to write his famous hymn, 'Onward Christian soldiers, marching as to war'. It became a universal favourite, but the same could not be said locally for its author. Some churches on leylines had such a special attraction that rectors stayed for half a century, but Baring-Gould left after only ten years, and apparently it was not a moment too soon – for his parishioners' too.

'In all ten years,' he wrote, 'I cannot say I liked the place or became attached to the people. The peasants were dull, shy, reserved, suspicious. I never managed to understand them, nor they me.' And in one of his books he went so far as to descibe the average East Anglian as 'a man of small reasoning power, moving like a machine, very slow in mind, only slightly advanced in the scale of things above the beast.' I hope he got off the island safely.

Other stories attached to this Angliaphobe rector may seem more promising to the seeker after leyline connections. It is recorded that he used to tell his children that a 'kelpie' lived in a ditch they had to pass on the way to church. It was an evil water spirit that enjoyed drowning small children and eating them. He also spoke of a ghostly orchestra in the church which groaned and squeaked during the hymns.

Alas, I am afraid that even Miss Slader would fail to detect a link with these mysterious manifestations. The kelpie was pure invention by this Victorian father to keep his children properly subdued, and the ghostly orchestra was just the wind howling in the outlet pipe of the church stove. But happily, St Edmund's has enough ancient connections without these embellishments, and this moated church makes a fitting end to the Mersea Island Line. As far as the East Anglian section is concerned, it is time to recall the other well-known hymn by Sabine Baring-Gould: 'Now the day is over ...'

KENT

LIKE many thousands of pilgrims before them, ley-hunters are inclined to converge on Canterbury if they find themselves in Kent, in the hope that leylines converge there too. The odds are in their favour. In addition to its long history, it has a number of ancient churches as well as the cathedral itself, all likely markers. *The Ley Hunter's Companion*, for instance, has a Canterbury ley that starts at Chartham church, a few miles to the south-west, passes through the cathedral and two city churches, and ends at Fordwich church, to the north-east.

However, for those of us who prefer to avoid the middle of busy cities, some alternative focal points are suggested in Alfred Watkins' *Ley Hunter's Manual*. Two of them are very well known, Minster church and Walmer Castle. Stick a pin in either of them, says Alfred, and a ruler will reveal 'several' leylines.

I tried it on both of them, but Alfred's ruler may have been a bit more flexible than mine — or distance was no object. I failed to find any within a reasonable range of twenty miles or so that had my minimum of five markers. Anyway I would have thought Walmer Castle was a rather suspect marker itself. It was one of the coastal forts built by Henry VIII in case of a French invasion, and I have never seen it suggested that he built them on prehistoric sites. Maybe Alfred knew something that most of us have missed.

His third recommendation, however, turned out to be a real winner, even though its name may be unfamiliar. Harbledown is a little village right on the edge of Canterbury, and in spite of the close proximity of such a famous neighbour it retains its own individual character.

And it deserves to do so, because its history goes back to prehistoric times when it was the junction of two great trackways, one from the west along the North Downs, the other from London and the north. There was a cluster of settlements around it, and the remains of probably the largest one, on Bigbury Hill, are still impressive. The Romans made Canterbury the main site instead of Bigbury, and Harbledown became a key point on the route linking the

Canterbury Cathedral.

Roman port of Richborough, with the rest of England. Much later, in medieval times, it was on one of the main pilgrimage routes to Canterbury.

The village has been left with two early Norman churches and a holy well. Alfred doesn't say which he had in mind as markers, but they provide a useful choice for ley-hunters looking for lines that avoid Canterbury.

I found one linking Harbledown with the Iron Age fort on Bigbury Hill. Beyond it the line reached another ancient earthwork in Perry Wood, and in the other direction it passed through the outskirts of Canterbury and ended at Fordwich church, which significantly is also on the leyline in *The Ley Hunter's Companion*. I was going to call mine the Harbledown Line, but Chaucer's pilgrims were familiar with the village under its local nickname. In 'The Manciple's Tale' they were told: 'Don't you all know where stands a little town, the one that people call Bob-up-and-Down, near Blean Woods on the way to Canterbury?' I am not too sure what the nickname meant, but if Chaucer thought it worth mentioning, that is good enough for me.

THE BOB-UP-AND-DOWN LINE (15)

Harbledown parish church may well stand on the site of a Roman temple. That is not just my view; the church guide says so. 'They were often built on hilltops and when converted to Christian use many were dedicated to St Michael, the killer of devils' – and a popular figure in leyline literature, because the devils he killed were portrayed as dragons. The church still has a visible link with those earlier days: a Mithraic carving on the wall of the Lady Chapel shows two bulls fighting, with the sun god apparently acting as a referee. Mithras was originally a Persian god, but the Romans adopted him and that is probably how he found his way to Harbledown.

Further down the hill there is another Norman church as a bonus – though the locals probably didn't

Above: *The pagan Mithraic carving in St Michael's Church, Harbledown, with the sun god watching two bulls fighting.* Left: *The Prince of Wales's holy well, highly regarded by the Black Prince.* Right: *'St Augustine's Tomb' in Fordwich church. It is actually Norman but may have had much earlier connections.*

think so at the time, because it was attached to a leper hospital. St Nicholas's Church was built about seventy years before St Michael's, and in spite of its connections it was still a great draw for the pilgrims heading for Canterbury, because it had two advantages over the parish church. It had a sacred relic of St Thomas and a holy well.

The well is still there, at the foot of the hill. It is set in an arched niche in the wall, and at the apex of the arch are carved the Prince of Wales's feathers, a reminder that this holy water was the favourite medicine of the Black Prince. It is said he regarded it so highly that he drank a flask of it each day. In spite of that he still died at an early age of an unpleasant disease – but at least it wasn't leprosy.

From Harbledown the line continues just north of Canterbury, to what is marked on the map with the symbol for 'church with spire'. Unfortunately, it turned out to be an elaborate Victorian chapel attached to the municipal cemetery. It certainly has a lofty spire, but the cemetery was consecrated only in the 1850s, and there was nothing much there before. It might be argued that the architect erected such an ostentatious landmark because he knew it was on a leyline, but that may be pushing it a bit.

The line then passes through an equally unproductive church on the A28 Margate road, but finishes up in the much more encouraging St Mary's Church at Fordwich. Since it featured in the *Companion* it has been made redundant, but it still has some of its treasures, and its pedigree goes back at least to the time of Edward the Confessor. The remains of a Saxon arch still survive in the tower above the present doorway.

'Perhaps the townspeople hurried into the tower with their household treasures,' the guidebook speculates romantically, 'when the Danes came plundering and burning up the estuary to sack Canterbury.'

It was not the Danes, however, but probably a tidal wave that undermined the church's foundations and gave the north side of St Mary's its slight tilt. Or perhaps it moved a little bit because it wasn't quite on the line. 'But, undaunted, the sturdy little church settled down again to carry on through the centuries,' says the guidebook, now really getting into its stride.

St Mary's great treasure is the Fordwich Stone, known locally as St Augustine's Tomb, a name for leyhunters to conjure with. Unfortunately, there is no evidence to connect him with the stone, which is actually Norman and dates from about 600 years after he died. Undeterred, the guidebook says, it is 'reasonable to suppose' it may have formed part of some saint's shrine, with sacred relics buried beneath it. Alternatively, one might say it was reasonable to

St Nicholas's Church, Harbledown.

it, the Penitent's Chair, but this time it seems they were on to a loser. Penitents, I am told, were never allowed to sit down. It was taken to Fordwich Town Hall for greater security. Nobody is sure of its history, but the guidebook gamely has a go. 'Did it come over in some Viking ship?' it ponders. 'Is it flotsam from some raider's wreck which drifted ashore to find sanctuary at last beside the Fordwich river?' Better still, could it have been used by St Augustine? The guidebook can have the last word. 'Who can say?'

Surprisingly, the *Ley Hunter's Companion* mentions none of this in its reference to Fordwich church, apart from saying it is mainly Norman with Saxon fragments. But it does come up with some information that makes the guidebook's lyrical approach seem very tame. 'In 1966,' it recalls, 'many witnesses saw a brilliantly lit egg-shaped UFO circle over Fordwich. Lights on the object changed from red to green, and it sounded "like a lathe".' St Augustine piloting a space-ship with port and starboard lights and a noisy engine, returning to check on his chair? Who can say …

Back in the less exotic pages of Alfred Watkins' *Ley Hunter's Manual* I found one more site in Kent to investigate. He mentions a group of three tumuli near the coast north of St Margaret's at Cliffe, and suggests a leyline from the middle one which passes through four churches, one called St Nicholas's and the others at West Langdon, Coldred and Shepherd's Well.

Again, Alfred's ruler and mine seem to operate, one might say, under different rules. I could not make any straight line go from any of the tumuli through all four churches – nor indeed did all four churches seem in line. For instance, a line through St Nicholas's and West Langdon does not go through either of the others. The best I could do was a line from the most southerly tumulus, nearest to the delightfully named Otty Bottom Cott. It misses St Nicholas's (which seems isolated on private land anyway) but passes through the site of Langdon Abbey, Coldred church, Shepherdswell church (its current spelling) and Broome House, which Alfred doesn't rate as a marker but mentions on his line.

suppose that local people in earlier times associated St Augustine with it because he was advised by Pope Gregory to erect churches on pagan sacred sites, and they knew – even though the guidebook doesn't – that this is what happened at Fordwich.

An ancient wooden chair, thought to be even older than the Stone, was found embedded in the wall behind the pulpit. Once again the locals had a name for

THE ST MARGARET'S BAY LINE (16)

Like Sandwich Bay, the coast here is largely occupied by golfers, and the tumuli are not exciting enough to risk their wrath. The remains of Langdon Abbey, however, are slightly more accessible. From the entrance to Langdon Abbey Farm I was able to see the grass-covered hummocks in a field by the farm buildings and remnants of ruined wall. The present 'Langdon Abbey' is out of sight beyond a gateway and obviously private.

St Pancras's Church at Coldred was locked, but happily this is one of the many Kent villages in which the local authority has provided an excellent information board on the green, which gives some basic history plus some extra titbits to gladden the heart of the frustrated ley-hunter.

According to Coldred's noticeboard, the church stands on the site of a fortified Saxon camp. It is mostly Norman with Saxon fragments, like many other Kent churches, but its foundations are said to be Roman, and they probably occupied the site first. Certainly, Roman remains have been found just outside the village.

Legend has it that St Augustine himself dedicated the original church to St Pancras. It adjoins Coldred Court Farm, originally an ancient manor house owned in Dover until the Reformation by the Maison Dieu Hospital.

All this is evidence of Coldred's long history, but its most significant feature for the ley-hunter is its name. Alfred was very keen on place names involving Cole or Cold, because he links them with the Celtic 'coel', an omen or belief, and 'Coelcerth', an omen of danger,

St Margaret's Bay, a popular starting point for ley-hunters.

beacon, bonfire. He says there is also a connection with tumuli and cairns, 'some solemn appurtenance of a religion now quite forgotten'. It all ties in with pre-historic sites on leylines and the beacons that lit them.

Add to that the position of the village, on one of the highest points in Kent and a good place for a beacon, plus the former local industry of charcoal-burning, and Alfred's cup in Coldred would be full. I hesitate to jog his arm, but the noticeboard also suggests the village was named after an eighth-century king of Mercia called Ceoldred, who helped the Kentish Men fight the Saxons. That rather spoils the link – unless of course he came from a family of beacon-lighters.

The present St Andrew's Church at Shepherdswell was dedicated only in 1863, but there was a church on the site in 944. Certainly the two yews in the church-yard are very ancient, perhaps a thousand years old.

Alfred may have hopefully adjusted the village's name to Shepherd's Well because in his view ancient wells were as significant as beacons. Unfortunately, the spelling on the noticeboard is Sibertswold, which suggests a rather different origin.

Never mind, I have a bonus for Alfred. He did not regard Broome House, just outside Barham, as a marker, perhaps because it was only built in the seventeenth century on what was, literally, a green field site. But many ley-hunters have a high regard for ghosts and secret tunnels – and Alfred may not have known that Broome House is reputed to have both.

It is currently a golf and country club, perhaps not the ideal atmosphere for ghostly appearances, but I heard about them from June O'Shaughnessy, who has worked at Broome House for many years and has delved into its history. It was built in the 1630s for Sir Basil Dixwell, one of the signatories to Charles I's death warrant, although the beheaded monarch is not among its spectral visitors. There is reputed to be a mysterious girl in a long dress and with plaited hair who wanders the upstairs rooms. A First World War soldier, still in his army greatcoat, is said to have been seen in what used to be the cellar and is now, perhaps appropriately, a bar known as 'Dizzy's'. And in the magnificent Great

Above: *Shepherdswell bell-cote.* Right: *One of the leafy faces in Shepherdswell church – a 'Green Woman'.*

Hall a ghostly butler moves majestically from the library to the reception desk – perhaps to check who is due for a scare tonight.

The Great Hall was restored and enlarged by Broome House's most famous owner, Lord Kitchener, with the unofficial help of a squad of Royal Engineers under his command. He made sure his guests knew what an important chap they were visiting: the Great

Hall is decorated with portraits of him in action, his coat of arms, his 'K.K.' monogram, and his appropriate motto: 'Thorough.'

But he was not sufficiently thorough, it seems, to have uncovered much information about the tunnels that existed under his property. These perhaps have a greater significance to the ley-hunter than do ghosts, because tunnel stories are sometimes linked with the supposed energy currents in leylines. There is a short tunnel from the main house to one of the outer buildings, and I was shown its narrow entrance. It didn't look very inviting. But more importantly there is also said to be a tunnel from Broome House to Barham church. If, indeed, the house is linked in this way with the church, it would make a possible leyline link with other churches that little bit more likely.

Incidentally, Kitchener designed two fountains in the gardens of Broome House, one with the water gushing from the beak of a mythical bird, the other decorated with nymphs and sea monsters, which all have a nice folklore flavour. The second fountain, in the rose garden, also has sculpted figures at each corner, described as 'young boys in pairs, wrestling, running, dancing, embracing …'. Another reference to pagan times, perhaps? According to June O'Shaughnessy and other students of Lord Kitchener's personal preferences, probably not.

That is the end of my St Margaret's Bay Line, but seventy years after Alfred Watkins included Coldred in his, it appeared again on another leyline – on the Internet. To many of us the Internet seems an even stranger phenomenon than leylines, but others seem to have got the hang of it, including ley-hunters, and their new improved leylines sometimes manifest themselves on the screen, if you know which buttons to press. I can't do it, but I know a man who can, and I have seen the results of their research.

I have to say that no matter how clever they are with computers, they don't seem quite as skilful with an old-fashioned ruler. There is, for instance, a ley which runs for some fifty miles from Eastbourne and through Bexhill and Hastings in Sussex – not my kind of rural ley-hunting area – to the remains of Sandown Castle on the Kent coast. This is the one that passes through Coldred, not through the church but the village pub. On my map, however, these do not line up with the next two markers, the remains of a chapel on St John's Farm near Swingfield Street and the White Gate crossroads.

That is the bad news. The good news is that the crossroads and the chapel ruins do line up with Coldred church, which is a rather more likely marker than the pub, and also with St Augustine's Church, Northbourne, instead of Sandown Castle. This, too, is a change for the better, because the castle, like its counterpart at Walmer, only dates back to Henry VIII, whereas St Augustine's dates back very nearly to St Augustine himself. So let us give him the credit for this revised line.

THE ST AUGUSTINE'S LINE (17)

There are ancient burial sites at Northbourne, which indicate it has been inhabited for nearly 5000 years. The Roman cemeteries found nearby seem almost modern in comparison. But its more important period was in the early seventh century, only a few years after St Augustine landed on the Kent coast five miles away.

In AD 618 King Edbald gave land at Northbourne to St Augustine's Abbey in Canterbury as a penance for marrying his stepmother, thereby thoroughly confusing relationships between other members of the family. On part of this land was built Northbourne Abbey, and close by it, in AD 640, the parish church of St Augustine. The abbey itself did not survive after the dissolution of the monasteries, and some years later its remains were incorporated into the manor house of Sir Edwin Sandys. That burned down in 1750, and the servants' quarters became what is now Northbourne Court.

Throughout all these misfortunes, the nearby parish church continued to function, and fragments of the first Saxon church can still be seen in the wall of the present one, nearly 1400 years later.

The most imposing feature of St Augustine's, and perhaps the most significant to ley-hunters, is its massive central tower. It was built as a village refuge in case of invasion, and its original entrance halfway up the tower is still visible. It had a beacon on top, perhaps continuing a practice dating back to a much earlier era, but instead of illuminating a marker on a prehistoric leyline the medieval beacon was part of a chain along the coast to signal any invasion. It was last lit in 1457, when the French attacked Sandwich, but the tower served a similar purpose in 1940, when an observer kept watch from the parapet to act as spotter for a field gun below.

From here the line runs to Coldred, where it crosses the St Margaret's Bay Line. It is perhaps a pity that this does not happen at the Carpenter's Arms, which would be a convivial meeting place, but the church has good leyline credentials, and like a much later 'St Pancras', it seems an appropriate junction for lines to meet.

After Coldred the St Augustine Line joins the Internet version, passing through the chapel ruins on St John's Farm and the White Gate crossroads. It ends on Tolsford Hill, which fortunately has a number of tumuli to choose from and both lines pass through one – though not necessarily the same one. These last three markers are not too exciting, but they round off a convenient little line of some fifteen miles.

The Internet version continues across the border into Sussex, but before we leave Kent I found another line on the Internet which is too tempting to ignore because it ends at Pluckley, 'the most haunted village in England'. So that is where I shall start.

St Pancras's church, Coldred – like a much later St Pancras, an appropriate junction for lines.

THE HAUNTED VILLAGE LINE (18)

According to legend – and to some of the more imaginative villagers with an eye to the tourist trade – Pluckley has such a large population of ghostly residents that it makes the average haunted house on a fairground ride seem like a rest home. They range, it is said, from a gypsy woman who fell asleep smoking her pipe and burned herself to death, to a highwayman who was pinned to a tree by the sword of an intended victim. Down at the disused brickworks there is a 'screaming man', who had good reason to do so – he fell into a revolving mixing trough filled with knives. Up at the Black Horse Inn there is the ghost of a girl who was killed by a ball in a skittle alley. And just when you think it is safe to go out in the street, a phantom coach may hurtle by.

Inevitably, in such an apparition-packed environment, the parish church of St Nicholas has its share of restless spirits. The Dering family were squires of Pluckley for thirty generations, and it would be surprising if they were not represented. Sure enough, while the White Lady Dering lingers among the remains of their burned-out mansion, the Red Lady Dering is roaming the churchyard in search of her unbaptized child. Instead, she may encounter the 'smiling monk' among the tombstones; he was executed at Tyburn but manages to stay cheerful.

These manifestations are not mentioned in the church guide, but I am sure ley-hunters would consider them significant. They would also note that the name of the village is derived either from 'pluke', a plough, and 'ley', a pasture, or from 'Pluccan's leach', Plucca's clearing. Either way, the second syllable must be encouraging.

What the guide does tell us is that the church dates back to Saxon times, and the present building is thirteenth century. Its unusual feature is the font, carved with coats of arms, one of which is disconcertingly described as 'three left bloody hands'. It is not a

Pluckley churchyard, the most haunted area of 'England's most haunted village'.

reminder of another gruesome death but a rather painful pictorial pun, or rebus. A local manor is called Malmains. Think of the French for 'bad' and 'hands', and you've got it.

St Nicholas's marks the northern boundary of the Weald of Kent, and there is a splendid view of it from the churchyard (if you can get Lady Dering and the smiling monk to move over). It makes an impressive start to the line, which heads off down the hill to Fir Toll, the next marker on the Internet ley. This would seem to be just a road junction flanked by new houses, with no sign of a fir or a toll, though there is a clump of trees on the central triangle. My hopes rose when I spotted a bright circular object glinting in the branches, but it turned out to be a convex mirror to help drivers leaving the gateway opposite.

The Internet ley seems to rely rather heavily on road junctions, because that is all I could find at the next marker, named Middle Quarter. Its only feature seemed to be its name. Middle Quarter lies south of Further Quarter and east of Stede Quarter. Logically there should be a fourth one to make up the set, but the map is quite merciless: it gives no Quarter.

My faith in the Internet choice of markers was not strengthened when I found that the next one, New House Farm, was apparently just another farm, but 'St Michael's (west well)' sounded more promising. St Michael's turned out to be not just a church, but the name of the village, and very unusually it had acquired that name by an Act of Parliament.

Originally it was called Boreside – perhaps because King Charles went boar-hunting in the area and the village was the only safe 'hide' for the boars. It had no church, and any services were conducted in a wheelwright's shop. But in the 1860s a local squire, Seaman Beale (not a sailor: it was actually his name), built a school and a church for this growing community – and for the benefit of his son, who happened to be the curate.

The church of St Michael and All Angels was consecrated in 1863, and the village adopted its name perhaps as a thank-you to Seaman Beale – or perhaps as a tribute to St Michael, slayer of dragons and a popular

Above: *The river at Castle Toll, on the Kent–Sussex border, the site of a Roman fortress.* Left: *St Nicholas's Church, Pluckley.*

saint among ley hunters. However, that hardly qualifies the church as being on an ancient site, and although there used to be a village pond – it was filled in to provide a site for the village hall – I could find no trace of a 'west well'.

From here the Internet led me to Cold Harbour Farm, no doubt selected as a marker because of its name – anywhere beginning with 'Cold' is welcomed by the ley-hunter, for reasons explained earlier at Coldred. I was interested to find that the Internet line also goes through Friezingham Farm, but it is not the temperature that counts.

After two crossroads, two farms and an unhistoric church, my faith in the Internet was at last restored with its next marker, Castle Toll at Newenden. The village itself has a fascinating history, not least because it claims that the first recorded game of cricket was

played here in 1300, during a visit by its earliest recorded fan, King Edward I. For non-cricketing ley-hunters, however, Castle Toll is rather more interesting. This knoll overlooking a tributary of the River Rother is thought to be all that remains of the Roman town and fortress of Anderida, built on the site of an earlier earthwork covering nearly twenty acres. A more recent theory is that it was the Saxon fort of Eopeburnen, one of King Alfred's strongholds.

Whichever version is true – and perhaps they both are – Castle Toll makes a convincing end to the fourteen-mile Haunted Village Line, just as it reaches the county boundary. The Internet ley continues through Sussex to Lord's Rock at Bexhill, but the markers along its route are mostly crossroads or farms, and the last section is through the suburbs of Bexhill, not renowned for its antiquities (unless, as its unkind detractors might say, you include the residents). There is nothing, in fact, to match Castle Toll – so let's quit while we're winning.

SUSSEX
AND SURREY

IF ley-hunters want an appropriate emblem to reflect the unanswered questions that surround leylines, they could well turn to Sussex and adopt the Long Man of Wilmington, the 200-foot hill figure on the South Downs. No one knows who he is supposed to represent, how old he is or why he was put there in the first place. As a result, he has generated an assortment of theories and conjectures – and, appropriately for a Long Man, plenty of tall stories, too. Notice any similarity with leylines?

But the most obvious link is what he is holding. Those staves have had many different explanations. They could represent the doors of the underworld being opened or perhaps the gates of Heaven being shut. More mundanely, they may have been a pair of spears, or a rake and a scythe, from which the blades have long since disappeared. Or they may have been standards held by a Roman soldier. More logically, in view of the proximity of nearby Wilmington Priory, they may be walking sticks carried by a pilgrim.

But to Alfred Watkins and his ley-hunters they can mean only one thing. These are the staves used in prehistoric times to line up all those 'old straight tracks, which he called leys, and the Long Man himself is a 'dod-man', one of those early road surveyors.

It is, therefore, not surprising that *The Ley Hunter's Companion* features him in its only Sussex leyline. Unlike the Long Man, the line that goes through him is unusually short, a mere two miles, and the *Companion* very fairly observes that it is not claimed to be the best. Thus encouraged, I put my rule on the line of the ley and gave it the faintest of wiggles to see where it went.

Fortunately, the area in which it starts, south of the Long Man, is liberally sprinkled with tumuli, and the ruins of Wilmington Priory to the north of it cover quite a substantial area, as indeed does the Long Man himself. So I found that the wiggle extended the original ley for another five miles to an attractive alternative marker, Michelham Priory.

The Long Man of Wilmington:
heavenly gatekeeper, medieval pilgrim or leyline surveyor?

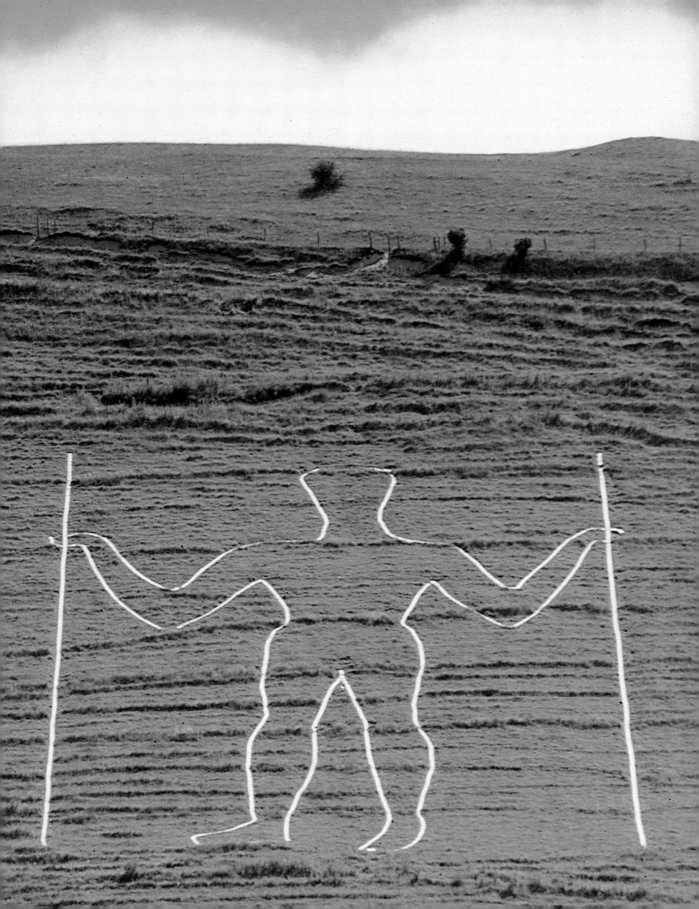

The Longer Long Man Line (19)

The *Companion* ley starts from a barrow in the heart of Friston Forest, not an easy place to penetrate nor an easy marker to find. There is a long barrow on the map to the west of the forest, which is more accessible, albeit none too exciting – just a useful alternative marker to start off the longer line. Much more interesting is the area the line passes through next. Windover Hill is one of the best stocked archaeological sites in Sussex. There are Bronze Age barrows scattered all over it, humps that are thought to be refuse tips from Stone Age flint-mines, and running across the hill is a steep terraced track, which probably dates from the Romans.

One of the largest round barrows, 135 feet across, 'apparently contained a cremation in an urn, placed in a pit under a pile of flints,' according to *The Guide to Prehistoric England.* The *Companion* ley passes through it; mine goes through a more modest barrow nearby.

Both lines then descend the hill to the Long Man, passing through slightly different parts of his anatomy. There is no cause for embarrassment, however, because the Long Man is not as generously endowed as the famous Cerne Abbas Giant; in fact he is not endowed at all. The *Companion* suggests that when it was cleared of undergrowth by the Victorians and transformed from the Green Man into the Long Man, its outline was marked out by an antiquarian 'of somewhat puritanical taste' – so we'll never know what we may be missing.

The rest of the Long Man is clear enough, but no one knows whether it is the outline of a giant who fell down the hill, or a Viking god, or a Roman hero, or even a prehistoric skier who has lost his skis as well as his other equipment. I rather like the theory that the Long Man was the work of commercially minded monks, who wanted to attract wealthy pilgrims to the excellent accommodation they were offering at the priory nearby. Was it, in fact, an enormous medieval Bed & Breakfast sign – or is it really Alfred Watkins' original Dod-man? I just don't know.

Both lines then pass through Wilmington Priory itself, but while the *Companion* ley goes right over the crypt, mine only clips the edge of the ruins. I hope that still counts. Certainly the whole site must be very ancient, probably much older than the priory, which was built by the Benedictines in the twelfth century. It was seized by Richard II in 1380 and closed down about thirty years later – so for once no one can blame Henry VIII.

Later it became a farmhouse, and tales were told of hauntings and other strange happenings. Then it was taken over by the Sussex Archaeological Trust, which turned it into an agricultural museum; I imagine that soon put a stop to such goings-on.

The *Companion* leyline ends at Wilmington church, which is close by, but mine misses the church and

continues to Michelham Priory. It is near the former home of the notorious political wheeler-dealer Horatio Bottomley, who finished up in jail.

The Augustinian monks would not have appreciated having such a character on their doorstep, but by the time he arrived they had long since gone. They did last longer than their Benedictine brethren at Wilmington, but inevitably Henry VIII caught up with them in the end.

Gilbert d'Aquila, Lord of Pevensey, built the priory in 1229. It stands on a bend of the Cuckmere River, which provides it with a very splendid moat, a luxury not usually associated with priories, but it makes Michelham all the more convincing as a ley marker. The massive gatehouse that looms over the moat, looking more like a castle keep than the entrance to a religious house, was built rather later, about the time that Richard II was taking over the priory at Wilmington. Maybe the monks of Michelham were determined not to share that fate.

Like Wilmington, however, their priory finished up as a farmhouse, and like Wilmington it is now run by the Sussex Archaeological Trust as an agricultural museum, but instead of displaying old farm implements it has a working watermill, a forge and a wheelwright's shop. Its origins are not forgotten. On its 750th anniversary in 1979, the flagpole on the gatehouse proudly displayed the standard of Gilbert d'Aquila. Ley-hunters may be disappointed to know that it did not feature a dragon or a Green Man, just a red eagle – but you can't have everything.

Another ancient site in Sussex which has always fascinated me is Chanctonbury Ring, that dramatic circle of trees on Chanctonbury Hill – although, alas, many of them were brought down in the 1987 gales. Like the Long Man, it is conveniently close to the long-distance South Downs Way. The clump of trees marks the site of an Iron Age hill-fort, and, more significantly for the ley-hunter, the Romans put a small temple in the centre of it.

Chanctonbury does not get a mention in the *Companion* or in Alfred Watkins' books, and when I

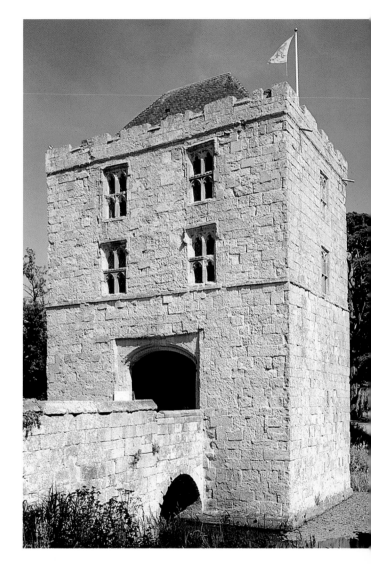

Above: *The gatehouse of Michelham Priory and its ancient moat.* Left: *An ancient wall carving in Wilmington*

tried the ruler on it I could understand why. There is a distinct shortage of churches and castles up there on the South Downs, and the few barrows all seem to be in the wrong places. But there are some impressive indentations called cross-dykes, which might have some earlier significance, and they offer a conveniently broad target for the ley-hunter. So here we go.

THE CHANCTONBURY RING LINE (20)

The line starts to the west of Chanctonbury, from the cross-dyke on Barnsfarm Hill. It goes through a tumulus and across another cross-dyke, and then reaches Chanctonbury Hill.

The famous ring of trees was planted in 1760 by a youthful Charles Goring, whose family owned the hill. The fort was actually much larger than the clump of trees, covering about four acres, and the bank and ditch that protected it still surrounds them. He chose to plant beeches, which may have put off ley-hunters, who attach more significance to Scotch firs. Perhaps firs would have been more used to the strong salt-laden winds that sweep across the hill, but Goring nurtured his trees carefully and lived long enough to see them mature. He wrote a grateful little verse:

> *Oh! Could I live to see the top*
> *In all its beauty dressed.*
> *That time's arrived, I've had my wish,*
> *And lived to eighty-five.*
> *I'll thank my God that gave such grace*
> *As long as e'er I live.*

As the trees grew, strange stories grew with them. It was generally believed that they were uncountable – which was just as well, because according to one legend anyone who succeeded might encounter the ghosts of the Roman soldiers who manned the fort and worshipped at the temple. Other manifestations include the sound of thudding hooves, as invisible horsemen ride by, and a white-bearded Druid searching for something he forgot a thousand years ago. It used to be frequented by witches, too, but if you are really looking for trouble, walk backwards round the Ring at midnight on Midsummer Eve. The Devil will appear and offer you a bowl of porridge, but if you eat it he will take your soul. There is no such thing as a free breakfast.

Above: *Chanctonbury Ring, the scene, according to legend, of many strange manifestations.* Right: *Poynings church, tucked away beneath the evocatively-named Devil's Dyke.*

With all these weird tales attached to it, coupled with the eeriness of the Ring as darkness falls, small wonder that it makes quite a distinctive ley marker. As a bonus, close by is a rare example of an ancient dewpond, one of a handful on the chalk hills of southern England. These man-made pits were lined with flints and stones first, then a layer of straw and, finally, a coating of clay. Once they had filled with rainwater they seldom dried out. The age of this one is uncertain, but they can date back to Neolithic times.

From here the line goes through a sewage works (I don't think Neolithic man had thought of those), just misses a permanent Scout camping site near the oddly named Small Dole, and ends at Holy Trinity Church, Poynings, under the shadow of Devil's Dyke. This great cleft in the Downs, so it is said, was another work of the Devil. He was digging this trench so the sea could flood the Weald, when an old lady appeared holding up a candle behind a round sieve. By a happy chance, a cock decided to crow at the same moment. The Devil saw the circle of light, heard the cock and thought the sun was rising, so he made an excuse and left.

A great story, but difficult to tie in with a leyline. Poynings church, however, is rather different. A wooden Saxon church is believed to have stood there first, and like many other Saxon churches it may well have been built on a pagan sacred site. The Norman church that succeeded it gets a mention in the Domesday Book, and the present building goes back to 1369, built by the lord of the manor, Michael de Ponyngges. He and his wife are buried beneath it, and their coats of arms are carved over the porch and the east window. It is sad to think that if the old lady with the candle and sieve had failed to turn up in time and the Devil had finished his trench, Poynings church would have been the first to go.

Surrey is not the most encouraging county for ley hunters. *The Ley Hunter's Companion* ignores it altogether, and Alfred Watkins can offer only a rather depressing line through the London suburbs.

I had higher hopes, however, of another leyline I found on the Internet, contributed by some enthusiastic students at the University of Surrey. They reckoned that four leylines crossed on their campus, which is on Stag Hill, just outside Guildford. 'There is no known prehistoric site on the hill,' they admit, 'despite its suggestive name, and the site of the crossing-point is unmarked today.'

I am not sure why they thought the name suggestive, but it certainly is to me. Remember that delightful theory I quoted earlier, that leyline crossings are favourite places for deer to mate? Hence, perhaps, Stag Hill. It might be promising.

THE STAG HILL LINE (21)

The line starts at Byfleet, where, according to a drawing made over a hundred years ago, a large mound stood against the side of the thirteenth-century church, carrying a staircase to a private gallery. Large mounds near churches, with or without a staircase, always delight a ley-hunter.

Wisley church, the next marker, has a stone by the porch, 'said by some to be a meteorite but more than likely a sarsen stone'. This is another plus point. Sarsen stones, which are a kind of pulverized sandstone from prehistoric times, were associated by the early Christians with pagan worship – 'saresyn' has the same origins as Saracen, and meant heathen. The line, reported the students, goes right through the stone.

So far so good. In fact, very good. But their next marker is Newark Priory, an Augustinian house of the twelfth century, and according to my ruler the line skirts the edge of the ruins. However, the priory buildings may have extended further than the ruins; we could still be in business. Somewhere between Newark and Guildford – they don't say exactly where – they found 'a striking hilltop clump of Scots Pines'. I failed to spot it on the map, but I am sure it is there.

Once the line had gone beyond Stag Hill into quieter countryside I found the last two markers, the churches at Shackleford and Peper Harow. St Mary's Church, Shackleford, is indeed on the line, and very handsome it is too, designed by George Gilbert Scott. But Scott was a Victorian architect, so the church was built in the nineteenth century. The man who paid for it, the Rev. Buttermere, became its first rector. Until then Shackleford was part of the parish of Godalming and had no church of its own, so there was no earlier church on that site. The students did their best to explain why it was on the leyline. 'We feel there must be an element of subconscious siting here,' they observe bravely.

In the same optimistic vein, I could note that the church contains carvings of wild flowers and plants, so having subconsciously chosen the site of the church on a leyline, perhaps Scott subconsciously chose decorations for it that could be reminiscent of pagan nature worship. He actually designed more than 700 churches, plus the Foreign Office, and I wonder if the students could discover how many have floral carvings and are thought to be on leylines. If they found the Foreign Office qualifies, and we ever get a Foreign Secretary called Dodman, who walks with two sticks, their cups would surely be full. But so far as Shackleford church is concerned, I fear that – to change the metaphor – they are on a losing wicket.

The line ends on a rather more convincing note, however. St Nicholas's Church, Peper Harow, is up a drive to what used to be the manor house, and the entrance gate is clearly marked 'Private', with no indication that the church is up there too. But even from the outside it is obviously a lot older than Shackleford church, with what looks like a Norman archway over the door. There was indeed a church here before 1311 – but beware of drawing conclusions from that archway. The whole place was 'restored' in the nineteenth century by Augustus Pugin, who mixed his usual imitation-Gothic style with various other periods, including a 'Norman' arch over the chancel. The nave is 'Early English', the chancel itself is 'Decorated', and he added a medieval-style mortuary chapel to confuse visitors still further.

In the seventeenth century the Peper Harow estate was acquired by the Brodrick family, who later took the name of Midleton, and the church became their family chapel, until the last earl died after the Second World War, leaving no heirs – both his sons were killed in 1945. The church is full of their family memorials, but there is also an unusual one to Bridget, wife of Robert Holdsworth. 'She had a grievous fitt of the stone, and voided one in weight near two ounces on July 12th 1724.' Her relatives obviously felt they should put this achievement on permanent record.

Out in the churchyard there is a less clinical memorial to Elizabeth Sheridan, who died aged only thirteen months. She lies beneath a heart-shaped grave, and a carved angel stands guard, 'made for my sweet Elizabeth by her loving mother'.

Adjoining the churchyard is an elaborate sixteenth-century granary, which looks even more imposing than the church itself, and the former manor house round the corner makes an impressive picture too. This peace-

Above: *The 'Norman' archway at Peper Harow, actually a Pugin imitation – to confuse ley-hunters?* Left: *The sarsen stone outside Wisley church, which is associated by some with pagan worship.*

ful setting seems a lot more than fifteen miles away from the start of the Stag Hill line, alongside the M25 – and it provides an attractive end to this chapter too.

HAMPSHIRE

AKE a cathedral city with a good sprinkling of ancient churches, add a large prehistoric camp to the north and a hill-fort covering twenty-three acres to the south, and it would be an unkind desk-ruler that failed to produce a straight line going through some part of the cathedral, the camp and the hill-fort, and one or two churches too.

The Ley Hunter's Companion has an excellent example, with a couple of barrows for good measure. It starts at Tilbury Ring, the prehistoric camp, passes through St Bartholomew's Church and the site of Hyde Abbey in Winchester, before clipping the eastern tip of the cathedral, and finishes up at the Iron Age hill-fort on St Catherine's Hill.

Paul Devereux added an intriguing footnote when he included the line again in his *New Ley Hunter's Guide* fifteen year later. He recalled that William Wykeham, founder of the college, decreed that twice daily the scholars should ascend St Catherine's Hill, and they should do so 'in an orderly line'. Says Mr Devereux: 'This was perhaps, just perhaps, some fragmentary memory of this alignment (the leyline). Wykeham was, after all, the king's surveyor.'

In Alfred Watkins' *Ley Hunter's Manual* I found an interesting alternative, which avoids going near the centre of this busy city, something with which I entirely agree. A Major Tyler contributed two possible leylines, each of six churches, intersecting near a ford on the River Itchen, where the old church of Itchen Stoke once stood. One ley starts at Kingsworthy, just to the north of Winchester, the other passes through St Cross, in the southern outskirts.

I checked Major Tyler's leys on the map. They were indeed straight, and for much of their routes they followed the attractive valley of the Itchen. They seemed my kind of leylines – and yes, I was Itchen to go.

Old Alresford church with its 'knobbly' tower.

THE ITCHEN VALLEY (KINGSWORTHY) LINE (22)

There must have been a time, not too long ago, when King's Worthy – as they like to spell it locally – was a delightfully peaceful village, but these days St Mary's Church stands within a triangle of three busy roads,

one of which is the M3 motorway. I therefore admire the honesty of those who designed the splendid panel in the porch, depicting the more attractive old houses in the village, because they have not ignored the changes around them and the motorway bridge looms at the top of the panel.

St Mary's has changed too since the Normans built it, and only the original tower remains. There is still a Norman doorway, but these days the best view of it is from inside the boiler-house. The church was 'restored' three times by the Victorians, who added a six-sided vestry with that final Victorian touch, a replica Gothic chimney. If there were any links with earlier days I failed to notice them, but if you have had any problems with the parcel post you can go and scowl at the memorial to Lord Eversley, who founded it.

With great respect to St Mary's, I rather wish the line started from her sister church of St Swithun at Headbourne Worthy, just down the road – a delightful little Saxon church, 'set within a noble woodland deity of graceful trees', as the church leaflet describes it – an interesting choice of phrase to a ley-hunter in search of an early pagan connection. It is encircled by the moat-like waters of Hyde Bourne, another bonus point for a ley marker.

St Swithun's is thought to date from the time of King Canute in the early eleventh century, and amazingly the original rood still survives – probably because it is carved into stone instead of being made of wood. It did get badly mutilated in the sixteenth century, but the outline of Christ on the Cross with Mary and John on each side is still quite clear. Above Christ's head the hand of God is emerging from a cloud.

The rood is not where you might expect it. The carving is on what used to be the outside west wall until the vestry was built onto it, largely to protect the rood from the weather. The wind and rain are not the only threats to St Swithun's; it has also had problems

Above: *The ancient river crossing at Itchen Stoke, where the line crosses it, too.* Left: *Kingsworthy as it used to be (except for the road bridge) as shown on the panel in the church porch.*

from below. The setting of the church is idyllic, but it is very boggy too, and in 1910 they actually called in a professional diver to advise how to strengthen the foundations. His advice must have been good, because it stands there still – and although it is not on this leyline, it deserves to be on another.

The line actually heads east from St Mary's to Easton, a village of pleasant thatched cottages and a late Norman church. The Victorians restored it, but in this case in its original style, and experts say the water-leaf capitals are outstanding, but I was more impressed by a memorial to a lady called Agatha Barlow. If indeed a leyline runs through Easton it must have imbued Mrs Barlow's family with a very strong religious bent, because all her five daughters married clergymen, and all five sons-in-law became bishops. St Mary's Church, Avington, the next on the leyline, is very different from the previous two. It is a splendid Georgian church, paid for by the then lady of the manor, Margaret, Marchioness of Caernarvon. But as the lengthy epitaph on her monument notes: 'It pleased God to remove her to a better world a few months before it was begun.'

The French-style parish church at Itchen Stoke, built away from the line – and redundant.

The good news for ley-hunters is that there was a Saxon church on the same site – 'an old low building, dark and incommodious for the parishioners, ruinous and decayed,' according to the application to knock it down. It was in the Domesday Book, and the land was granted by the Saxon King Edgar to the Priory of Winchester as far back as AD 961, so it has impeccable religious credentials.

When the new church was built, nothing of the old one survived, but St Mary's has been untouched since and remains an unspoilt product of the eighteenth century, with high box pews (some still equipped with wig or hat pegs on the walls above), a three-decker pulpit, a musicians' gallery and the arms of George III above the font. The barrel organ in the gallery can still play over thirty hymn tunes.

From here the line continues along the river to Itchen Stoke, where it crosses the other Itchen Valley Line. The original church did not stand on the main road like the present one, which is an incongruous building based on the church of Sainte Chappelle in Paris. Opposite this is Water Lane, an ancient track running down to what used to be an important ford on the Itchen, where the original settlement lay. Nothing remains of the earlier church except an overgrown churchyard beside the lane, and the ford has been replaced by a footbridge, the start of a popular riverside walk.

I can't help wondering whether the later churches would have fared better if they, too, had been built down Water Lane on the leyline, because they have not had an entirely happy history. Lord Ashburton, a nineteenth-century squire, gave the new site and had the old church pulled down, but its successor lasted only thirty-five years.

In 1857 a new parson arrived, the Rev. Charles Conybeare, who complained that the new church was cold and damp – in spite of its elevated position above the river – and announced that rather than repair it he wanted a new one. He had the money, his brother was an architect, and the squire didn't seem too bothered, so down came the church and up went the new one, but because of high costs it is redundant.

Finally, the leyline goes to the churches at Bishop's Sutton and Ropley. It runs alongside a better known line, the Mid-Hants Railway, which was closed in the 1970s but is now run privately and successfully as the famous Watercress Line.

THE ITCHEN VALLEY (ST CROSS) LINE (23)

Major Tyler's second line in the *Manual* starts at Holybourne church, which unfortunately is on the far side of the busy town of Alton and anyway makes the line rather long, so I prefer to start at the second church he names, St Andrew's at Medstead – not least because some ley-hunters associate its name with the Celtic god Grannus. The theory, as I have mentioned earlier, is that the names sound similar, so pagan worshippers wouldn't notice the difference.

It is rather a bizarre conception, but it is almost matched by the story behind one of the church bells at Medstead. Apparently the local cricket team had an away fixture at West Meon, and one of the players spotted a bell lying in a farmyard near the ground. He suggested it should be awarded to the winning team, and rather surprisingly the West Meon team agreed. Medstead won the match, carried the bell home in triumph, and it now hangs in the church tower, along with two others acquired in more orthodox ways.

The other curious feature of St Andrew's is an unusual stone bracket beside the south door. The church leaflet agrees it seems very ancient – 'more like fourteenth century French work than anything English' – but it cannot explain how it got there.

For ley-hunters it's interesting because of the foliage carved on it, which always provokes thoughts of earlier forms of worship. On the other hand, is it possible that a Medstead team of petanque-players was playing in France, saw the bracket in a farmyard and won that too?

New Alresford on the River Itchen is not all that new, founded in about 1200 when Bishop de Lucy of Winchester dammed the river and laid out one of the country's first 'new towns', mainly, one gathers, to obtain the rents from the building plots. Old Alresford, on the other hand, is very old indeed, and that is where

The curious leaf-covered bracket in Medstead church; its purpose is obscure.

the leyline goes from Medstead, to St Mary's Church. The church itself is not immediately encouraging to the ley-hunter. It is an eighteenth-century building of red brick, remarkable only for the rather jaunty stone balls perched on the four pinnacles of the tower, like balls on the noses of performing seals. However, 'there is much to suggest,' as the church leaflet nicely puts it, that the site has been a place of worship for over 1000 years. Indeed, there is a local legend that after a victory over the Danes, the Saxons erected a shrine to the Virgin Mary on this site, and her name is retained.

Dr John Hoadley, the rector who built the present St Mary's, left a curious little legacy behind as well as the new church. A memorial he erected to his housekeeper, Anne Davenport, features a dog with a face that looks strangely human – and female. I wondered hopefully if this might be a link with some obscure pagan animal god, but the church guide makes a rather different suggestion. Is it the face of Anne herself, 'good friend and faithful servant'? I doubt she would appreciate the comparison, but the rector might have had a whimsical sense of humour. Perhaps he was also responsible for perching those balls on the tower.

This small but sincere memorial
of his good friend and faithful servant
Mrs ANNE DAVENPORT spinster:
was erected by Dr IOHN HOADLY Rector of this Parish.

She was the youngest daughter of the Rev Mr Basil Davenport,
Vicar of Broadhinton in Wiltshire:
Born Iuly 24. 1705,
Died May 23. 1760,
And was buried in the Church-Yard,
Near the south-east corner of this Chancel

Outside the church is a Portland stone sundial, which would have been of particular help to much earlier leyline travellers, because a plate on it explains the mysteries of solar time, and the sundial itself is said to be accurate to thirty seconds. From the churchyard there is a splendid view westwards along the river valley and the line of the ley towards Itchen Stoke. In the foreground are some of the beds that gave the nearby Watercress Line its name.

After crossing the other leyline at Itchen Stoke this one continues to St Cross Hospital, the oldest almshouse in England, founded by King Stephen's brother, Bishop Henry de Blois, in 1136. As the line goes through it, I assume he chose a site with an even earlier religious significance.

The Hospital chapel has a couple of odd features to catch the ley-hunter's eye. One of the windows in the north transept is decorated with an unusual pattern of bird beaks, which I am sure Alfred Watkins could find a theory for; and talking of bird beaks, take a closer look at the lectern. It has the standard body of an eagle, but a rather peculiar head. Was it just the work of a carver who was not very good at eagles? No, the authoritative *Blue Guide to Churches* confirms my first impression. It is undoubtedly the head of a parrot. I wonder if Alfred would find a theory to fit that.

The almshouses were built to accommodate thirteen old men and provide enough dinners every day for a hundred more. Bishop Beaufort extended it three centuries later to include fifteen members of his Order of Noble Poverty, but the free dinners continued. Needy ley-hunters will be glad to know that travellers can still claim the Wayfarer's Dole at the porter's lodge; a piece of bread and a mug of beer. That should be just enough to get them to the last marker on the St Cross line, All Saints' Church at Hursley.

There was an Iron Age fort just outside the village, and Henry de Blois, the bishop who built St Cross Hospital, erected a castle on the same site. Successive lords of the manor built successive mansions, but for the past forty years the current one has been occupied by an unlikely squire, the IBM company.

There have been almost as many successive parish churches as manor houses, and the earliest one was Saxon, so the usual possibilities of its being built on a pagan site apply. By 1752 the church had become ruinous, and there had been so many burials that the churchyard was nearly level with the windowsills. A new church was built by the Heathcote family, typical of its day, with high-sided box pews and a solid screen between nave and chancel, so the altar could not be seen by the congregation.

FALSE TRAILS

In *The Old Straight Track* Alfred Watkins extols the leyline potential of Silchester, a Roman town built on the site of an earlier British settlement. He seemed to have good reason for his enthusiasm. Silchester had no fewer than four pagan temples, an amphitheatre and an early Christian church as well as the present parish church of St Mary's, and he sketched four lines that linked them all up.

Unfortunately, there was a maximum of only three markers on any one line. He may have tried to extend the lines to take in some more, but he gives only one example. It goes through just one temple and St Mary's, but it extends to a moat in the south-east direction, and Mortimer West End church to the north-west. I tried to extend it further, but no other markers appeared.

Oh well, I thought, let's stretch a point for Alfred and follow up this final four-marker line. There was no

doubt about the authenticity of the pagan temple, and the guidebook says of St Mary's: 'It stands by chance on a spot enclosed as sacred in pagan times.' Alfred would argue it was not just 'by chance'.

A nearby pond used to be the town's defensive ditch, which could qualify as a moat. So far, so good. But I could not find the other moat Alfred mentions to the south-east, either on the map or on the ground, and when I got to Mortimer West End church the last hope for this leyline died. St Saviour's was built in only 1856, and no church stood there before. The local worshippers went to Silchester and were allocated pews in the north aisle, which became know as 'Mortimer's Hole'and Alfred, I fear, fell into it.

The Roman wall at Silchester, where four leylines cross – or do they?

WILTSHIRE
AND DORSET

W,ILTSHIRE has four of the best known prehistoric sites in England: Stonehenge, Avebury, Old Sarum and Silbury Hill. Whole books have been written about each of them, and so many leylines have been drawn through them that there are few gaps left to fill. *The Ley Hunter's Companion*, for instance, has leylines covering them all. Indeed, the famous stone circle at Avebury is featured twice, once on a ley linking it with Silbury Hill, the other with some lesser known hill camps and barrows. I confess it is Avebury that fascinates me most. Old Sarum is the best of the rest, an Iron Age hill-fort that became a Roman town, then a Saxon settlement, then the hilltop site of the first Salisbury Cathedral. From here you can look down on the present cathedral and beyond to another Iron Age fort, Clearbury Ring. All three are in a convenient straight line and form the basis for the Old Sarum ley in the *Companion*.

Of the other two sites on my list, unless you can get inside Silbury Hill it looks just another artificial mound, albeit a big one, and what is there left to say about Stonehenge? After watching a long television programme explaining how it was a prehistoric fertility symbol, with the lengthening shadow of one stone entering, phallic-like, into the uncomfortably unyielding stonework of an earth goddess's personal parts, I felt my own modest powers of imagination had been convincingly dwarfed. By the same reasoning, Silbury Hill has been interpreted as 'an earth sculpture of the pregnant earth goddess, a fertility symbol par excellence'. Gradually the mind starts to boggle.

But Avebury has a homely charm about it that no deep-thinking archaeologist can destroy. Its mysterious prehistoric stones intermingle comfortably with a traditional English village. And even though the shapes of the stones have been interpreted in various sexual ways, the whole arrangement of banks and ditches and standing stones, covering twenty-seven acres, still defies the experts – and long may it do so.

The *Companion* leyline through Avebury and Silbury Hill starts to the north, at a motte and bailey called Bincknoll Castle, then goes through a well

Maiden Castle, an ideal ley marker.

and the churchyard at Broad Hinton. After that, however, it jumps straight to Avebury, which I found interesting, because there are three churches in between and the line misses them all. One of these is at Winterbourne Bassett, a name that caught my eye because there is a Winterbourne Steepleton on another leyline in Dorset, and it is also mentioned in another book I came across, *Prehistoric Avebury* by Aubrey Burl.

On the whole Mr Burl is rather scathing about leylines. For example: 'Leyliners draw impossibly accurate alignments from Avebury through Silbury Hill to a random barrow or church or mile-wide hill that God happened to place in the correct position.'

But he also recorded that Winterbourne Bassett had huge concentric circles, two-thirds the size of Avebury circle, plus an earthern long barrow close by, and less than a mile west there were nine sarsen stones covering prehistoric burials. He did point out that nothing is left now except a few random stones, but with such a range of potential markers to choose from, it seemed worth looking for an alternative Avebury line to the one in the *Companion*. It is ironic that such a leyline sceptic should put me on to it.

THE WINTERBOURNE BASSETT LINE (24)

The precise positions of the circles, the barrow and the burial mounds at Winterbourne Bassett are not shown on the average map, so there is a certain leeway – or leyway? – as to where the line can start. The choice could even include the church of St Katherine and St Peter ad Vincula, an interesting combination of patron saints, which has never been explained. Originally, it was just dedicated to St Katherine; the date of the additional dedication, says the church leaflet, is not known.

The church itself is built largely of sarsens, the same kind of stones that covered prehistoric burials and that have long been associated with pagan sacred sites. The leaflet mentions that the Winterbourne valley must once have been thickly strewn with them – 'scores of rejects have been moved off the lower fields'. Or, as the archaeologist Aubrey Burl put it: 'Time and the indifference of local farmers have destroyed the prehistoric rings.'

The line continues from Winterbourne Bassett, almost parallel to the ley in the *Companion*, through the medieval village of Richardson – now apparently just one house – to the well-concealed church of St Nicholas at Berwick Bassett. It is now redundant and seems to have few visitors. Its only decoration is a lonely candlestick on the pulpit. But one can picture it as it was in the fourteenth century when it was built, and, according to the Churches Conservation Trust's leaflet, 'the font suggests a previous structure'. Its proximity to the ancient Ridgeway suggests that its origins may be even earlier.

Like the leyline in the *Companion*, this one goes through the western edge of Avebury Circle. It is a pity

Above: *Winterbourne Bassett church.* Left: *Avebury Circle.*

that neither of them passes through Avebury church, because I found in it an early Norman font on which are carved two serpents with twisted tails, gazing hungrily at a bishop. They no doubt symbolized sin to the early Christians, but to the ley-hunter, as I have mentioned before, they have a quite different significance.

From here, again like the *Companion* ley, the line crosses Silbury Hill, but because of its slightly different alignment it crosses the eastern instead of the western flank – illustrating the convenience of having a ley marker that covers over five acres! Archaeologists

agree it was built in three stages, starting in about 2500 BC, but theories about its purpose range from a massive burial ground to a solar observatory and, of course, there is always the pregnant earth goddess school of thought, though a casual glance at a photograph of it might bring to mind the goddess's breast, rather than her swollen tummy.

Both lines then cross the conveniently lengthy Wansdyke, and the *Companion* line finishes up at Marden Henge, believed to date back to Neolithic times. It is an even bigger marker, covering thirty-five acres, the largest henge yet discovered, but regrettably my line still managed to miss it. Instead, it finishes up on Milk Hill, a name that seemed to have no particular relevance, until I remembered the earth goddess and the suggestive shape of Silbury Hill – an appropriate note on which to move on to Dorset, home of the ostentatiously equipped Cerne Abbas Giant.

Not even *The Ley Hunter's Companion* insists that the giant is a Neolithic or even an Iron Age figure. It very fairly records one theory that it was just a seventeenth-century folly. But it notes that in the eighteenth century the giant was referred to as Helis, and an earlier writer had found that the god Helith was worshipped in the area, which indicated that the giant might be Hercules. 'If this is so,' reasons the *Companion*, 'a number of researchers would agree that such a Roman import was located on the site of an earlier fertility cult.'

It does have a Cerne Abbas leyline, starting at Holwell church (a name based on 'holy well' is a great attraction to ley-hunters) but it does not actually pass

Two early fertility symbols? Above: The pregnant tummy – or is it a breast? – called Silbury Hill. Left: The well-endowed Cerne Giant.

through the giant itself. Instead, it goes through the Trendle, an earth enclosure believed to date from the Iron Age. The Trendle is just above the giant's left arm, but the *Companion* admits that the connection between them is something of a mystery.

Everyone is agreed, however, about the genuineness and the significance of Dorset's other famous ancient site, Maiden Castle near Dorchester. It started off in about 3000 BC as a Neolithic encampment, and a little later a burial ground was added. Then came a gap of about 2500 years while the site was abandoned, until an Iron Age fort was built on it about 350 BC. This is what ley-hunters call 'an evolved site', though sceptics say these different structures were built for different purposes at widely differing times, and there is no connection between them except the leylines.

Either way, one writer rates it in any list of 'The Seven Wonders of Ancient Britain', and the leyline in the *Companion* is an excellent excuse to go and see it.

THE FIRST MAIDEN CASTLE LINE (25)

As always, the line in the *Companion* is impeccably straight, starting at Holy Trinity Church, Warmwell, and ending with a tumulus at Winterbourne Steepleton. However, I had the temerity to see if my ruler could extend it further, as it was only about eight miles long. Perhaps I use a thicker pencil, but I found an extra marker in each direction, still within a total distance of only ten miles.

Instead of starting at Warmwell, I went a mile or so further east, to St Michael's Church at Owermoigne. St Michael is, of course, associated with dragons, always a good start, and the name of the village turned out to be a bonus too. Before the le Moigne family arrived it was just Ower, derived from a Saxon settle-

ment called Ogre – splendidly evocative of strange and frightening apparitions. Actually the village was renowned not for ogres, but for other figures which appeared and disappeared mysteriously in the night: it was a great centre for smuggling. At one time it is said the squire and the parson were both involved, and a bricked-up window in the rectory cellar is supposed to be the route by which the parson's tobacco and brandy arrived. Other smuggled goods were hidden in the orchard by the church and in the tower of the church itself.

Owermoigne rectors may have strayed from the strict letter of the law in other ways too, because the

The secluded church at Winterbourne Steepleton.

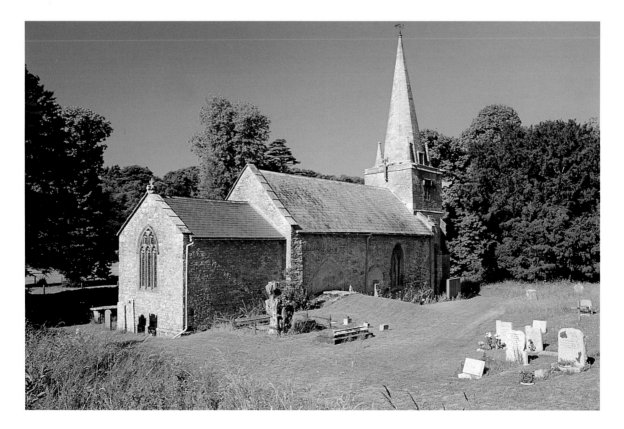

handsome eighteenth-century font, carved in Portland stone, mysteriously disappeared during rebuilding work in 1883. It was rediscovered later, filled with flowers in the rectory garden.

But if the rectors could be a bit dodgy, the squires could be far worse. In Tudor times Lord Charles Sturton, whose family had married into the le Moignes, was hanged for the murder of a man named Hartgill. The excellent church booklet does not say what Mr Hartgill had done to offend him, but it does note that as a concession to his nobility and his Roman Catholic faith, Queen Mary allowed a silken rope to be used for his execution. He must have found that a great consolation.

None of this has much to do with leylines – which may be why the *Companion* ignored Overmoigne – but the stories were too good to miss. At Warmwell the churchyard is roughly circular, which indicates an early origin, but the most striking feature of it is the double line of military graves – aircrew from the nearby RAF station who died in the Battle of Britain.

Above: The Nine Stones, a prehistoric stone circle. Right: Sculptured angel at St Michael's Church.

The thirteenth-century tower of St Martin's at Broadmayne is built onto the south side of the church, and the leyline passes through the join – the *Companion* is always very precise about this sort of thing. I did wonder therefore if there was something significant about the tower not being in the usual position at the west end, but the church leaflet soon cleared that up. The ground drops away sharply to the west, it points out, and the south side offered a firmer foundation.

The church was extensively restored and enlarged in the nineteenth century, and the only ancient relic is a thirteenth-century stone coffin lid, which was rescued when the road was widened. I could find nothing to link the church with an earlier period, nor apparently could the *Companion*.

Maiden Castle, however, is linked with so many ancient periods that ley-hunters can take their pick.

The *Companion* line runs along part of the Iron Age bank, on the northern edge of the site. The critical book I mentioned before, points out what a large target Maiden Castle provides and what a long period it covers, starting with a Neolithic enclosure and bank barrow. It comments: 'We would expect the Neolithic ley to cross the earthwork in such a way as to pass through at least one of these Neolithic structures, but it goes nowhere near either of them. It only touches the very latest Iron Age defences.' For the average ley-hunter, though, the Iron Age is probably sufficiently prehistoric.

The leyline ends, rather disappointingly from a pictorial point of view, at a couple of tumuli just north of Winterbourne Steepleton. Using my thicker pencil, I found it could take in the attractive little church of St Michael's – that significant name again – in the village itself. It stands in a glade, and according to one gazetteer it has a very special feature. 'Built into the exterior of the south wall is a sculptured angel which, if the dating of 950 is correct, is one of the oldest pieces of church sculpture in England.'

All I could see in the wall, however, was the empty niche. I gather the angel has been moved inside for greater protection, and perhaps for that reason the church is kept locked. So I never saw it, nor the Anglo-Saxon font of about the same period, but there seems no doubt about the church's antiquity.

My thicker leyline did not stop there. I continued it along the valley and near the main road there are the Nine Stones, a prehistoric stone circle. They are probably of a totally different period from the Iron Age defences at Maiden Castle, but they are good enough to provide the final marker on my revised line.

Just to prove it is possible to find a line in the Dorchester area which does not pass through the all-embracing Maiden Castle, I followed up a leyline in Alfred Watkins' *Ley Hunter's Manual*. It had the attraction of not only avoiding the castle but of starting at Tolpuddle, a village I had read about since my school-days but had never actually seen. A place that could produce the Tolpuddle Martyrs must surely be something special.

THE TOLPUDDLE LINE (26)

The village is well aware of its famous sons, and you can hardly miss the reminders of them, from the Martyrs Inn to the TUC memorial cottages bearing their names. In the churchyard is the grave of James Hemmett, the only Martyr to resettle in the village following their transportation to Australia for trying to found a trade union.

But there is more to St John's Church than memories of the Martyrs, and it goes back a lot further. King Canute had a servant who was married to a woman called Tola. She owned the village of Pidela. She gave it into the care of the monks of Abbotsbury, and in due course Tola's Pidela evolved into Tolpuddle. It is not known whether the monks built the first church in the village, but the present one dates back some 800 years.

Its oldest relic is a carved stone effigy depicting the full-length figure of 'Philip the Priest', which dates from the time the church was built. It was found earlier this century in two pieces, one embedded in the turf outside the chancel, the other built into the chancel wall. The Latin inscription reads: 'If any lover of Christ should see this tombstone, let him say, Grant rest, O

Above: *A pagan survival in St Peter's Church, Dorchester?*
Left: *Tolpuddle's Philip the Priest rescued and reassembled.*

Christ, to Philip the Priest.' The couple who located the pieces, the Rev. H.R. Long and his friend William Prideaux, did rather better than that. They re-assembled the effigy and installed it in the church.

From Tolpuddle the line follows the Roman road towards Dorchester – a logical route, since many ley-hunters argue that the Romans did not design all those nice straight roads themselves, they just laid them along the existing prehistoric tracks. When the Roman road – or its modern successor – swerves to avoid Puddletown Forest, the leyline naturally continues straight on into it, to what are marked on the map as Rainbarrows – presumably of the prehistoric variety.

However, Alfred does not mention the Rainbarrows in the *Manual* – so perhaps he knew something I don't. His next marker is Dorchester church, and although I normally try to avoid large town centres, St Peter's is worth the effort. Dorchester

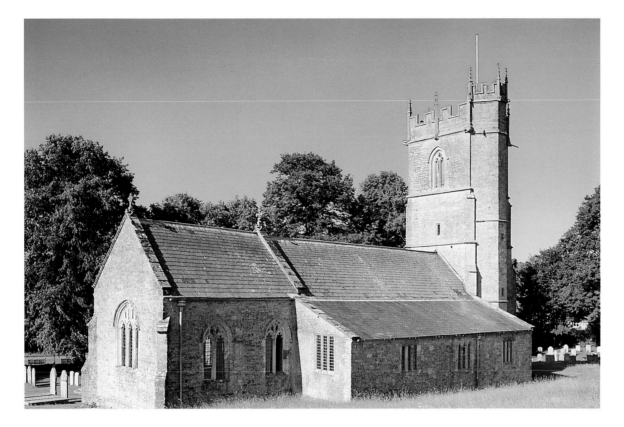

Above: *St Martin Church, Winterborne.*

was a Roman town, and although there is no evidence that the church stands on the site of a Roman temple, it may still have very early origins. And the church leaflet points out that it is the only one of the town's three medieval churches to survive. 'The other two are nineteenth-century rebuilds,' it says rather sniffily.

Actually, St Peter's was restored by the Victorians too, but there is an extenuating circumstance, because the architect had a sixteen-year-old assistant called Thomas Hardy, and the plan of the restoration work drawn by Dorset's most famous writer now has a place of honour in the church.

More interesting to the ley-hunter, though, are the gruesome gargoyles outside, representing a variety of unidentifiable creatures. When the *Companion* came across similar gargoyles on another church it commented, 'probably another sign of pagan survival', and that could well apply to St Peter's as well.

From here, alas, the *Manual* line seems to go slightly awry. Its next marker is St Martin's Church, Winterborne, but however thick a pencil I used, I could not line up St Martin's with the churches at Dorchester and Tolpuddle. It is a pity, because St Martin's is one of those fascinating churches where the chancel is out of line with the nave, a curious phenomenon that ley-hunters associate with leylines. The church guide quotes the popular theory that the angled chancel symbolizes the drooping head of Christ on the Cross, but it adds, very fairly: 'There is no historical evidence to support this tradition.'

So, even though the line misses it and finishes up in a couple of tumuli instead, I think St Martin's provides a more intriguing note on which to leave Wiltshire and Dorset.

SOMERSET
AND DEVON

OMERSET has a rather special ancient site. It is where the Faery King had his palace, where the enchantress Ceridwen kept her cauldron of poetic inspiration, and where King Arthur came to rescue his wife Guinevere from Melwas, King of Somerset. It is also one of the many places where Arthur was buried. There are so many ancient versions of the King Arthur story that it is no wonder he has been linked with leylines in several areas. Actually, the oldest Arthurian legend originated in Wales, where he was a superhero who killed a giant in Snowdonia, hunted a massive wild boar in Builth and left behind at least two Arthur's tables, at Llansannan and Cefn y Bryn. But the most credible King Arthur lived in the sixth century and held back the Saxon invaders in a dozen victories. The most popular legends are set in the Age of Chivalry, when Arthur and his gallant Knights of the Round Table rescued maidens in distress, slew an assortment of unpleasant predators, and behaved like jolly good chaps. They managed to cover a fair amount of ground, no doubt assisted by Merlin's magical powers, but Arthur's best known beat was the West Country, and inevitably his name has been linked with Glastonbury Tor.

Local tradition also has it that Jesus came here with his disciple, Joseph of Arimathea – an occasion not to be confused with Joseph's later visit to hide the Holy Grail in the Chalice Well. It could have been the place of the earliest Christian worship in England, and certainly there was an earlier chapel on the site, which was destroyed in the thirteenth century by an earthquake – not exactly an everyday occurrence in Somerset.

In more recent time it has been a favourite observation point for spotting unidentified flying objects and a gathering place for what used to be called the Flower People. It is still the venue for perhaps the best known open-air festival in the country. With all this wealth of fairytale folklore, early religious connections and unconventional activity, ley-hunters find Glastonbury Tor quite irresistible. Certainly it provides a most dramatic leyline marker, its eerie silhouette with the tower of St Michael's Chapel perched on top, matched by

The ruins of Glastonbury Abbey.

the atmosphere of mystery that you can experience when you are actually on it – a sense of being surrounded by the inexplicable. *The Ley Hunter's Companion* does, of course, have a Glastonbury Tor leyline but – perhaps surprisingly – it is rejected in a later book by Devereux. It starts several miles to the north, at Brockley church (which has since been made redundant), continues through Burrington church, Burrington Combe (where the famous Rock of Ages was cleft for the hymn-writer), the Neolithic Gorsey Bigbury henge and the Bronze Age Westbury beacon camp. They all seem admirable markers to me.

After crossing the Tor it ends further south at St Leonard's Church, Butleigh, which seems an even better marker, because Butleigh lies inside the Glastonbury Zodiac, a pattern mysteriously formed by natural features like streams and field boundaries. But there is much scepticism about these 'ground zodiacs'. One writer commented: 'There are so many features on any Ordnance Survey map that the chances are you can find the outlines of a zodiac just about anywhere, if you look hard enough and are prepared to bend the rules.'

Perhaps this was one reason why the leyline to Butleigh was rejected. Whatever the reason, I looked for other lines through the Tor – and Alfred Watkins came up with one in his *The Ley Hunter's Manual* that seemed worth a try.

THE GLASTONBURY TOR LINE (27)

This is longer than most of the lines I have described, about twenty-eight miles, and it relies questionably on a crossroads for one of its markers, but the others are much more productive.

It starts at the Tor and heads west to St Mary's Church, Woolavington, which has an impeccable pedigree for a leyline. It is set out very convincingly in the church leaflet, which says that although the first known church was built there in 1088, there is no evidence of another burial place in the area, even though it had Roman and early British sites all around. And when the Saxon village was built it seems that the site of the church in the centre of it was left vacant.

'We can only surmise,' says the leaflet, 'but it does seem quite likely that our church was built on the traditional place of worship in the village.' And this of course could well extend back into pagan times.

The imposing oak door is still fitted with its original sanctuary knocker, perhaps the church's most unusual relic is the Hody Stone, named after John Hody, the son of a fifteenth-century serf who rose to become Chief Justice of England. Could the leyline perhaps have helped? The stone bearing his initials was found in the floor of the tower during restoration work and is now set in an archway in the wall. In his will he asked to be buried at Woolavington and made bequests to the local priests 'for the love that he had to it, for there he began his first learning'.

He was fortunate, in fact, that St Mary's had a chantry chapel staffed by three additional monks. It was built onto the church in 1285 by a pious and wealthy squire called Gilbert de Woolavington, who was also vicar of Huntsmill but chose Woolavington for his chapel. The primary duty of the monks was to pray for Gilbert's soul, but apparently they still found enough time to educate young Master Hody. He was one of the last to benefit from their presence; the monks of St Mary's chapel were pensioned off after the Reformation.

The stone head of a tonsured monk, thought to have been dug up in the churchyard, sits on a window-ledge in the chancel. Nobody knows whom it repre-

Above: *The chapel in the deserted village of Lilstock.*
Left: *Glastonbury Tor, the haunt of the Faery King, Arthur and Guinevere, Joseph of Arimathea – and ley-hunters.*

sents, but perhaps this was one of the teachers who provided John Hody with his 'first learning'.

From Woolavington the line goes through Alfred Watkins' road junction marker in Pawlett, crosses the estuary of the River Parrett and reaches St Mary Magdalene Church at the confusingly-named Stockland Bristol – it is nowhere near Bristol. I was mildly encouraged by the double row of gargoyles round the tower – 'probably an unconscious

reminder of long-forgotten paganism', to borrow a memorable phrase from *The Ley Hunter's Companion*.

Alfred's final marker on this line is much more intriguing. He just describes it as an 'ancient church on coast', and when I continued the line from Stockland Bristol it did indeed hit a church in the middle of nowhere, not far from the sea. It turned out to be the delightful little chapel of St Andrew, at what used to be the village of Lilstock, and it has a fascinating tale to tell.

There has been a church on the site since at least the tenth century, and its dedication to St Andrew, as I have explained elsewhere, could indicate a pagan predecessor. The present little building is fourteenth century,

By then it had been derelict for forty years and the original village had virtually disappeared. The parish was first amalgamated with Kilton, then absorbed into the united benefice of Quantoxhead. There seemed little point in preserving it. However, the district council opposed the application, and the rector of Quantoxhead, the Rev. Rex Hancock, came to the rescue of the little church with a dramatic offer to pay the £3000 needed for its restoration. It is the sort of thing that wealthy Victorian parsons quite often did to acquire themselves a nice newly restored church, but it rarely happened on the salary of a twentieth-century rector who was due to retire shortly anyway. He asked only one thing in return: 'I would like my body to lie in state there before being buried in Kilton.'

So St Andrew's survives, and happily its door is kept unlocked. There is not a lot to see – the twelfth-century font was moved long ago to another St Andrew's at Stogursy, and an imposing memorial stone to the Luttrell family has been moved to East Quantoxhead. But it has not been all one-way. St Andrew's was given a bell from the chapel over Watchet Museum, other well-wishers gave an altar cloth, and the Bishop of Bath and Wells gave permission for one service to he held there each year. The main credit must go though to Rex Hancock, who retired in 1993. 'Thanks to his generosity,' says the church leaflet, 'it was possible to bring this chapel back to life'.

That is where the *Manual's* Glastonbury Tor line ends, but it is not the end of Glastonbury so far as ley-lines are concerned. Among others there is one that takes in, not only the Tor, but the Abbey remains and St John the Baptist Church with its Holy Thorn – a complete set, as it were, of Glastonbury's three notable religious sites. It is part of a 200-mile ley I found on the Internet, which runs from the Sussex coast to the north coast of Devon. According to my ruler it has a number of kinks, but certain sections of it are straight enough, and Glastonbury lies on one of these 'mini ley-lines'. In this case the section is about fifteen miles long, and like the *Manual* line it runs roughly from east to west, but at a slightly different angle.

Pagan reminders on Stockland Bristol church tower?

but in Victorian times it was partly demolished and 'remodelled', and only the chancel arch survived. 'The rest is Victorian twee,' said the Somerset county historian rather scathingly in 1991, supporting an application by the Church Commissioners to destroy it.

THE GLASTONBURY 'THREE SITES' LINE (28)

I picked up the long-distance leyline at West Pennard church, a few miles east of Glastonbury. St Nicholas's was originally a chapel of the mother church of St John's in Glastonbury, and the manor belonged to the abbey, so it could almost be regarded as a fourth Glastonbury site, but the connection ended with the abbey's dissolution by Henry VIII.

The church is built on rising ground, which gave the medieval architects a few problems. The building follows the slope of the ground and the windows are on a slant, but the roof of the south aisle is level, so one end seems much lower than the other. 'Adding greatly to the confusion,' as the guidebook puts it, the arches

of the south arcade vary considerably in size and span. It is always nice to find little eccentricities like these in churches on leylines.

The outside south wall is also rather odd; the lower part, unlike the rest of the church, has a smooth ashlar facing. But that oddity does have a rational explanation. In the early nineteenth century it was adapted for use in the newly introduced sport of fives. Not surprisingly, the church authorities were not entirely happy about fives balls being thumped about in churchyards, and in due course separate courts were built, but not before some churches had had to erect shutters on the windows to stop them being smashed by stray balls. It did mean, however, that St Nicholas's may have been one of the few places where you could play fives on a leyline.

From West Pennard the line runs to Glastonbury Tor and on into the town itself. All that remains of the Abbey is the curiously-shaped Abbot's Kitchen, where meals were prepared over open fires in each corner, and the four chimney flues converged on the central stone lantern in the roof. The lantern might have been mistaken for a lookout tower – until it started gushing smoke.

Many people believe the abbey stood on the earliest Christian site in Britain, where Joseph of Arimathea built the first wattle-and-daub church, long before a monastery was built in the sixth or seventh century. Legend had it that King Arthur and Queen Guinevere were reburied there, but that did not stop Henry VIII from dissolving the abbey along with the rest.

St John's Church was provided for the town by Abbot Dunstan in about 950; he may well have followed Pope Gregory's advice and built it on a pagan sacred site. The present fifteenth-century building has many reminders of Glastonbury's long religious history, from a stained-glass window illustrating the

Inside the Abbot's Kitchen at Glastonbury Abbey.

legend of the Holy Grail to a Glastonbury thorn bush in the churchyard, a 'clone' of the one that is said to have grown where Joseph of Arimathea's staff took root. A spray of flowers from it is sent to the Queen and the Queen Mother when it blooms at Christmas. The original bush, incidentally, was chopped down by a Roundhead soldier – who hacked off his own leg in the process.

From Glastonbury the line continues westward to a holy well at Edington, where Alfred is said to have won a great victory over the Danes. The well is on a bend in the road that runs out of the village from the church of St George (the well-known dragon-slayer). It was restored in the 1930s.

According to the Internet line, the next marker is St Edward's Church, Chilton Polden. I found I needed a particularly thick pencil to get the church onto the line, but it has some interesting tales to tell. It stands on the site of an ancient chapelry, which is mentioned in a charter of Ina, King of Wessex, who gave Glastonbury its first monastery. In the 1880s it was in danger of collapse, but enough money was raised to rebuild it, and a Bridgwater lady gave a fourteenth-century chancel arch, chancel windows and the ancient

Above: *The Joseph of Arimathea window in Glastonbury church.* Left: *The holy well at Edington, where King Alfred is said to have fought the Danes.*

stonework of a window from a former church in the town, which were all incorporated in the Victorian restoration. The Internet main line continues to Watchet and beyond, but the markers are not too convincing. I shall pick it up again in Devon.

Meanwhile, *The Ley Hunter's Manual* has one more Somerset ley, contributed by a Mr Robert Rule, which takes us to the Devon border and the unexplained ancient stones called the Whitstones.

THE WHITSTONES LINE (29)

The line starts at Monksilver church, four miles south of Watchet, though Mr Rule might have extended it further eastward, to an ancient crossroads at Combe Cross. But All Saints' Church is a good starting point, because among the carvings on the bench-ends is a Green Man, that familiar reminder of a pagan past. The first rector was recorded in 1324, but the church, the original part of the preaching cross beside it and, indeed the ancient yew in the churchyard are probably earlier.

It was run by the monks of Goldelive Priory in Monmouthshire, which perhaps accounts for the 'monk' in Monksilver. The 'silver' does not refer to their money; it more probably came from 'sylvan', a wooded clearing. After the Reformation the living was given to the Dean and Canons of Windsor to benefit education, so Monksilver's actual silver may have sub-sidized Eton School.

The medieval gargoyles on the tower are very similar to those on Wells Cathedral, and it is not just a coincidence that one of them seems to be having trouble with its mouth. In the thirteenth century Bishop Button of Bath and Wells was regarded as the patron saint of toothache sufferers. But then again, gar-goyles are 'unconscious reminders of long-forgotten paganism', and no doubt pagans got toothache too.

The church booklet notes that the chancel arch is somewhat out of line and speculates about the reason for it. Ley-hunters would no doubt suggest that it was an adjustment to get into alignment with the ley. It is not so easy to explain the odd window arch in the south aisle. The former rector who wrote the guidebook says some people think that the mason was drunk – 'but I think he just wanted a change – and why should they be all the same anyway?' He has a point.

Instead of the pulpit being reached by the usual little stairway, it has to be entered, rather dramatically,

Monksilver church pulpit, entered through a hole in the wall.

through a hole in the wall. The effect must be rather like a royal box – or a cuckoo clock – but no doubt the congregation is well used to it, and as that former rector might have said, 'Why should they all be the same anyway?'

chapel is built on an area of solid rock, so no burials can take place in the churchyard, but when the church floor was being relaid a skeleton was discovered underneath, and the guide makes a significant point. 'It was curled up in the manner customary with pagan interments, suggesting that the site could have been a centre of pre-Christian worship.'

The present building dates from about 1250, and it still has its musicians' gallery. A lady preparing the church for the annual flower festival told me that her mother remembered farm-workers playing their fiddles up there to accompany hymns during services, and it is still used by the choir.

In contrast, there is a very modern metalwork sculpture beside the altar, the work of a local sculptress,

Outside the church door is the 'murder tombstone' of Mrs Elizabeth Conibrer and her two daughters, found murdered in nearby Woodford. It is inscribed: 'Inhuman wretch, whoe'er thou art, That did commit this heinous crime, Repent before thou doth depart, To meet thine … [illegible] … Divine.'

Our friend the former rector writes: 'There are many tales about this event, but I do not care to pen any of them here. They no doubt give interest to some people, which perhaps is a fitting commentary on our society!' And he has one final comment about the church itself. 'We worship Him who lives for ever, not wood and stone. The Church sees to the former, perhaps it would be better if the Ministry of Public Buildings and Works saw to the latter.' It really is a very refreshing kind of guidebook.

On the way to Mr Rule's next marker, I came upon another church, quite by accident, exactly on his line. It is curious he missed St Bartholomew's Chapel at Rodhuish, and remarkable that I should find it, because as the church guide says rather ruefully: 'The Chapel is sometimes called "the hidden gem", because it is so tucked away among the lanes, and it is not mentioned in Mee's "Somerset" or in Pevsner's work.' But they weren't following a leyline.

It turned out to be a fascinating discovery. The

Rachel Reckitt, who also carved the wooden angels with their trumpets above the altar. Her father was the architect who helped restore the chapel, and her mother provided the embroidery. The flower lady told me their family was involved in quite a substantial business in Norfolk. It was indeed. These were the Reckitts of Reckitt & Colman, whose mustard is one of Norfolk's best known products. With my own Norfolk connections, this was the final cherry on the St Bartholomew cake. A small world, and it seems the leylines help to make it so.

From Rodhuish I followed the line over the hills to Mr Rule's next marker, Timberscombe church, which turned out to be a much more prominent church in a much larger village, with its own special appeal. It is dedicated to St Petrock, and legend has it that the first church was built on this site in the sixth century under the supervision of Petrock himself. He was one of the Welsh missionaries who came to the West Country during that period, and Timberscombe church shares his patronage with the rather grander one at Bodmin in Cornwall.

When the Victorians restored the present church they fortunately reused many of the old timbers and bosses in the roof. Ley-hunters will soon spot the carved head surrounded by leaves on the boss nearest the chancel, another representation of the pagan Green Man.

There is a long gap before the next marker, the aptly named Ley Hill, and so we come to the Whitstones, which I finally located in a boggy field alongside the coast road. Fortunately, they are nearly opposite a car park named after them; there is no other clue. They are not white stones but distinctly grey; they look somewhat out of place and their significance is obscure. Keen eyes may spot two parallel banks some eighteen inches high and about thirty feet apart, but alas, they have no prehistoric connections. They are all that remains of an abortive attempt to build a railway from the iron mines inland to the coast. The mining company pulled out of the project in 1858 and the track was never laid.

A curious little tale, but it hardly explains the

Above: *Whitstones.* Left above: *One of the bosses from the original church at Timberscombe.* Left below: *Rodhuish chapel.*

Whitstones. So they continue to provide a baffling marker to end this line – and to start another, which picks up that long-distance leyline from Sussex and continues into Devon.

The North Devon Coast Line (30)

The last mention of the Internet line was when it reached Watchet. From there it makes one or two discreet little wriggles, according to my ruler, in order to get back on course again at the Whitstones.

I have mentioned the theory that deer like to mate where leylines converge, and I suppose the location of the Whitstones, on the edge of Exmoor, gives it a little more credence than some of the leyline crossing points I have found – particularly those on motorways.

Continuing westward, the line crosses Robber's Bridge at Oaresfoot, not mentioned by the Internet but a river crossing in that isolated area could well have been a gathering point in much earlier times. The name itself is not surprising, because this is Carver Doone country, and the line crosses the Devon border near Oare, where he shot the lovely Lorna during her wedding in the village church.

The next marker is St Bartholomew's, Barbrook, a small, simple building with a wooden bell-cote and containing just the basic furnishings, none of it very old. Barbrook is on the coast road, the first village after the steep and twisting climb in and out of Lynton and Lynmouth, and St Bartholomew's may offer a peaceful haven for fraught motorists to calm their nerves.

Perhaps the leyline contributes to the soothing atmosphere, but I could find no early connections.

The next marker was much more productive. The Internet just says 'Martinhoe tumuli', and the tumuli are certainly there, on top of the hill overlooking Woody Bay, but there is a lot more to Martinhoe than that. Martinhoe beacon was a Roman fort and signalling station, garrisoned by sixty soldiers keeping watch for Silurian ships from South Wales. In AD74 the Romans attacked and conquered the Silurians, and the beacon became redundant and was abandoned. The fort was on the site of Old Barrow, and it seems probable that such a large garrison had some place of worship for their gods on what was already a sacred site.

The Saxons had a settlement there, and St Martin's Church is mentioned in the Domesday Book. Fans of R.D. Blackmore come to see the memorials to the writer's ancestors, and the gravestones in the churchyard to the Ridd family, whose name will always be linked with the Doones. It was linked even more closely by Lorna Doone Ridd, who was named after the heroine in the book and died in 1955, aged 75.

Finally, a precarious drive into a deep combe and out again, then a half-mile walk up a near-vertical lane marked 'Unfit for Motors' to the last marker, St Peter's Church at Trentishoe, 'the fort on the ridge'. There is, in fact, a perfectly good road to the church from another direction, and the other visitors could not understand why I was so out of breath.

St Peter's too is associated with R.D. Blackmore's forebears. His great-grandfather's sister married the rector, and one of his novels, *Clara Vaughan*, is set in Trentishoe. Until the church was enlarged in the nineteenth century it was claimed to be the smallest in Devon; it is still pretty small. The earliest reference to it is in the thirteenth century, and it doubtless goes back much further, but its most interesting feature, oddly enough, is its quite modern little organ.

The church organist, 'Dick' Turpin, went on the final cruise of the *Mauretania* and was so impressed by its organ that when the ship was broken up he asked to buy it. The owners made it a gift, telling him it would be very suitable for a church on the North Devon coast 'because it was constructed to withstand all climates'. Mr Turpin died in 1979; his tombstone by the church door bears his real name, David. And the organ plays on.

Ley-hunters may believe this fortuitous acquisition did not happen just by chance. Indeed the fact that the church has survived at all is quite remarkable. In 1959 the rural dean reported that it was 'obviously redundant', and moves were made to close it. At the time Trentishoe had forty residents, and they rallied to its defence, quoting a biblical conversation between Abraham and the Lord in the Book of Genesis. Abraham said, trying to avert another kind of tragedy: 'Peradventure there shall be forty [righteous ones] found there?' And He said: 'I will not do it [destroy it] for forty's sake.'

Actually they were talking about the impending destruction of Sodom, so I imagine the good folk of Trentishoe did not pursue the analogy too far. Even so, the church still stands and is still in use, the final marker on the 200-mile leyline from Sussex, and on this twenty-mile North Devon coast 'mini-leyline'.

I have to say that the main hunting ground in Devon for ley-hunters is, of course, Dartmoor, so liberally bespattered with cairns, stone crosses, tumuli and menhirs – standing stones that often date back to the Bronze Age. The snag with Dartmoor, for the less energetic ley-hunter, is that so much of it is inaccessible by any form of transport. There is also such a wealth of markers that, not only is it a little too easy to line up five or six chunks of stone or mounds of earth in quite short distances, but they can also get a little boring to the non-archaeologist, no matter how ancient they may be.

There is an example in *The Ley Hunter's Companion*, the Western Beacon ley in a virtually road-less area of South Dartmoor. It starts with a cairn on Butterdon Hill, then there is a standing stone known as the Longstone, followed by the Black Pool and a couple

Above: *Trentishoe*. Left: *Robber's Bridge at Oaresfoot, an ancient river crossing in Lorna Doone country.*

more cairns before reaching the beacon. It finishes up at a crossroads, the only roads in the area, all within a distance of two miles.

To prove my point I extended the line northwards and came across so many markers in the next twenty miles that it was almost embarrassing: Hobajon's Cross, hut circles, Hangershall Rock, Three Barrows, Knatta Barrow, Petrie's Corner, Clapper Bridge, a cairn called Petrie's Round Stone.

My thoughts are echoed, I am afraid, in that scourge of the ley-hunters, *The Ley in Question*. Black Pool, it says, has every appearance of being natural, there is no evidence of the crossroads being a prehistoric site, and the Longstone is probably just a boundary stone on the parish border between Ugborough and Harford. 'So it turns out to be an alignment of four cairns. They fall into two kilometre squares on the National Grid, and this area includes no less than eighteen mark points. It is not surprising that some align.'

Do join in the arguments between the experts, and pursue the leyline and beyond if you wish. I shall make an excuse and leave – for Cornwall.

CORNWALL AND
NORTH-WEST DEVON

SOUTH-WEST Cornwall is just as rich in ancient stones as Dartmoor, but for the unathletic ley-hunter they are mostly more accessible, and they also have far stranger legends attached to them. Perhaps the Cornish are more inventive than the Devonians, but dour old Dartmoor has little to match the dramatic appearance and the far-fetched folklore of ancient Cornish standing stones like the Hurlers, the Men-an-Tol and the Cheesewring. As a bonus, there are a couple of prehistoric villages and an assortment of holy wells. Most striking of all, perhaps, is St Michael's Mount, once joined to the mainland but now accessible only at low tide. It was the site of a Benedictine monastery in Saxon times. It is thought to have been a sacred site before that, and probably the longest ley in Britain starts there, according to ley-hunting gurus like John Michell and Paul Devereux.

It passes through the Cheesewring, a rock formation looking like a cheese-press, where you can sit in a natural stone chair and have a chat with the Devil. Then it heads off to the famous sites at Glastonbury and Avebury, via various churches all dedicated to St Michael (well-known dragon-slayer), like the Mount itself. Eventually it reaches East Anglia and ends, rather less spectacu-larly than it began, by disappearing into the North Sea among the holiday camps and caravan parks north of Lowestoft.

That leyline is a little too ambitious for me to pursue, and certainly *The Ley Hunter's Companion* does not attempt it, though it does refer to it as 'a stroke of pure geomantic genius'. Instead, the *Companion* stays in the far south-west for a rather shorter one – less than four miles, in fact – which takes in the pre-historic settlements at Chysauster and Mulfra, an Iron Age hill-fort called Castle-an-Dinas, a standing stone and the strange wheel-shaped stone known as Men-an-Tol, the 'Stone of the Hole'. Altogether a very rich harvest on one short leyline, and I could not hope to better it.

The Men-an-Tol is particularly folklore-laden, credited with powers that range from curing scrofulous children – who were passed three times through the two-foot hole, then dragged around the stone three times, anticlockwise –

St Michael's Mount, the starting point for England's longest leyline.

to acting as an oracle. Brass pins were laid on it, and in answer to questions they mysteriously vibrated to provide the answer. Again, how could that be bettered?

However, I had a go. Two notable sites, the Hurlers and Trethevy Quoit, are quite close to a famous holy well at St Cleer. Unfortunately, they are not on the same line, but it was not difficult to find two possible leylines to include them. The one involving the Trethevy Quoit is the shorter, starting at St Cleer's church with its lofty tower, then going through the well and the Quoit before reaching a collection of tumuli on Caradon Hill and the aptly named Ley Mill. This is just over four miles, and although one can continue it to an earthwork on Castlepark Hill, some nine miles away, the only markers really of interest are the well, which is also on the other line, and the Quoit.

This is an imposing chambered tomb, with the merit of being only about twenty yards from the road. There are eight stones, of which seven form the sides and the eighth is the capstone. One of them divides the chamber into two, and originally the whole thing was inside an oval mound about sixty feet high, which existed until the last century. Experts date it from around 3000 BC. So the Quoit is well worth a quick fling up the lane from St Cleer, but I found more to look at on the alternative St Cleer line, to the Hurlers.

THE HURLERS LINE (31)

The line starts at the holy well in St Cleer, with the ancient stone cross that stands beside it, some 200 yards down the road from the church. The well is inside a fifteenth-century stone shelter, which looks rather like a miniature church itself, with elegant pillars and arches and stone pinnacles on the corners of

the roof. The shelter was restored in 1864 and still looks in good shape.

This was considered to be a healing well, like many others in Cornwall, and thus a place of pilgrimage, but it is not St Cleer's only claim to medieval fame. The ceremony of Banishing the Witches is still performed in June on the Eve of St John. Various herbs and an oak sickle are thrown on a bonfire, and sometimes the effigy of a witch is burned. It would be nice to think that the water from the holy well was used eventually to put out the fire, but I suspect the good St Cleer would not approve.

From the well the line passes through another roadside cross – there are quite a number about – to the Hurlers, that imposing trio of Bronze Age stone circles near the village of Minions. The line passes through all three of them. The experts say there were up to thirty-five stones per circle, but now there are seventeen in the large centre circle, and thirteen and nine in the others. At least, I think so. But legend has it that they cannot be accurately counted, and each time you try, you get a different total. As one seventeenth-century writer put it: 'A redoubled numbering never eveneth with the first.' I did not have the nerve to try counting them twice.

Some say the circles have an astronomical significance, but nobody is quite sure. There is no doubt though that the builders did a good job, some 4000 years ago. The stones stand in pits, wedged upright by granite blocks. They were carved into various shapes like diamonds, and the tops were levelled off. The area inside the north circle seems to have been paved with granite slabs, but again, no one knows why. In fact, only one thing is certain about the Hurlers. The legend that they were people turned into stone for playing the game of hurling on a Sunday is not true. Sorry …

After the non-Hurlers, the line continues northwards through a tumulus to Nodman's Bowda, and ley-hunters will doubtless argue that Nodman is

Above: The Bronze Age Stone circles, the Hurlers. Left: *St Cleer's well under its ecclesiastical shelter and, alongside, its ancient stone cross.*

derived from 'dod-man', the name given by Alfred Watkins to his prehistoric leyline surveyors. A pity that Bowda does not sound more like Beacon – but perhaps it was the Bower where the dod-man had a snooze between surveys.

The line just misses the church at North Hill on the edge of Bodmin Moor, but goes through Example Cross, a curiously named road junction, which Alfred might suggest was named as a good example of a ley marker. It ends on the edge of a hill-fort north of Tregadillett, near Launceston, thirteen miles north of where it started at St Cleer.

From here ley-hunters can continue northwards into a very different part of Cornwall, which is comparatively short on standing stones but has its full quota of holy wells, some remarkable old churches and rather easier terrain in which to get about, compared with the rugged remoteness of the far south-west.

I had been told that the strongest leyline in Cornwall was situated in this area, based on Bude. It had been traced by using a bent wire coathanger as a divining-rod. The secret was to encase the wire in long strands of spaghetti, to eliminate other forces that might distract it from the ley. The lady who used it had passed the information on to a friend of mine in the locality, but insisted she remained anonymous – and my friend was not keen to try it out for himself.

'Much as I love you,' he wrote, 'I am not going to walk down Bude High Street holding a spaghetti-covered coathanger'. I am afraid I felt the same way, and I never did trace the Bude leyline. But I fared rather better – just using a spaghetti-free ruler – with two churches I knew of.

One is the church of St Morwenna and St John at Morwenstow, a place I have visited – and written about – many times before, but never in search of a leyline. The other is the much smaller St Swithin's Church at Launcells, which I had never seen but heard much about, including its famous holy well. So I put a ruler between the two – and there it was.

THE ST SWITHIN'S HOLY WELL LINE (32)

No one knows the origins of St Swithin's Church, but it seems agreed that churches were often built where there was spring water, and that probably applied to places of pre-Christian worship too. Either way, there is no doubt the holy well, which is actually a spring feeding the River Neet, was there first, and it still produces a steady supply of clear water inside its little stone shelter. Worshippers have to pass it as they cross the brook to the church, in its delightful woodland setting. The well is just by the bridge, a convenient source for the holy water stoup in the church porch.

The church was not always dedicated to St Swithin. Its first patron saint was St Andrew, which ley-hunters would consider significant, because, as already noted, the early Christians often dedicated their churches to him if they were built on a pagan sacred site. St Andrew remained the patron saint at Launcells until the church was re-dedicated to St Swithin in 1321 – nearly 500 years after Swithin was around.

St Andrew is still remembered on one of the splendid fifteenth-century bench-ends. It is carved with the cross of the saint and three tears. Did it express sadness about the re-dedication, perhaps? Ley-hunters will also

note, among all the biblical subjects carved on the benches, a rather incongruous portrayal of a huntsman and hounds – and a dragon.

Apart from possible leyline links, the church also has two memorials of particular interest. One is a tombstone, which was brought into the belfry from the churchyard, presumably to preserve its curious epitaph:

> 'Life is an Inn (think man this truth upon),
> some only to breakfast and are quickly gone.
> Others to dinner stay and are well fed,
> The oldest man but sups and goes to bed.
> Large is his debt who lingers out his day,
> Who goes the soonest has the least to pay.

No matter how much I 'think this truth upon', I still cannot fathom what it is driving at. The benefits of an early death, perhaps – surely not.

I prefer the other memorial, which is still in the churchyard, not because of the epitaph but because it commemorates a man who challenged the biblical warning not to build your house upon sand – and got away with it. Sir Goldsworthy Gurney built Bude Castle on sand in 1839, and it still stands on Summerlease Beach – but only because he was shrewd enough to lay a concrete raft on the sand first. The raft 'floated', and the system has been widely adopted since on sandy or boggy building sites. It was the nearest anyone had got to creating a 'castle in the air'. These days it is occupied by the local council; one hopes it will not sink under the paperwork.

On the rising ground behind St Swithin's is Launcells Barton, a mansion built on the site of a former holiday home of the early abbots of Hartland; the remains of their fish ponds can still be seen. It was largely rebuilt by Sir John Call, wealthy brother of an eighteenth-century vicar, and the church guidebook notes that the polished marble reredos behind the altar

hers is below the cliff on the site of her cell, where she was able to look across at her native Wales, whereas St John's is in an orchard in the vicarage garden.

When the famously eccentric Rev. Robert Stephen Hawker built the vicarage, with its distinctive chimneys modelled on his favourite church towers (except the kitchen chimney, which was a copy of his mother's tomb), the holy well of St John the Baptist conveniently provided him with a gravity-fed supply of holy water, which must have helped to keep him so healthy – he remained vicar there for over forty years.

The well had already been providing water for baptisms since at least the thirteenth century, and the little stone shed that houses it was probably built in the 1500s. As well as being useful, it also an appropriate final marker for the St Swithin's Holy Well Line.

But that is not the end of the connection with wells. Parson Hawker was also the curate of St Nectan's Church at Welcombe, and St Nectan has a holy well too. It provides the basis for another Morwenstow line.

Above: *The interior of Launcell's church.* Below left: *St Swithin's holy well at Launcells.* Below right: *Morwenstow church.*

was given by his architect, as a thank-offering for the work being completed without any accidents – 'a fact which seemed to surprise him.' it adds dryly. Maybe he should not have worried. The leyline from the holy well runs right though it. It continues on to an ancient settlement in Stowe Wood, overlooking the beautiful Coombe valley. Stowe is the Saxon word for holy place, and coupled with its commanding position on the hillside this has all the makings of a pagan sacred site.

Appropriately enough, the line next passes through Ley Wood, and then through two privately occupied old manor houses, Eastway and Tonacombe. Finally, it ends as it began, at a holy well, this time St John's well at Morwenstow. St Morwenna has a holy well too, but

THE MORWENSTOW LINE (33)

This line starts at the church itself, which perhaps has been overshadowed by the fame of its Victorian parson, the remarkable Robert Stephen Hawker. How can anyone ignore a priest who discards the standard cassock and wears either a fisherman's jersey and seaboots to sit and meditate in the hut he built on the cliff, or a yellow blanket with a hole cut in it for his head to tour his parish on a mule, carrying his pet pig? He used to say the blanket was a replica of the garb worn by early Cornish saints. As for the pig, he just happened to be very fond of animals – his cats had the run of the church during services, until one was excommunicated for catching a mouse during the sermon.

Yet his parishioners were devoted to him, he helped to save many shipwrecked mariners from the treacherous waters below the cliff (that hut was for observation as well as meditation), and he is credited with founding the Harvest Festival service, to restore the religious meaning of what had become an end-of-harvest drinking party. He may also have been the first to advance the now popular theory – though not accepted by ley-hunters – as to why some churches, including Morwenstow, have a chancel out of line with the nave. Hawker told his flock: 'As Christ hung upon the Cross His head inclined, so his sanctuary is built with an inclination to one side.'

Small wonder that if Morwenstow is mentioned in Cornwall, it is not the church but Parson Hawker whom people remember – not least the lines from his ballad about a Cornish hero; 'The Song of the Western Men': 'And shall Trelawny die? Here's twenty thousand Cornish men will know the reason why!' But the church of St Morwenna and St John is remarkable in its own right, particularly to the ley-hunter.

According to the church guide, there is reason to believe that a Celtic chapel or oratory stood on the site as early as the sixth century. 'And before that,' it adds, 'a pagan shrine with its holy well may have attracted humble devotees, for there is remarkable continuity about places with sacred associations.'

The site must have been a very special one for the Normans to erect such a grand building in so remote a place. Its most significant feature for the ley-hunter is the pattern of beak-heads round the doorway and more clearly round the central arch in the north aisle. Only one other Cornish church, at nearby Kilkhampton, has this kind of decoration, though it does crop up occasionally elsewhere, and it seems nobody is quite sure what it signifies. Even the guidebook cannot solve it – and this is no ordinary guidebook, but written by an MA of both Oxford and Cambridge, a professor of literature and philosophy and author of several works on philosophical subjects; he just happened to live in Morwenstow.

'The iconography [of this Norman beak-headed decoration] remains a mystery,' he wrote. 'It may have something to do with warding off evil ...'

The arch in the north arcade has twenty-six faces, some representing bearded old men but most of them 'deliberate caricatures of birdmen'. The beaks overlap the edge of the moulding beneath them, for all the world like ancient versions of Mr Chad, that wartime cartoon character who was always pictured peering over a wall. In the phrase of their twentieth-century successor, they may well be saying: 'Wot, no explanation?'

Robert Hawker, I am sure, would have read something significant into the beak-heads. He had a great interest in legends and the supernatural. He claimed to

Above: *Morwenstow's Celtic cross. There was probably an earlier pagan shrine here.* Left: *Some of the beak-heads in Morwenstow church. No one is sure of their significance.*

have seen a vision of St Morwenna, and he recorded a curious experience while riding between his two churches of Morwenstow and Welcombe, which may be of particular interest to ley-hunters, because he was riding his horse Carrow along the same route that this line takes to St Nectan's holy well.

He had to pass through the deep combe that leads down to the sea at Marsland Mouth, near Marsland Manor, which is also on the line. Later he wrote: 'As I entered the Gulph between the Vallies today, a Storm

leaped from the Sea and rushed at me roaring. I recognized a Demon and put Carrow into a gallop, and so escaped.'

He still had problems with the Devil, however, which gave rise to another tradition for which Hawker can claim the credit. When carrying out baptisms at St Nectan's Church he always insisted that the north door, normally kept shut, should be open during the service 'for the escape of the Fiend'. In many churches today the north door is still referred to as the 'Devil's Door'.

On his regular rides to St Nectan's Hawker not only crossed the Devil-haunted combe – where, after his unpleasant encounter, he always sang hymns as he rode to avoid repeating it – but also crossed the county border, which made the name of his second parish all the more appropriate. As Arthur Mee put it in one of his guides: 'It is as if it were saying to the traveller

Above: *Marsland Mouth, the end of the coombe where the rector encountered a Demon.* Above right: *St Nectan's well at Welcombe.* Below right: *Welcombe's welcoming church.*

coming from Cornwall, "Welcome to Devon".'

The church is welcoming too. I found the door open – the south door, that is – and inside is the eleventh-century font in which Hawker carried out his baptisms, and what is believed to be the oldest screen in Devon. St Nectan's was originally a chapel attached to Hartland Abbey, and like Launcells church it was probably built on an existing holy site by a well, which was later named after St Nectan. It is just across the road, protected by a similar stone structure to the one at St Swithin's, and although it is high on the hillside it is said to continue producing fresh water all through the year.

North of Welcombe is Firebeacon Cross, and with

un- exciting tumuli and a crossroads, plus a corrugated-iron chapel, which was not quite in the same league as the churches at either Morwenstow or Welcombe. I decided to leave the field clear for the local dowser and to seek leylines in pastures new – or in this case, pastures very old.

a name that qualifies it as a ley marker twice over – a beacon and a crossroads – the line ought to go through it. Unfortunately, not even my thickest pencil could include it, so the next marker is another holy well, at Philham. Here the welcome is not so evident, because the well must be on private land at St Clare's Farm, and there is no indication of its existence to the passer-by.

The line ends at an ancient settlement on Windbury Heath, overlooking Windbury Point on Bideford Bay. It can be reached only by the coastal path, but it has the merit of covering a substantial area and provides a large target for leylines.

Indeed, it is also at the end of a line that I attempted to base on Kilkhampton church, in view of its rare beak-heads. I had also been told that a local dowser had detected a ley in the churchyard. However, the only possibility I could find was the line to the Windbury settlement, which relied almost entirely on some rather

HEREFORD
AND WORCESTER

I VENTURED into Herefordshire with some trepidation, because this is Alfred Watkins' country. He was born and bred here; this is where he first noticed the alignment of ancient sites and evolved his theories about leylines and their terminology. It is, in fact, an area in which one would expect to find no leyline unturned – or rather, unstraightened. However, there are still gaps to be filled. For instance Alfred generally gives very little information about any churches on his leylines except their name. Some of the other markers are merely identified as 'homestead' or 'cross-roads' or 'barn'. And the alignments he mentions in *The Old Straight Track* sometimes have only three markers, even over quite long distances. Some of them – dare I say it? – do not appear on my map to be in a straight line.

One of his favourite sites is Arthur's Stone, on a hilltop overlooking Golden Valley. Golden or gold is significant for Alfred because he notes that it often appears in place names on leylines. It could be something to do with the gold-smiths who used to travel along them, he thinks, or connected with the golden rays of the sun. He quotes several alignments that pass through Arthur's Stone, but I could not find any that clearly came into my category of five markers within twenty miles.

One goes through Newton Tump to the west and Bodcott Barn to the east. The Tump is, indeed, another mound, but he does not explain the significance of the barn. Another line runs from Dorstone church to the Knapp, 'a well-known point of 700 feet elevation'. A third goes through Eardisly Castle moat, Snodhill Castle and 'ancient homesteads'. And his final suggestion is Bredwardine Castle, the Golden Well, the Gold Post and Cefn Hill, which does make five markers but on my map I could only find the castle and Cefn Hill. The well must still be there, but perhaps somebody has been a little unfair and moved the Gold Post. So with apologies to Alfred, here is my attempt at an Arthur's Stone Line. It is sixteen miles long and takes in three churches, a ford and a motte and bailey. I hope he would have approved.

Inside the ancient tree at Much Marcle.

THE ARTHUR'S STONE LINE (34)

Arthur's Stone is not just a stone, it is a chambered long barrow with other stones around it. There is no record of who was buried there, or why, but one thing is certain: it wasn't King Arthur. This is a Neolithic mound, dating from about 3000 BC, but in this part of the world any ancient site, particularly if it is on a hilltop, is likely to be given an Arthurian connection.

The line starts to the west of it, at a motte and bailey known as Mouse Castle near Hay-on-Wye. No doubt, with his local knowledge, Alfred could have explained its curious name and even linked it with ley-lines, as he did with the snail, but it baffles me.

Having passed through Arthur's Stone the line reaches the church of St Michael (slayer of dragons) and All Angels at Moccas Court. Moccas is another odd name, but this time it can be explained. It comes from the Welsh words meaning 'pigs' and 'moor'. However,

the church guide also mentions that the Celts had a mythological god called Moccoss, and Alfred might have suggested that he could have had a shrine here before the church was built. I like to think he also had the power to impose bad luck on a project, hence the term 'put the mockers on something'.

Either theory may be difficult to prove, but it is 'almost indisputable', as the guide puts it, that a Christian community was established here in the fifth century by the Welsh saint Dubricius, a predecessor of the better known St David. He founded a monastery and spent much of his time here. The present church was built in about 1130, using the curious local stone called tufa, which looks rather like petrified sponge or even grey Gruyère cheese. When the building was restored in the nineteenth century by George Gilbert Scott, he went to great lengths to obtain similar 'holey'

stone for the walls, and St Michael's still looks much as it did in Norman times.

It stands on rising ground in the park that surrounds Moccas Court. A fortified castle used to stand in what is now the deer park, but in 1650 the manor passed into the hands of Edward Cornewall, and in the eighteenth century the Cornewalls built the imposing Moccas Court, which can be seen from the churchyard. It is still owned by a descendant of the original Edward Cornewall, who is buried in the church under the organ loft where the family pew used to be.

Over the south door is a tympanum which is said to represent the Tree of Life, with human figures clinging to it for protection from the wild beasts attacking them. I am always intrigued by early portrayals of wild beasts – just in case they include a dragon or a serpent, which feature in some leyline theories – but the tympanum is so worn that I could not identify any of the creatures. There is also an upright stone by the church that I hoped might be a ley marker, but it is just a remnant from an earlier wall. Nonetheless, the church is a fascinating marker in itself.

The line goes over the River Wye at a point where a track leads down from Monnington on the far bank, an indication that this used to be a crossing point. These days one has to drive a couple of miles upriver to the nearest bridge, then drive back to the next marker, St Mary's at Monnington on Wye, where the churchyard, perhaps significantly, is surrounded by a ditch.

St Mary's was originally thirteenth-century, but it was rebuilt in 1679, and there is not much earlier work to see. Indeed, the most interesting sculptures I spotted were not in the church or the churchyard but in the private garden next door. There is a circle of heads on stone pillars which look like members of the Churchill family. It is just a coincidence, I am sure, that this modern version of a stone circle is uncommonly close to the line from Arthur's Stone.

The final marker is another St Mary's, this time at Credenhill. Apart from the fifteenth-century porch, I could see very little, but on the hill above it is a substantial Iron Age hill-fort covering some fifty acres.

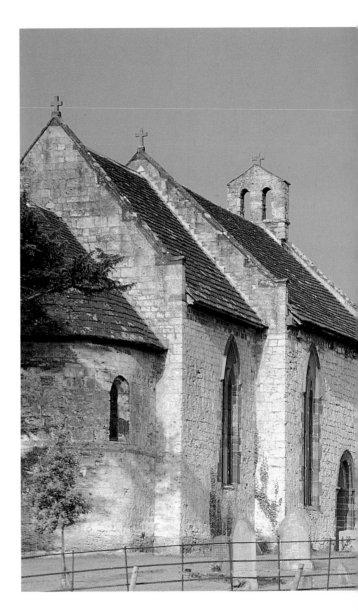

Above: *Moccas church, possibly built on the site of a Celtic shrine.* Left: *Arthur's Stone, high above Golden valley.*

Experts say it was constructed about 400 BC and was occupied continuously until the Romans came.

However, Alfred Watkins seems to prefer the Iron Age camp at Aconbury, so I tried out one of his Aconbury lines.

THE ACONBURY CAMP LINE (35)

Alfred's markers for his line include three churches and Castle Farm, Madley, which were easy to locate, and a house called Hill of Eaton, which was not. He linked the house with Eaton Tregor Castle, but here again his local knowledge was more detailed than my map, and I could find no trace of either name. But we have enough markers without it.

St Mary's Church, Tyberton, was originally twelfth century, but the oldest features these days are probably the preaching cross and the ancient yew in the church-yard. Ley-hunters may be briefly encouraged by the squirrels that feature in various parts of the church, including a handsome modern book-rest on the altar. Could they be a subconscious link with pagan wood-land rites? Alas, no. A squirrel is part of the coat of arms of the Lee Warners, who married into the squire's family. There is not even the customary eagle holding up the lectern, to encourage thoughts of the wild; at Tyberton it is supported by a sturdy angel.

Alfred identifies Castle Farm at Madley as 'proba-bly' on the site of Cublington Castle; Cublington village lies between Tyberton and Madley. He says that an earlier gazetteer mentions the castle without indi-cating its site, so Alfred reckons it could just as well be this one. He detected signs of a moat around it, and from the centre of the mound 'a narrow, straight, cobbled causeway crossed the moat site, and this is sighted on Aconbury Camp, seven miles distant'.

The farmhouse certainly stands on a mound, but I could see no sign of a moat, and the 'cobbled causeway' looks like part of a normal farmyard. I also failed to spot the distant Aconbury Camp, but maybe the intervening vegetation has grown a lot higher in the seventy years since he was there. He also quoted legends about an underground passage to Madley church and the discovery of a 'pipkin of gold' in the cellar. But the current farmer told me he knew very little about the farmhouse's history, except that it was built in the six-

Above: *An owl on a leyline ought to be significant, but at Castle Farm the farmer's mother just happened to like owls.*
Right: *The stone pillar outside Aston Ingham church.*

teenth century. I was intrigued by the stone owls on the gateposts, but like the squirrels at Tyberton they have no pre-Christian significance. It just so happens that the farmer's mother liked owls.

Alfred's next marker is Cobhall Court. He says its name comes from being on an ancient cobbled way – the one from Castle Farm, no doubt – and for all I know, it was. But I felt on safer ground with Aconbury Camp itself, which is well documented by archae-ologists. The site covers about seventeen acres and was occupied from a rather later date than Credenhill

Camp, again until the Roman occupation. Alfred's line runs along the edge of it.

St Mary's Church, Little Dewchurch, his next marker, has four medieval gargoyles on the tower, always a welcome sight for the ley-hunter. One is recognizably a lion, two are unidentifiable beasts with mouths menacingly open, and the fourth has a man's face with his hands holding the mouth wide – perhaps trying to look as menacing as his neighbours.

Ley-hunters should not be deceived by the emblem of an open flower that features on the door hinges, the roof beams and other parts of the church. It is not a reference to a nature-worshipping past, just the 'signature' of the eminent Victorian architect who carried out the restoration.

St John the Baptist's Church at Aston Ingham, the final marker, is just inside the county border. It was here that, for the first time, I found a leyline mentioned in a church guide. 'It is believed by many leading authorities', it says, 'that somewhere lies a long barrow or tumulus, possibly beneath the church, for Aston lies in a direct line or ley from the Camp on May Hill [just outside the village] to the Camp at Aconbury'.

One of those 'leading authorities', I suppose, was the well-known local 'ley preacher', Alfred Watkins, though surprisingly he does not mention May Hill.

It is easy to spot the first likely evidence of the ley, a stone pillar in front of the church, 'believed to be that from a Celtic cross'. Aston used to be in the heart of the Forest of Dean, and the ley-friendly guide explains how travellers would have left gifts to the gods of the Forest at the cross. But it adds rather bitterly: 'One authority denies us the antiquity of even the pillar of our churchyard cross, and calls the cross itself "modern".' I am sure ley-hunters will refuse to be discouraged.

There has been a church on the site since Saxon times, and although the Norman church had to be largely rebuilt in the 1890s, the red sandstone and local rubble that were used make it look much older. Its main attraction is the seventeenth-century lead font, with its rather jolly heads as decoration and the initials W.M. – probably William and Mary. Again a slightly bitter note creeps into the guide: 'Indeed in most guides to churches and to Herefordshire the font is the only reason the authors give for mentioning Aston Ingham at all.' Not any more.

The line could extend into Gloucestershire, to a moat at Mote Farm, Taynton, but there is more to pursue in Herefordshire, including Alfred's other leyline through Little Dewchurch.

THE LITTLE DEWCHURCH (SIX CHURCHES) LINE (36)

There are only four churches on Alfred's leyline, but with the help of a ruler I found another, and the sixth one appeared quite unexpectedly, without any help from me. *The Old Straight Track* has so many leylines in this area, linking so many churches, that it is a little surprising he missed these two.

Alfred's version starts at Woolhope, but I was able to extend the line further back to Putley church, which perhaps he missed or just left out because it apparently has no patron saint. No name is mentioned at the church itself, and *Crockford's Clerical Directory* confirms that the dedication is 'not known'. However, the font offers a helpful choice. It is carved with the animal and bird emblems of the four apostles, and for good

measure there is a Noah's Ark carved on it too, which presumably contains all the symbols of the other saints. Alternatively, there is a large selection of half-lifesize disciples on the splendid reredos.

Woolhope does not have this problem. The church is dedicated to St George, another popular saint among ley-hunters because of his dragon-slaying. The next church on the line, St Mary's at Fownhope, is mentioned in *The Ley Hunter's Companion*, which comments on the 'strange beasts' on Fownhope's Norman tympanum. The church leaflet, however, says they are just an eagle and a beast, emblems of St John and St Luke.

St Mary's has other notable features from days long gone. A stone with a Communion chalice carved on it

nothing at all. Alfred Watkins can be forgiven for missing it, because it lies behind some farm buildings, almost invisible from the road and accessible only with the farmer's permission. This is St John's Church, Bolstone, derelict and deserted since the last service was held there in the 1980s. The farmer told me he kept the grass in the churchyard cut for twelve years,

Above: *The meticulously accurate milepost at Fownhope.*
Left: *The Norman tympanum in Fownhope church.* Right: *The abandoned church at Bolstone.*

is believed to have marked the grave of the last Norman vicar of Fownhope. There is an ancient parish chest carved out of the trunk of an oak tree, and two fonts, one Tudor, the other a portable version, which always used to be carried into the porch for baptisms. The leaflet explains that in this way the baptized child can then enter the church literally as well as spiritually. As a bonus there are some stocks by the churchyard wall and a remarkably precise milestone by the flagstaff inscribed: 'Hereford 6¼ miles and 56 yards.'

St Mary's, in fact, has a great deal to offer the curious visitor, but the next church on the line has

but nobody seemed to care, so he gave up. It is now just a wilderness, and the church has holes in the roof and goodness knows what kind of a mess inside.

But sad little St John's is not entirely forgotten. When I reached the final church on the Six Churches line, St Mary and St Thomas à Becket's at Much Birch, I had two pleasant surprises. For only the second time. I found a reference in a church leaflet to a leyline, and it also mentioned Bolstone church. Writing about Much Birch church, it says: 'The present building took over ancient pagan sites and is probably on an old straight line to Little Dewchurch, Bolstone, Fownhope and Woolhope from pre-Christian days.' Obviously the influence of Alfred Watkins has had a lasting impact; here is one prophet who is not unknown in his own country.

A Victorian cherub swoops above the chancel at Much Birch.

The church was rebuilt in the nineteenth century and there is little evidence left of its early origins, apart from a fourteenth-century preaching cross. Its most unusual feature is the ceiling in the chancel, painted blue with cherubs peering out of the clouds. The cherubs seem to have very Victorian faces; perhaps one of them is a youthful Alfred, gazing down benevolently on a church where his *Old Straight Track* must be remembered so well.

As a final tribute to him in his home county, I followed a leyline described in his *Manual*, which starts and finishes conveniently close to the border with Gloucestershire, and that is where my ley hunt takes me in the next chapter.

THE ROSS-ON-WYE LINE (37)

The line starts at the Iron Age hill-fort at Wall Hills, about a mile west of Ledbury. There is not a lot to see, apart from some banks and ditches, but like most hill-forts it has the great merit as a ley marker of covering some thirty-six acres. And when the line reaches Much Marcle, a lot more starts happening.

It passes through Hellen's House, a sixteenth-century mansion that owes its name not to a lady called Helen but to the much earlier de Helyon family. They are represented in St Bartholomew's Church by a rare fourteenth-century effigy carved in oak, believed to be Walter de Helyon. More interesting to the ley-hunter, though, are the carved decorations on the pillars in the

nave, an assortment of strange beasts, heads and foliage, including a man's face with foliage coming out of his mouth, reminiscent of our old pagan friend, the Green Man.

In the churchyard are the base and stump of an old preaching cross and one of the oldest yew trees in the country, possibly 2000 years old. Glaring down on them from the tower are some gargoyles, another reminder of pre-Christian days.

Before leaving Much Marcle the line passes through Mortimer's Castle, a motte and bailey some fifty yards north of the church. The line misses the famous Marcle Hill, where a terrifying landslip in 1575 swallowed up a vast area of countryside, including Kynaston Chapel; only its bell has survived. I can't resist the thought that, if the chapel had been on the leyline, perhaps it might have fared better.

In Ross-on-Wye, the *Manual* says, the line goes through the 'Corpse Cross' in the churchyard, erected in memory of 315 victims of the plague who were buried in a pit nearby in 1637. Any link with a leyline seems rather tenuous, but St Mary's Church has some intriguing features for the ley-hunter.

John Kyrle, known as 'The Man of Ross', worshipped here and planted an elm tree outside the window by his pew. After his death in 1724 two elm shoots sprang up through the floor under the pew, and this was regarded as so significant that they were allowed to grow – an unconscious reminder of long-forgotten paganism perhaps, to repeat the now familiar phrase. Unfortunately, they caused dry rot in the wooden floor and had to be destroyed, and the tree itself was felled in 1878 during the restoration work. However, as a happy compromise, two climbers were planted in a stone trough near to the window, and they are growing there still.

The stump of an old preaching cross at Much Marcle.

pre-historic sites, but Alfred says it is a fine example of a marker stone indicating the direction of the leyline. It stands upright, about seven feet high, and there are grooves running from top to bottom. 'It seems quite impossible that they should result from any natural cause,' says Alfred. An indication of the distance to the next marker? He doesn't say.

The next marker is St Dubricius's Church at Whitchurch, dedicated to the saint who founded the monastery at Moccas Court, on the Arthur's Stone Line. The church stands close to the river – in fact a little too close at times. It has been seriously flooded twice in the last fifty-odd years. The river is also the basis of a delightful legend about the saint's birth. The local king found his daughter was pregnant and ordered her to be put in a sack and drowned in the

St Mary's other unlikely invaders are hedgehogs, which feature on various items around the church. Like the woodland creatures I have found in other churches, such as squirrels at Tyberton, there would seem to be a logical explanation. The church leaflet says hedgehogs are also know as 'urchins', and they may be a pictorial pun, or rebus, on the name Archenfield, on John Kyrle's coat of arms. I find that a little convoluted; why not just an arch-in-a-field? I think Alfred might devise a more convincing explanation that would link hedge-hogs with elm trees and leylines.

His next marker is the 'ford at Goodrich', which presumably is where a path goes down to the river below Goodrich Castle. It is a pity the line misses the castle, which is on a mound where castles have stood since Saxon times. From Goodrich the line goes through the Queen Stone, which is well away from the road in a horseshoe bend of the Wye. It is not mentioned among

Wye, but she was washed onto a sandbank unhurt. So he ordered her to be burned, but she wouldn't burn, 'presumably because she was still wet,' as the church leaflet comments – drily. The next morning her baby was born and named Dubricius, or Dyfrig in Welsh, meaning 'water baby'. He became a great teacher, bishop and saint.

The church goes back to Saxon times, and in the churchyard is the base of an old preaching cross, which is not very unusual, and a tulip tree, which is. The species was brought over in the seventeenth century from America, where it was known as 'canoe wood' because a canoe large enough for twenty people could be hollowed out of its trunk. They grow to a height of 150 feet; the one at Whitchurch is said to be 300 years old – and still growing. The North American Indians and their sacred rites have been linked with leylines, so perhaps it is not just coincidence that this unlikely import should have been planted here.

The line next passes through a maze, but one that was planted only in the 1970s to mark the Queen's silver jubilee. It follows a tradition, of course, that

Above: The ruins of Goodrich Castle look down on the River Wye. Left above: Rare to find climbers growing inside a church at Ross. Left below: Rarer still to find a tulip tree in the churchyard at Whitchurch.

dates back to pagan times, so it is interesting that, like the tulip tree, it should be placed in that position.

The final marker is described in the *Manual* as Gt Doward Camp, but even Alfred agrees that it is not marked on the Ordnance Survey map. There is, however, an Iron Age hill-fort, plus some Bronze Age barrows, on the adjoining Little Doward, and in the same area is Arthur's Cave, which is, in spite of its name, the oldest prehistoric feature in Herefordshire by many thousands of years. It was inhabited from the Ice Age onwards, from the time when Palaeolithic hunters lived there in about 12000 BC. Inevitably, legend has it that the cave was one of the innumerable hiding-places of the ubiquitous King Arthur. Having started the Herefordshire leylines at Arthur's Stone, Arthur's Cave seems an appropriate place to end them.

GLOUCESTERSHIRE

GLOUCESTERSHIRE is represented by only one leyline in *The Ley Hunter's Companion*, but it is a particularly interesting one because it contains what I think must be the ultimate in leyline churches – St Nicholas's Church, Saintbury. There are so many extraordinary features about it, either linking it with pre-Christian days or posing unanswered questions. The church seems to have become something of a place of pilgrimage for ley-hunters, because I found a recent entry in the visitors' book by someone who had been attending a ley-hunters' conference some distance away. He had made a point of visiting the church and wrote that he was deeply impressed by the atmosphere that he experienced in it.

To me the atmosphere seemed fairly average, but I found its ancient curiosities quite fascinating. Only a few of these are mentioned in the *Companion*, which treats it as just another marker on 'A Cotswold Ley', but I think it deserves the leyline to be named after the church instead.

Carving in the niche of Chavenage Chapel.

THE SAINTBURY CHURCH LINE (38)

I am perhaps influenced by the fact that, as a layman, I found the other markers on this line rather unexciting. There is a roadside cross, a couple of barrows, both now flattened, a Saxon pagan cemetery, not marked even on the map used by the *Companion*, and Seven Wells Farm, which is private. Happily, there is ample compensation at St Nicholas's Church, Saintbury.

Even the name of the village has an unexpected story behind it, as the church guide explains. It does not mean 'Borough of the Saint', the obvious interpretation.

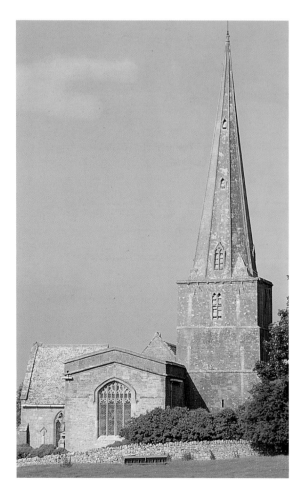

Instead, it comes from 'swain', meaning a village, and 'burg', which also means 'fort'. It is thought to date from the period when there were Roman camps in the area, and the guidebook says it means the 'Fort or Town of Villagers'. Anything involving an ancient fort is likely to whet the appetite of a ley-hunter.

The most obvious unusual feature of the church itself is the position of the tower and spire on the south transept, instead of at the west end or in the centre. The *Companion* notes it, but offers no comment; nor does the guidebook, except to agree it is unusual. The *Companion* also notes a Saxon sundial and some gargoyles, again without comment. Inside the church it takes more interest in a curious octagonal stone table in the south transept. It says this is commonly known as 'the pre-Christian altar', because some believe it predates even the Saxon church on this site. To be fair, there are also some who don't, including the esteemed Pevsner. He says it was simply a 'dole table', used for distributing the bread dole on Sundays. The guidebook takes a middle road and says its origin is obscure, though it does quote the theory that it was a heathen altar on which sacrifices were offered. Take your pick.

The last feature mentioned in the *Companion* is a stone slab under a Jacobean table in the north transept, said to be the medieval altar that was hidden there when the Puritans ordered stone altars to be destroyed.

But there is a lot more to St Nicholas' than these. I was attracted first of all, if attracted is the right word, by the quite hideous face carved over the Norman doorway to the church. Perhaps because it can be seen at such close quarters, it looks a lot uglier than the average gargoyle, and one wonders if, like gargoyles, it is 'an unconscious reminder of long-forgotten paganism'. The guidebook reckons it is probably just a dreadful warning to the congregation not to misbehave in church. I would think it is just as likely to be there to frighten away evil spirits.

Inside the church there is quite a range of unusual features to choose from, some of them unexplained, like the identity of a female saint in the east window and the picture of a bishop in the sanctuary. 'He might be St Nicholas, the patron saint of the church, though the inscription "San. Nicholas priest W" is puzzling,' muses the guide.

Another inscription it draws attention to is on the memorial to William Warburton, a former rector of what is called 'St Burie'. Obviously, whoever wrote it had not seen the guidebook's analysis of Saintbury.

But for a ley-hunter the most fascinating discovery is a figure portrayed on the south wall, in the splay of a window. The guidebook does it full justice: 'For a long time no one seemed to know how it came to be there or why it should be lying on its side in that particular part of the church. However it is now thought that the figure is a "sheila-na-gig", a Celtic fertility object.'

That indeed is what it looks like, a distinctly pagan representation of the Earth goddess which has occasionally crept into Christian churches.

I have come upon a sheila-na-gig in a church only once before, at Whittlesford in Cambridgeshire, where it is carved much more elaborately over an outside door, and indeed the *Companion* contains a photograph of it. The Saintbury version is not only plainer but in a

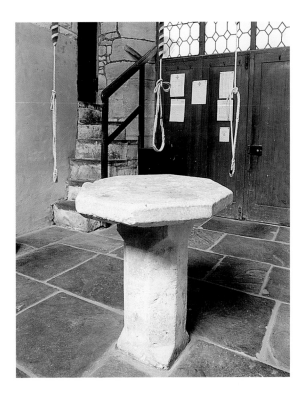

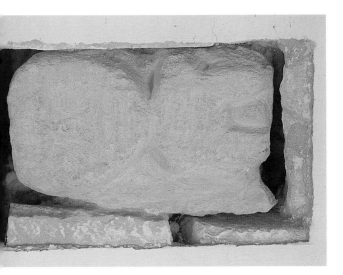

Above: *A pre-Christian altar or a medieval dole table?*
Left: *The tower of Sainbury church, sited over the south transept.* Below: *A sheila-na-gig.*

much less prominent position; which is why it fails to get a mention in the *Companion*. Indeed, I would not have spotted it myself without the help of that invaluable church guide.

The other marker on the Saintbury Church Line that proved unexpectedly fruitful, if only indirectly, is Seven Wells Farm. The *Companion* goes into the significance of the name in some detail, but as it is private property and the wells are not visible anyway I did not go into the farm. It occurred to me, however, that if 'seven wells' means so much in ley-hunting, there is another group in Gloucestershire that still exist and are easily accessible.

Out of curiosity, I put a ruler on the Seven Wells at Bisley church, and with a few wiggles, I found an alignment with four other markers within nine miles.

THE BISLEY SEVEN WELLS LINE (39)

Bisley has earned some unfortunate nicknames over the centuries. After the collapse of the wool industry on which it depended it became known as 'Beggarly Bisley', and shivering travellers have referred to it as 'Bisley God-Help-Us', not because of any supernatural threats but because of its exposed and windy position. It is mainly notable these days, however, for the semi-circle of springs outside the churchyard, the 'Seven Wells', where the Rev. Thomas Keble, brother of the better-known John Keble, instituted the custom of well-dressing.

It is now a common practice in some rural areas, particularly in Derbyshire where I go ley-hunting later, but it still seems ironic that a Church of England cleric should reintroduce an entirely pagan ceremony of making peace offerings to the water gods. Perhaps it is appropriate that it should be revived on a leyline.

The 'Seven Wells' were restored as a memorial to Thomas Keble, and the water now gushes out of elaborate little gabled recesses in the stone churchyard wall – though confusingly there are only five of them.

It seems agreed that the Romans probably had a pagan religious site where the church now stands, and there has been a Christian church here since Saxon times. When Bisley was a prosperous wool centre, the mill owners constructed their own staircases and doors to their private galleries in the church, so they did not rub shoulders with their workers, but the energetic

Above: *The manticore at North Cerney.* Left: *Bisley's 'Seven Wells', where Thomas Keble revived the pagan custom of well-dressing.*

Thomas Keble removed them all. He also heightened the church roof, which had apparently been supported only by a fir pole.

With his usual thoroughness he must have reshuffled a great many other features of the church. There are medieval stone figures in the roof of the north aisle, and stone coffin lids set in the wall below. But on the plus side he did retrieve a Norman font that was found in the churchyard. It not only has decorative carvings around it, but also two fish carved inside the bottom of the bowl – a disconcerting sight for any sharp-eyed baby as it is held over the font for baptism.

The strangest feature at Bisley church, however, is outside in the churchyard. It is shaped rather like a six-sided stone rocket, and it was variously known as the

Well Head, the Boneyard or the Poor Soul's Light, where candles were lit when prayers were said for the poor and alms were left for them. Normally, a poor soul's light is inside the church, which seems logical if the candles are to stay alight. The one in Bisley churchyard is said to be unique.

It also covered the church well, and it earned its title of the Boneyard or Bonehouse because it is said bones were dumped into it when old graves were broken open. The term took on a new significance after a priest was called out one dark night to give Communion to a dying parishioner and accidentally fell down the well. His body was not discovered until some time later.

Tradition has it that the Pope was so irritated at the loss of one of his priests that he excommunicated the entire village, and burials were forbidden in the churchyard for two years. Funeral parties had to walk the fifteen miles to Bibury to bury their dead in a corner of

The splendid cross on North Cerney's rood screen, picked up for about £10 in an Italian shop.

part of the defences of the Dobunni tribe's capital before the Romans arrived.

The final marker is All Saints' Church, North Cerney. Like Bisley, it has a history going back to Saxon times, and like Saintbury church it has an assortment of unusual features with odd tales to tell. For instance the central figure on the rood-loft of Christ on the Cross dates from about 1600, but it has been there only since earlier in the twentieth century, and it was acquired in a most fortuitous way.

While the present rood-loft was being constructed, the parish priest, a churchwarden and the architect made a shopping expedition to Italy. They were in an antique shop when the priest stumbled against a packing case, dislodging the lid. The others went to his assistance and discovered inside the case this splendid figure of Christ. The shopkeeper said it was of little value and sold it to them for about ten pounds. Visitors to All Saints' can see what a bargain they got. Just a happy accident? For the ley-hunter, though, the most intriguing feature at All Saints' is North Cerney's answer to the Saintbury sheila-na-gig, an outline of a manticore on the outside wall of the south transept. The manticore was a mythological beast with the body of a lion, the head of a man, a scorpion's tail – and an reputation for eating people, as well as other manticores. One early Greek scholar described it as 'the most noxious animal that ever infested the earth'.

What it was doing on the wall of a quiet country church in Gloucestershire has never been explained. There is a more worn outline of another one nearby, perhaps its mate – or its dinner. The church leaflet says optimistically that manticores 'do not appear to hold any significance'. Perhaps Alfred Watkins would not agree.

Encouraged by all these bizarre discoveries, and lacking any guidance from Alfred on Gloucestershire leylines, I put a rule on another ancient landmark that I have come across before, the Long Stone near Minchinhampton, not far from the entrance to Gatcombe Lodge. I pointed the rule vaguely southwards – and up came an alignment that I have called the Minchinhampton Long Stone Line.

the churchyard known as Bisley Piece. The route they took, known as Dead Man's Lane, is also the route of the Seven Wells Line, which seems to confirm a recent theory that some leylines may also be corpse trails.

The mourners had to go past the next marker on the line, the Giant's Stone, where there were tales of hauntings by headless spectres, just to add to their depression. The stone itself is thought to be all that remains of a long barrow.

The line then passes through an earthwork on the slopes above Edgeworth, it just misses the Hoar Stone long barrow, and finally reaches Scrubditch, an Iron Age ditch with a bank still ten feet high, which was

THE MINCHINHAMPTON LONG STONE LINE (40)

The Long Stone dates back before 3000 BC. It is one of the oldest prehistoric sites in the county and is thought to be all that remains of a long barrow. It is a chunk of oolite, a kind of limestone with holes in it, which stands nearly eight feet high and probably goes down the same amount into the ground. It is about 300 yards from the second marker, a more complete barrow of about the same period. A little further south, opposite the entrance to Gatcombe Park, is another stone called the Tinglestone, for no obvious reason unless it ties in with a legend that has been applied to the Long Stone as well. It is said that if a child suffering from rickets is passed through a hole in it, it will be cured. Maybe it feels a tingle in the process

On the face of it, the next feature on the line looks much more dramatic: a Neolithic long barrow in the glebe field at Avening, containing three stone burial chambers. Alas, it is a trap for the unwary ley-hunter looking for confirmation of a straight line. The stones are genuine enough, but they were all moved to this site *en bloc* in 1806 from a field nearby. We are assured they have exactly the same relationship to each other as they had on the original site, but to the meticulous ley-hunter they have rather lost their significance as a ley marker – unless, of course, they realized in 1806 that the old site was off the line.

However, Avening church provides ample compensation. Here is another ancient church on a Saxon site, in an area where ancient tracks met, and ley-hunters will enjoy the carving on a pillar that looks like a beast with one head and two bodies peering out of some foliage. An 'unconscious reminder', perhaps?

The church itself has a fascinating history. Before the Conquest, Avening was held by a young nobleman called Brittric, who was sent on a mission to Flanders by Edward the Confessor and there met an attractive

young lady called Matilda. She fell in love with him, but he did not reciprocate, and perhaps on the rebound she went off and married William of Normandy. When he became King of England she had her own back on the man who had spurned her. She persuaded William to confiscate his estates and put him in prison, where he died.

The 3000-year-old Long Stone near Gatcombe Lodge.

This was rather more drastic than she had intended, and in her remorse it is said she rebuilt Avening church so that Mass could be said for his soul. Ironically, she and the king lived in Brittric's former home at Avening Court while they supervised the restoration. The church was dedicated to the Holy Rood on Holy Cross Day, 14 September, either in 1070 or 1080, opinions differ. To mark the occasion, Matilda gave the workmen a feast of boar's head, and the Avening Feast is still celebrated on what is called, rather unkindly, Pig Face Day. It must have been great fun for the village, and one hopes some consolation for the unfortunate Brittric.

Perhaps as a further act of repentance William and

Above: The family chapel at Chavenage, built as a folly but said to be haunted by a geniune monk. Right: Westonbirt Arboreteum, where the line ends.

Matilda gave Avening and Brittric's other estates to Caen Abbey a couple of years later. It meant that, for the next 300-odd years, Avening was sent French priests from Caen. Such are the long-term repercussions of unrequited love.

The next marker is the imposing chapel at Chavenage, an Elizabethan stately home now opened to the public in the summer months by its owner, Colonel David Lowsley-Williams. The chapel is conveniently linked to the rear of the house by a narrow passage, and it contains memorials to the colonel's grandfather and uncle. There is a Saxon font, a sixteenth-century altar, some rather jolly gargoyles and a most imposing tower. But all is not quite what it seems.

The Saxon font was retrieved from the foundations of a barn on the estate, the altar probably started life as on overmantel on the fireplace in the main hall, the gargoyles are a little too jolly for a ley-hunter, and the imposing tower was actually built as a folly in the 1700s, with just a tiny 'body' attached to it – hardly big enough to be called a nave. It was replaced by the present building about 100 years later.

These days it can seat 100 people, and services are held regularly. In spite of its rather bizarre history, it is a genuine chapel – but is it a genuine ley marker? I clutch at one straw. According to the official guide to Chavenage: 'a robed monk is said to haunt the chapel and has allegedly been seen twice since the war.' So maybe the monk knows something we don't.

More routinely, the leyline then passes through a tumulus between Chavenage and Beverstone, before finally disappearing into Westonbirt Arboretum. This was founded by Robert Slayner Holford in 1829 and is generally regarded as one of the finest collection of trees in the world. It was obviously an ideal site to plant them, and, of course, trees used to be associated with pre-Christian forms of worship. Did Robert Slayner Holford know something too?

I feel I am pushing my luck. Time to move on …

WARWICKSHIRE
AND OXFORDSHIRE

THERE is only one Warwickshire leyline in *The Ley Hunter's Companion*, and half of that is in Hereford and Worcester. It goes through Warwick Castle and Shakespeare's burial place, Holy Trinity Church, Stratford-upon-Avon, but they are already so well known that there seems little left to say about them. I found one of the lesser known churches on the line much more entertaining: St Ecgwin's at Church Honeybourne. Apart from its unusual dedication – Ecgwin was a seventh-century Bishop of Worcester, not widely known outside his diocese – it has some delightful carvings of shield-bearing angels on the roof corbels. They look rather portly and are apparently seated, holding up their shields just like ice-skating judges with their scorecards. But Church Honeybourne's most endearing feature was much more unexpected: the rector's numberplate was HII REV.

Paul Devereux, co-author of the *Companion*, could not have been too happy with this leyline because it is rejected in his subsequent *Ley Hunter's Guide*. Anyway, Hereford and Worcester has had ample coverage already.

I felt that there must be a Warwickshire leyline somewhere and tried a rule on Nadbury Camp, one of the largest hill-forts in the county. Any fort that covers seventeen acres is a good starting point for a leyline, and, happily, one materialized, with five markers in seventeen miles.

The King's Stone, eight foot 'outpost' of the Rollright Stones, which are said not only to be uncountable but also liable to visit the stream for a drink.

THE NADBURY HILL-FORT LINE (41)

The line starts north of the fort at Bishop's Itchington church, dedicated to St Michael, who did slay dragons. It was built in 1872, but it stands on the site of the daughter chapel of All Saints' Church, Lower Itchington. The only unusual note is struck by the very pleasant house just across the road, which is incongruously called 'The Cell'. A reminder of an earlier hermit, perhaps, or a less homely kind of cell? I didn't like to enquire.

In contrast to a comparatively new church, the next marker is an old barn, which used to be a medieval chapel of ease. It is in Burton Dassett, some five miles to the south. It went out of use at the Reformation, but during the reign of Charles I the Roman Catholic lady of the manor, Lady Wootton, installed a Catholic priest and used it as her personal chapel.

The Puritans soon stopped that, and it became derelict until a farmer rerooted it and used it as a barn. Only the substantial stone buttresses on what is left of the original walls still have a distinct ecclesiastical flavour.

Nadbury Camp was an Iron Age hill-fort in a commanding position on a hillside. According to the *Guide to Prehistoric England,* it was defended by a bank, a ditch, and a counter-scarp bank, which is a bank outside the ditch. It adds, however, that the site has been 'badly denuded', and I failed to spot any ditches, counter-scarp or otherwise.

Above: *The view along the line from the golf club towards Tadmarton.* Left: *The buttresses of this barn at Burton Dassett survive from a medieval chapel.*

Soon after the hill-fort the line crosses the county boundary, near Hornton Hill Farm, and continues into Oxfordshire to join quite a network of leylines in the area of the Rollright Stones. It crosses one of these lines on what is perhaps significantly called Jester Hill. Is somebody not taking this seriously?

After passing through the handsome tithe barn on the other side of the road, the next marker on the line is Tadmarton church. St Nicholas's Church dates back to the thirteenth century and it still has its original font, decorated with some grotesque and unexplained heads.

Somewhere in the churchyard is a particularly large grave occupied by Coleman Samuel Shutford. Mr

Shutford was reported to weigh 36 stone, and according to the burial register, the coffin was more than seven feet long and the combined weight of coffin and corpse was eight hundredweight.

The line ends at a holy well on an area of Tadmarton Heath, which is now a golf course; the well is just behind the clubhouse. The club secretary knew nothing about its history or which saint was connected with it, but he told me it never dries up throughout the year and supplies water for the clubhouse and for irrigating the course. Before leaving Warwickshire I followed a line mentioned by Alfred Watkins in two of his books, which fortuitously links the area of the Battle of Edgehill with the area of the Rollright Stones, the next ley-hunting ground. It passes over a hill with a name that, for ley-hunters like Alfred Watkins, is a lot more encouraging than Jester Hill.

The Sun Rising Hill Line (42)

Alfred's line starts at Radway church, which is a little curious because the church was built on its present site only in 1866. The old one stood in quite a different part of the village and was demolished the year before. A lot of material from it was used in the new one, including a couple of gargoyles on the tower, and some of the effigies and monuments inside the church were transferred, which may have caused the confusion.

When the old church was pulled down, a Norman piscina and other fragments from an earlier church were found in the foundations, so if a leyline starts at Radway, it should surely start from here.

The locally based architect, Sanderson Miller, whose family vault is in the old churchyard, built a castellated tower on the spot where the king's standard-bearer stood during the Battle of Edgehill, which is now the Castle Inn. A stone pillar by the road commemorates the battle, and on its anniversary each year you may well see a ghostly Sir Edmund Veerney galloping around on his white charger, looking for his severed hand which held the royal standard. But the actual site of the battle is not accessible to the public; appropriately it is owned by the Ministry of Defence.

Alfred's leyline then passes over the summit of Sun Rising Hill, on the ridge above Radway. He has worked out that on midsummer day the sunrise is in line with two nearby churches when viewed from here – but Radway is not one of them. It is an impressive hill, over 700 feet high, but can be climbed without much effort by driving up the steep main road. The line then reaches the county boundary and follows it for a mile or so, continuing into Oxfordshire. On the way

Above: *Traitor's Ford, an ancient river crossing on the county border – and on the line.* Left: *Radway's old churchyard.* Right: *One of the strange faces – doing strange things – in Chipping Norton church.*

it passes through the sinister-sounding Traitor's Ford, which is actually a delightful little corner in a wooded valley and gives every indication of being an ancient crossing-place. It still has only a footbridge, and cars have to venture through the stream. For most of the year this is no problem, but a flood measurement pole is marked to a height of six feet, so it could be tricky. There is no hint how it acquired its name; perhaps it has something to do with its proximity to Edgehill.

The line just misses Great Rollright church, which is rather a pity because it has some of those beak-head mouldings on the tympanum above the south door which seem to be associated with leylines. One of its sixteenth-century rectors has a splendid memorial brass portraying him in full clerical garb holding a cup and paten, but the outline of a mitre on the hem of his robe apparently indicates that he was offered a bishopric and turned it down. Perhaps, even though the leyline just misses the church, it drew him so powerfully that even a bishopric could not tempt him away.

The final marker is St Mary's Church, Chipping Norton, a very grand building dating back to the Normans, with some curious faces carved in the porch. The church guide calls them demons' heads; they certainly seem to have a pre-Christian flavour. Inside there is another devilish face on a pillar, and other pillars are decorated with leaves, but unfortunately for seekers after the Green Man, the face and leaves do not coincide.

There is, however, an unexplained mystery above the north aisle: two sets of windows above each other, which seem to serve no useful purpose. They are of different designs, and between them is an unusual coat of arms and the outline of a church or some other large building.

'No convincing reason has been found to explain the windows' existence,' says the guide, and it invites suggestions. It is a tempting offer, but any link with a leyline is quite beyond me. Perhaps Alfred could have helped. He certainly had a high regard for St Mary's as a marker, because he included it on another leyline that passes through the Rollright Stones. But there is a rather more interesting line through the Stones in *The Ley Hunter's Companion* which merits a closer look.

THE ROLLRIGHT STONES LINE (43)

Cropredy Bridge, my starting point at an ancient river crossing, offers plenty of helpful information for the inquisitive visitor. One stone plaque explains that it was built by the Bishop of Lincoln in 1314, altered three times between 1691 and 1886, and rebuilt in 1937. A plaque on the opposite parapet recalls it was the site of a notable battle in 1644, and observes piously: 'From Civil War Good Lord Deliver Us.'

It omits, however, one of the curious repercussions of the battle, and so indeed does the *Companion*. Apparently, the villagers were so concerned about the safety of their church just up the road that they took the magnificent eagle lectern, their greatest treasure, and hid it in the river. After the Royalists had beaten off the Parliamentary troops and Charles I had retired for a little rest and recuperation at Williamscote, a nearby Elizabethan mansion, the villagers could not remember where precisely they had dumped the lectern in the river, and it was discovered only many years later. If a ley-hunter had come upon it meanwhile, what a splendid embellishment it would have provided for his leyline story.

The next marker is All Saints' Church, Wroxton. The *Companion* says it is fourteenth century, standing on the site of an earlier one, and leaves it at that, but All Saints' has another interesting tale to tell. A church was already there in 1217 when the rector, Michael Belet, decided to found an Augustinian priory nearby. In due course the priory took over the church for its exclusive use, and the good folk of Wroxton must have been delighted when Henry VIII dissolved the priory, along with all the others, and they got their church back.

The leyline reaches the Stones via the almost-obliterated Castle Bank Camp, which has no established history, and Madmarston Hill Camp, a much better documented Iron Age fort covering seven acres, with some substantial earthworks still standing. It contained a large pit in which, according to the official records, archaeologists found animals' bones and 'a gigantic stewpot'. If the animals were religious sacrifices, it seems they also provided some useful dinners.

Between these two camps the line crosses my Nadbury Hill-fort Line at Jester Hill. I commented

Above: *Copredy Bridge, scene of a Civil War battle – and a lost lectern.* Left: *Lord North – not everyone's hero in spite of Britannia guarding his memorial in Wroxton church.*

earlier that the name may be significant, and the *Companion* thinks the hill may be significant too, but for a different reason. It says it is presumably a natural feature, 'but with a most unnatural-looking regular slope'. It does not suggest what link there may be between unnatural looking slopes and leylines; I hope we are not just giving the jester another laugh.

I wonder if the same thought occurred to one of the *Companion*'s authors, Paul Devereux, because in his subsequent *New Ley Hunter's Guide* this is one of the leylines he has rejected.

There is no doubt however about the authenticity of the Rollright Stones, sometimes called the King's Men. This is another of those stone circles that tradition says cannot be counted, and even the *Guide to Prehistoric England* cannot make up its mind – it says '53–54'. The *Companion* does not quote any figure, and nor shall I – it might be the right one, which would spoil the fun. The circle is over 100 feet in diameter, and nearby are the solitary King Stone and the Whispering Knights, the stone uprights of a chambered barrow. Estimating the age of all these is even trickier than counting the stones, but it is somewhere between 2200 and 1400 BC.

Inevitably, legends abound. The stones, it is said, go down to a nearby stream for a drink, either on New

Year's Eve or when they hear the Long Compton church clock strike midnight, depending who is telling the story – and, of course, how thirsty the stones happen to be at the time. In more recent times, ley-hunters have claimed to detect energy being given off by them, in some cases so powerfully that the energy current travels overground to other ancient sites.

The Rollright Stones are on the northern border of Oxfordshire. Down in the south-west corner, on the Wiltshire border, there is another happy hunting ground for ley-hunters. The sites include Wayland's Smithy (a Neolithic long barrow), an Iron Age hill-fort known as Uffington Castle, Dragon Hill where St George is said to have slain the dragon, and the Uffington White Horse, which is – well, the Uffington

The Rollright Stones, reputedly uncountable.

White Horse, with as many legends attached to it as the Rollright Stones. Unfortunately, these four potential ley markers are so 'staggered' that even the most ingenious ley-hunter with the broadest pencil would have a problem getting them all on one line.

Alfred Watkins found one going through the Smithy and the southern earthwork of the castle, and the *Companion* has one going through the castle and Dragon Hill. Thanks to the size of the castle earthworks – they enclose about eight acres – I managed to find a line that touches the northern earthwork and aligns with Wayland's Smithy in one direction and the White Horse in the other.

THE UFFINGTON WHITE HORSE LINE (44)

The line starts a few miles across the Wiltshire border, in the churchyard of All Saints' Church, Liddington. It contains the remains of a Saxon cross which is said to have brought pilgrims from Shaftesbury Abbey, in the days when the church was one of the abbey's 'prebends'. That meant its income was used by the prebendary, not for the church but for the benefit of the abbey church and the nuns who lived there.

The title of prebendary continued to be used after the abbey had gone, and the church leaflet refers throughout to prebendaries rather than rectors. They include Prebendary Talbot, who became an eighteenth-century Bishop of Oxford, and later the same century Prebendary John Moore, who eventually became Archbishop of Canterbury. Perhaps the title – and a little help from the leyline – gave them a good start.

Above: *Liddington's Saxon cross.* Below: *Wayland's Smithy where a ghostly blacksmith was said to shoe horses overnight.*

The line continues through the village to Liddington Manor, an ancient manor house with the remains of a moat. It is privately owned and occupied and out of sight from the road. Next the line crosses the county boundary near Bishopstone and reaches the first of the principal markers, Wayland's Smithy. Wayland was a Saxon folklore figure, but the 'smithy' dates back much earlier than that – to about 3000 BC.

The original long barrow had a second one superimposed on it about 300 years later. The first one was a wood-lined tomb paved with stones; the second had six large upright stones at one end, leading into an ante-chamber and three burial chambers in which several skeletons, including a child's, have been found. Standing in a small isolated coppice beside the prehistoric Ridgeway, small wonder it gave rise to strange legends, and Wayland the Smith stars in most of them.

It would seem he was a talented young smith, well trained by the trolls, who was kidnapped and imprisoned in a cave by a king and forced to work for him. The king had him maimed to prevent him running away, but Wayland exacted a gruesome revenge. He murdered the king's two sons and fashioned their skulls into goblets for the royal table. Then he flew off, using wings he had made himself. After that he lived in assorted caves and mounds in whatever country decided to adopt his story, and the Saxons allocated him Wayland's Smithy. It is said that, in gratitude, if a horse needed shoeing and was left at the Smithy overnight, with a modest tip, it would be newly shod

Below: *The Uffington White Horse, the oldest of its kind in Britain.* Right: *At the sign of the Blowing Stone, yet another legend in this legend-rich area.*

in the morning. He did a brisk business – but there was not much demand for his goblets.

The line continues to the northern earthwork of Uffington Castle, on the summit of White Horse Hill. A coin of the Dobunni tribe was found just outside it, which confirms its antiquity, but a saucer-shaped UFO, spotted above it in 1969 (according to the *Companion*), has yet to be verified.

And so on to the White Horse itself, the best known and most dramatic of these ancient sites. It is the oldest white horse hill-figure in Britain, and with a length of 360 feet it is one of the biggest, but nobody is quite sure who cut it or why. Some say it was to celebrate King Alfred's victory over the Vikings, and indeed there is an Alfred's Castle not far away near Ashbury, but that is another Iron Age fort and has no connection with him – and nor, in all probability, has the White Horse.

Most experts say it dates back to pre-Roman times when horses were often featured on coins and utensils by Iron Age Celts. One authority says it 'seems likely' that it was cut in the hillside in the late first century BC as a tribal emblem; animal worship was prevalent at the time. Another refers to the Celts' numerous horse goddesses, including Epona, and suggests the White Horse was a tribute to one of them. But to add to the confusion, it also points out that the sweeping continuous line of the neck, back and tail is very similar to various Bronze Age rock carvings.

Ley-hunters would, I am sure, go for the Epona horse goddess theory. Perhaps it would help if they stand in the eye of the White Horse and make a wish to this effect. Legend has it that this is a lucky spot, and no wish has a greater chance of success than one in the eye.

The line ends at a tumulus opposite the cemetery in Kingston Lisle. This is not too exciting in itself, just a mound with some trees, but it is quite close to the Blowing Stone Inn, which commemorates another of those delightful legends that flourish so prolifically in this area. The stone, of which the village is very proud, has several holes in it, and if you pick the right one to blow through you can produce an impressive noise.

Some liken it to a bellowing calf, others describe it as 'a gruesome sound between a moan and a roar, a ghost-like awful voice'. One or two observers say it sounds like a monumental raspberry.

Inevitably King Alfred has become involved. It is said that the Blowing Stone is his hunting horn, used for summoning his men to battle. Another theory is that it was used by the Celts to call in their nomadic tribespeople when danger threatened. The stone was brought down from the hills in the nineteenth century by the local blacksmith and is still in the garden of his former smithy. I like to think that if anyone can blow the right note through the right hole, the White Horse will get up off its hillside, cancel its arrangement with Wayland, whom, of course, it visits every night for its MOT, and will come down to the smithy to be shod.

Back to leylines. So far all the ones in Oxfordshire have been round the periphery of the country. It seems appropriate to look for a more central one. I looked for a nice big hill-fort to give me plenty of leeway and found one on Castle Hill, in the Sinodun Hills near a stretch of the Thames between Shillingford and Dorchester. I lined it up with an Iron Age burial ground about a mile away, and the rest fell into place.

THE BRIGHTWELL BARROW LINE (45)

The line starts at the church of St Mary-le-More in Wallingford, a little town dating back to the Romans that stands beside an ancient crossing-place on the Thames. St Mary-le-More was rebuilt – rather more than less – by the Victorians, and its oldest feature is the seventeenth-century tower, but the church leaflet says encouragingly: 'It is generally thought that the first Christian building here was Norman in character, occupying the site of a pagan temple.'

From the church the line runs north-westwards to the substantial earthwork that was erected by King Alfred (the real one) to protect the town. It crosses it on the edge of the Kynecroft, a former cattle enclosure which is now a public park. It is still very high and steep at this point, with a path running along the top. Wallingford had a castle and priory in medieval times, and it was a Royalist stronghold in the Civil War. Then Cromwell flattened the castle and the priory has gone too, but this Saxon earthwork survives.

After passing Brightwell-cum-Sotwell, the line reaches Brightwell Barrow, on high ground about a mile outside the village. It is thought to be an early Iron Age burial site, and pottery has been found with incinerated remains. A circle of trees was planted in 1840 to replace an earlier one.

The line then enters an area administered by the Northmoor Trust, a body that promotes countryside conservation, so the next markers are particularly well preserved. There has been human occupation here for 6000 years, and the line passes through the two key points on this ancient site. They are twin hills crowned by trees, known as the Wittenham Clumps, but Castle Hill also had an early Iron Age fort, and the two hills are so symmetrical and so prominent in the landscape that the Trust says it is inconceivable they did not have some joint significance in pagan times.

At one stage the Wittenham estate was owned by the Dunch family, who were on Cromwell's side in the Civil War. This did not go down too well in Royalist Oxfordshire, and the two rounded hills were re-christened by the locals, 'Mother Dunch's Buttocks'. Perhaps it was to eliminate this memory and break up their smooth, curved outline that a later squire planted the clumps of beech trees in 1730, as part of a general landscaping plan.

There is one tree in particular on Castle Hill where bunches of flowers are often found in the large hole in the trunk, and sometimes polyanthus and daffodils have been planted round it. 'We have never been able to identify the origins of these rather touching tributes,' says the Trust. 'We assume they are in memory of persons or perhaps courtships conducted on the Clumps.'

Any ley-hunter worth his salt would surely suggest a quite different solution; a return to the days of pagan tree worship. But in fairness I have to say this tree is thought special because in 1844 a man called Joseph Tubb carved a poem on it, which was still legible until the tree died about ten years ago and the bark deteriorated. It gave a lyrical description of the view, and showed a fair knowledge of the area's prehistoric origins, thus:

Where the low bank the country wide surrounds
That ancient earthwork form'd old Mercia's bounds
In misty distance see the barrow heave
There lies forgotten lonely Culchelm's grave.

Mr Tubb could have been looking straight along the leyline. If that were the case the tree, or its predecessor, could have been a marker – and it deserves those flowers after all.

The line crosses the edge of Little Wittenham and ends at St Mary's Church, Long Wittenham. Like the other St Mary's at Wallingford where the line started, it is thought to stand on a pagan sacred site. It has

The Wittenham Clumps, the site of an Iron Age hill-fort.

managed to retain more of its early treasures, notably its twelfth-century lead font, which was saved from Cromwell's men by being packed inside a wooden case filled with rubbish. Like the lectern at Cropredy Bridge everyone forgot where it was hidden, and it was only rediscovered and restored by a sharp-eyed rector in 1839, nearly 200 years later.

Wittenham may be Long but the effigy of Gilbert de Clare, a thirteenth-century lord of the manor, is distinctly short by normal church effigy standards. It measures two feet from head to toe, small enough, in fact, to recline cross-legged on the edge of a piscina, the stone basin used for pouring away water after Communion. He took the oath of a Crusader, hence the symbolic legs, but it is not too certain is he ever went on active service. His devoted wife may have arranged to have them crossed for purely personal reasons.

St Mary's other notable treasure is a copy of Foxe's

Book of Martyrs, printed in 1579, which contains the name of a local man, John French, who died for his faith. The church leaflet comments: 'For a community as small and insignificant as our own appears to have been, to have had a Crusader (even if he never actually made it to the Holy Land) and a martyr in its historical past is truly something to be proud of!' Perhaps it had something to do with the leyline.

Actually, there may be two leylines involved. In the Cornwall section I mention the long-distance ley from St Michael's Mount to East Anglia. Its central section passes through Oxfordshire, heading roughly northeast from Ogbourne St George in Wiltshire. No other marker is mentioned until it reaches Bury St Edmunds, but as far as I can judge without putting large-scale maps all over the floor and using a six-foot ruler, it passes uncommonly close to Long Wittenham.

From Oxfordshire the long-distance ley goes into Buckinghamshire and Bedfordshire. I am heading that way too.

BERKSHIRE, BUCKINGHAMSHIRE, BEDFORDSHIRE AND NORTHAMPTONSHIRE

BERKSHIRE can claim probably the most illustrious 'lay ley marker' in the country – that extra 'lay' is to exclude cathedrals. Windsor Castle features prominently in Alfred Watkins' *Old Straight Track*, mainly because of its very large mound. Its other possible prehistoric connection is the dead-straight Queen Anne's Drive, which starts about a mile away and is directly aligned on it, suggesting that it was an ancient track. Watkins also lines up the castle mound with various churches in Bucking-hamshire, but all these leylines have to pass through Slough, which is a little off-putting.

The other famous landmark that he uses as a sighting point for much the same reason is Ivinghoe Beacon, which is a rather more obvious prehistoric site than Windsor Castle and enjoys rather more rural surroundings. Just its name would qualify it as a ley marker – Alfred was very strong on beacons – but it also has the remains of an Iron Age fort dating back to the sixth century BC.

Here again he is liable to jump quite a distance to his other markers. For instance, there is a line starting from the Beacon which runs for twelve miles before reaching the next one at Monks Risborough. But from there it goes along the foot of the Chiltern Hills, a pleasant area for ley-hunting, so I followed up this section of the line. Part of it is across the county border in Oxfordshire, so I will start at that end, then bid that ley-friendly county a final farewell.

The painting of the scene in the Garden of Gethsemane in Grafton Regis church, includes an incongruous jester-like figure.

THE CHILTERN HILLS LINE (46)

This line is as remarkable for the potential markers it misses as for those it passes through. For instance, Alfred starts at St Mary's Church, Pyrton, but on the hillside that overlooks it, just the other side of Watlington, is a curious triangular mark cut in the earth, rather like a pointer, which looks as if it ought to have some ancient significance. Further along the Chilterns and parallel with the line are two more marks on the hillside, Whiteleaf Cross and Bledlow Cross, plus two Beacon Hills.

All but one of these can claim some qualification as a marker. The Beacon Hills have their name, and some experts say the two crosses are contemporary with the Long Man of Wilmington, much respected by ley-hunters, though others say they were cut to mark a victory over the Danes. One enthusiast maintained the Whiteleaf Cross would align with the rising sun on the Celtic New Year's Day, 31 October, but had to adjust that theory when at last a cloudless 31 October dawned and he found the sun aligned with one of the Beacon Hills instead.

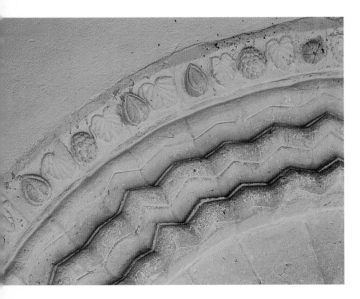

The only complete non-runner is the Watlington Mark, which I mentioned first. One writer did his best to prove it was carved 2500 years ago as a pointer for the equinox, but actually it dates from only a couple of centuries, when a local resident, one Edward Horne, who perhaps had more money than sense, decided that Watlington church would look better with a spire on top, and as no one else seemed to share that view he had the spire-shaped triangle cut on the hillside beyond it. The mark was certainly on an alignment with the church and his house, but that hardly qualifies as a leyline.

So I shall stick with Pyrton church, which was built in Norman times and has records going back to 1115. The mixed fruits, nuts and leaves around the 'zigzag' Norman archway over the door seem encouragingly reminiscent of earlier days.

The line misses the sham Gothic Shirburn Castle, which again is a potential marker because it was originally built in 1377 on a site that may well have had an earlier history.

Lewknor still has its traditional route to the church, through the playground of the thatched village school. St Margaret's, the next marker on the line, is another twelfth-century church, with a large and gloomy chapel devoted to the Jodrell family, whose main claim to fame, in my view, was its connections with Norfolk. It was curious to find the familiar names of Norfolk villages such as Salle and North Elmham so far afield in such sombre surrounding. Had they been attracted by the leyline?

Alfred's third marker, Kingston Blount church, alas is a church no longer, just a private house. Its bell was transferred to the next marker, the Church of the Nativity of the Blessed Virgin Mary at Crowell, where it acquired a dual role. An arrangement was made to share the church with the Roman Catholic community, so the bell summons Catholics to Mass as well as Anglicans to Communion.

Before reaching Alfred's fifth church the line misses another likely one, Holy Trinity at Bledlow, which has a sarsen boulder some four feet long incorporated in one of the buttresses of the tower. Alfred, I am sure, would have identified that as a marker stone. He would also have noted the profusion of carved and painted foliage that decorates the church, from the twelfth-century font to the pillars, and even the iron strap hinges on the thirteenth-century south door. There are more leaves included in some of the wall-paintings, and even the leafless painting of Adam and Eve shows Adam digging – to plant a tree, perhaps, and grow some more leaves? But amidst all this greenery I failed to spot a Green Man; the foliage was probably concealing him.

There are more leaves on the font at St Dunstan's Church, Monks Risborough, the final marker on the Chiltern Hills Line, but in spite of its promising name, there was never a monastery at Monks Risborough. It just happened to belong to the monks of Christ Church, Canterbury.

There is also no connection, I am afraid, between the tongs that feature in various parts of the church and Alfred Watkins' beacon-lighters on the leylines, who may have used tongs to handle the hot coals. In fact, they merely commemorate St Dunstan's method of dealing with unpleasant opponents. While St George was busy thrusting his sword into dragons, St Dunstan preferred to tweak the nose of the Devil with his tongs.

It was also due to St Dunstan, and not to any strange influence from the leyline, that the church held its Millennium celebration ahead of the rest of us. Dunstan died in AD 988.

So in the end there seems little to link St Dunstan's Church with leylines, yet I found that it could be a marker on a second line, too. As Alfred's line left so many potential markers unaccounted for, I thought I would try to include at least a couple of them in a line of my own. In particular, I thought that Cymbeline's Castle, the scene of an early battle against the Romans, was worth a try, and with the help of St Dunstan it worked.

Above: *A sarsen boulder in a buttress* of *The Bledlow Cross*. Left: *The fruit and leaves on the Norman doorway at Pyrton church.*

THE CYMBELINE'S CASTLE LINE (47)

It starts at the church of St Peter and St Paul at Ellesborough, the origins of which have caused almost as much conjecture as the castle itself, just across the road. It is often dubbed 'The Church on the Hill' – in fact, that is the title of the church guide – and it is the hill that prompts the debate. As the guidebook points out, this is one of the richest areas in Buckinghamshire for tumuli, burial mounds and Iron Age fortifications, and no one seems quite sure whether the hill is natural or man-made. Certainly the ground falls away steeply on three sides, and the remains of a ditch have been found, which could mean that it was a fortification or, as ley-hunters would prefer to think, a pagan sacred site. Indeed, the guidebook quotes one writer's description of the hill as 'a high mount resembling a tumulus or barrow'.

Above: *Cymbeline's Castle*. Below left: *Whatever it was, St Peter and St Paul have a good view of it*. Right: *From Ellesborough church from Cymbeline's Castle*.

The church seems to have had a mixed effect on the fortunes of its rectors. Some of them died quite early while still in office: John Hamilton, for instance, was thirty-seven, his successor Chaloner Leathes only thirty-five. Thomas Emery died of the Great Plague that swept London in 1665, in spite of Ellesborough's comparative remoteness; 'a wandering dog' got the blame. And one curate was lost prematurely, not through an early death but because of 'troubles with the patron's wife, Lady Frankland Russell'. On the other hand, Robert Walls returned after nearly thirty years to become rector for a second time.

Which one of these rectors, one wonders, is the ghostly figure who is said to walk the pathway to the church in the twilight? Is it the plague victim, wishing that infected dog had wandered elsewhere? Or the devoted rector who returned once and wants to return again? Or the banished curate, hoping for an assignation with Lady Frankland Russell? Or someone much earlier than any of them, just following the leyline?

Perched above the porch are the figures of St Peter with his key and St Paul with his sword. They have a good view of all the Prime Ministers and their houseguests who attend the church from nearby Chequers. And they can look across the road, along the line of the ley, to Cymbeline's Castle. According to legend, this is where Cunobelinus, King of the Britons, put up a fight against the Romans. Some authorities say it was a Roman fortification, others say it goes back to the Iron Age. Probably both are true; the Romans just took it over. But in the long term it was the Brits who stayed and the Romans who went.

The line continues to Monks Risborough church and on to the mount, by St Mary's churchyard in Princes Risborough. St Mary's is dismissed by a local historian as 'undistinguished', which is a bit unkind, but the mount alongside it, though it looks even less

distinguished today, has quite an impressive history. A plaque on it records that this was the site of the manor of the Black Prince, which is how the little town got its name. Previously it was called Earl's Risborough, but the prince's castle brought it promotion. Now the prince and the castle have long since gone, but the name remains – and any mound that had a medieval castle on it is useful to the ley-hunter too.

The line ends at a moat in Roundabout Wood, up in the Chiltern Hills. The name has nothing to do with the road adjustments caused by the M40 motorway that now slices through the Hills, and it is a peaceful way to avoid them. When Alfred Watkins was checking on leylines from Ivinghoe Beacon, he must also have realized the potential of Maiden Castle, a few miles away across the Bedfordshire border. It has a remarkable prehistoric pedigree, dating back to about 3500 BC, and better still, it covers some eleven acres, giving plenty of room for manoeuvre with a ruler. Alfred duly manoeuvred, and came up with a leyline.

THE SECOND MAIDEN CASTLE LINE (48)

Maiden Castle is sometimes called Maiden's Bower, but it looks even less like a bower than a castle. It started life as a Neolithic causewayed camp, built by the first farmers and herdsmen to reach Britain from the continent. Fortunately, they left behind some of their pottery to prove they were there.

In the Iron Age, about the fourth or fifth century BC, it was reoccupied and fortified with an eight-foot bank and a ditch ten feet deep and twenty-five feet wide. A double line of postholes shows that the entrance was closed by wooden gates, probably with sentry walks over the top. From the air there are signs of early fields outside the earthwork, and storage pits and hut circles inside. It was, in fact, a large and prosperous community until the Romans came. They may have taken it over when they built Watling Street, a mile or so away.

The line runs roughly parallel to the road, through the churches at Tilsworth and Great Brickhill. At Tilsworth the line first passes through Tilsworth Manor, which looks as if it had a moat and may well qualify as a marker in its own right, but Alfred does not mention it.

All Saints', perched on a hill overlooking the line and the manor, has a massive tower that is similar in period to the thirteenth-century tower of St Mary's at Great Brickhill. The only unusual feature at St Mary's is a small stone fish inserted in the window jamb to the north of the chancel, which gets a special mention in the church leaflet and is left unexplained, but I have failed to trace any link between small stone fishes and leylines. However, I like the way the avenue of lime trees lining the church path has been pollarded so thoroughly that they look like a row of giant knobkerries. They would surely make an Ancient Briton feel at home.

Alfred would have felt at home too so far, because the leyline has passed through countryside and villages

that are almost as peaceful as he would remember them, but he would be astounded – and probably horrified – at what comes next. The line enters the vast conurbation that used to be just Bletchley but is now the new city of Milton Keynes – and Alfred's next marker is slap in the middle of it.

On the face of it, Milton Keynes is just about the last place you would expect to find a leyline – or indeed a ley-hunter. But according to one of those intriguing messages that appear from time to time on the Internet, the sun rises and sets directly along Midsummer Boulevard on Midsummer's Day, and indeed, says the Internet message: 'the roads are thought to be planned along leylines, to draw in positive energy into the city.'

It adds casually that Milton Keynes is also the first city in the UK to give a dedicated plot of land to witches, and it quotes someone called Tim as saying: 'Milton Keynes makes you sad. I used to have lots of friends before I came here.' I hardly think leylines can be entirely to blame.

When Alfred Watkins was here seventy-odd years ago Shenley Church End must have been a tranquil little village surrounded by miles of green fields. Even on a 1977 map it is still three or four miles from the edge of Bletchley. To reach it now from the trunk road you have to thread your way through a maze of round-abouts, housing estates and shopping centres. But if you read the direction signs carefully – and follow the right leyline – you will see the tower of St Mary's rising reassuringly above the sea of red roofs.

The church that gave Shenley Church End its name is still surrounded by a peaceful churchyard full of old trees and older gravestones. I was interested to see on the roof of the south aisle the head of what looks like a large-eared pig, and there are other strange heads on the nave. Most interesting of all, inside the porch one

Above: *A pig-like gargoyle on the church roof at Shenley Church End.* Left: *Shenley Church End church.* Below: *A buffalo-shaped stain in the porch – or is it just damp?*

of the bricks seems to be stained in the shape of a charging buffalo. The porch was only added in 1637 so it cannot be the work of a medieval mason, but maybe some pre-Christian images on churches were still being added in the seventeenth century. Then again, it could just be the damp.

Alfred would maintain that the Romans built Watling Street upon a prehistoric track, which qualifies the straight stretch of the trunk road for the next eight miles as his final marker. There seems nothing unusual about it except its straightness, but it does pass close to a little place called the Gullet. I like to think it is a subconscious reminder of the dreaded swallowing power of the dragons associated with leylines in prehistoric times.

Not far along the A5 from the Gullet it crosses another ley mentioned by Alfred Watkins in his *The Old Straight Track* which runs from Buckinghamshire into Northamptonshire. He calls it 'The Six Churches Line', but unfortunately my ruler refused to connect with two of the churches he names, so I found a possible alternative to take their place.

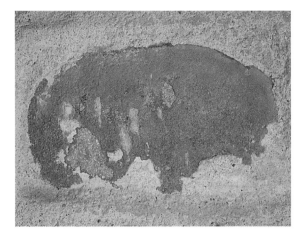

THE STOWE HALF-CASTLE LINE (49)

Alfred's line starts at St James's Church, Barton Hartshorn, an attractive little church with some really splendid brass candelabra. But this is one of the churches I could not line up with the rest, and my revised line starts at his next marker, St Mary Magdalene's Church at Tingewick. Parts of the original twelfth-century building survive, but I was more struck by the brass memorial to Erasmus Williams, a rector who died in 1608. It depicts him kneeling between two pillars of a temple. The one he faces represents his calling, the one behind him is festooned with geometrical instruments, representing what he gave up: 'Forget that which is behind,' is the message. Could he have been plotting leylines when the call came? Actually, there are some musical instruments round the pillar too, suggesting he had been a musician as well as a scientist, but that does not disprove my theory. He could have run a band in his spare time.

From Tingewick the line heads for Stowe School, former home of the Dukes of Buckingham and Chandos, where the incautious ley-hunter may be enthralled to discover in the grounds the Temple of Ancient Virtue – until he finds it is one of a number of temples and follies put there as landscaping features.

The line passes close to the Corinthian Arch at the entrance, which has as much to do with Corinth as that temple has with ancient virtue. In the process it crosses Stowe Avenue, which Alfred reckons is an alignment with Windsor Castle, so beware of rutting deer, which are said to favour leyline junctions. A cautionary road sign might be appropriate, but it is difficult to picture one which might not cause offence – particularly so close to a school.

My next marker, albeit a questionable one, is the curious building known as Stowe Castle. On the sides facing Stowe Park it really does look like a battlemented Norman castle, but on the other it looks like a

V-shaped country house. It is in fact just anther folly, though quite an elaborate one; the walls on the 'castle' side are over two feet thick. Stowe Half-castle, as I prefer to call it, was built in 1740 to provide the Duke of Buckingham with a view of a castle, just as the Tattingstone Wonder in Suffolk, half-church and half-cottage, was built for the local squire because he could not see the real parish church from his windows. But the duke had a vast area in which to choose a site for his 'castle'; was there anything special, one wonders, about this one?

These days the house is privately occupied, but there is a Stowe Castle business park beside it, and the stables have been converted into a restaurant and boutique.

Alfred's line should pass through Lillingstone Dayrell church, but this is the other church that does not seem to line up with the rest. However, his other Lillingstone marker, the Church of the Assumption at Lillingstone Lovell, is spot on, and it certainly looks the part. It stands on a steep hillside, so steep that at the east end of the churchyard there is a rather alarming seven-foot drop to the lane below. The church has an eleventh-century tower, and the nature of the site suggests that something was there before.

The most interesting church on the leyline is the next one, St Mary's at Grafton Regis, across the Maiden Castle Line into Northamptonshire. It is probably earlier than the eleventh century and it has a couple of interesting faces carved on the sides of the porch. The tower again is a massive one, and again it stands on a hill. On the chancel wall is a panel from a medieval rood-screen with a painting of the Garden of Gethsemane, and on the left of Christ is a figure

The Rev. Erasmus Williams rector of Tingewick, turning his back on his geometrical instruments. Had he been plotting a leyline?

dressed like a medieval jester, in red tights and doublet with a multi-pointed collar. There must be a logical explanation, but he seems a very incongruous intruder in this traditional biblical scene.

The village's main claim to fame is the secret marriage that took place in the parish in 1464 between Elizabeth Woodville of Grafton Palace and King Edward IV. She was the mother of the Princes in the Tower, and her daughter married Henry VII. The remains of the palace were built into Grafton Manor, next to the church, and it is now a hospital for accident victims.

There are tombs to the Woodvilles in St Mary's, including John Woodville, who built the tower. But it is primarily devoted to the Fitzroys, the junior branch

Above: *Stowe Castle, as seen from the stately home. The other side looks what it is, an eighteenth-century manor house, built as an elaborate 'folly'.* Above right: *Hartwell church needs no clock; there is one on the telegraph pole opposite.* Below right: *The sharp drop from the churchyard at Lillingstone Lovell.*

of the Duke of Grafton's family who still live there. It is a remarkably distinguished history for an otherwise obscure Northamptonshire village.

The final church Alfred names is St John the Baptist at Hartwell. I am sure he was much encouraged by the carvings around the doorway of the 'beak-head' faces so often linked with leyline churches, but there is bad news. The church was actually moved from its original site south of the village, and although some of its Norman materials were re-used, the faces round the door are uncommonly well preserved. They are probably modern copies of those at another church in the same benefice. I am afraid the old site does not appear to be on Alfred's leyline – but I suppose he might still argue that the church could have been moved for that very reason.

St John's has no tower, just a bell-cote for two bells, but an ingenious benefactor has installed a large modern clock on a telegraph pole just across the road. If there is no place for a church clock on a church, a telegraph pole must be the next best thing. In fact, it struck me as rather a good idea for a finishing post, and certainly it marks the end of the leylines in this region. The M1 motorway is now close by to lead the way into the North Midlands.

LINCOLNSHIRE,
LEICESTERSHIRE AND
NOTTINGHAMSHIRE

THESE three counties seem to have been largely ignored by Alfred Watkins. Maybe, like East Anglia, they are on the opposite side of the country to his Herefordshire stamping-ground and he rarely came over this way. But his lack of enthusiasm is understandable after a glance through *The Guide to Prehistoric England*. Nottinghamshire and Leicestershire have only three prehistoric sites between them, and sites are pretty thin on the ground in Lincolnshire too, considering the large area it covers.

Alfred does mention one Lincolnshire country church he rather fancies, but he does not suggest any leyline going through it, and I failed to find one either. His point about St Mary's at Stow-in-Lindsey is that, according to legend, St Etheldreda stopped here rest one summer's day, and planted her ashen staff in the ground before falling asleep. She planted it so successfully that it burst into life, and produced enough leaves in time to protect her from the noonday sun. She was so pleased when she woke up that she built a church.

I have to say the church guide is a bit dubious. It does not deny the miracle, but suggests it happened in a quite different Stow. Even if it was this one, I am not sure why it qualifies St Mary's as a ley marker. I thought Alfred usually argued that many Saxon churches were built on pagan sacred sites that had existed since prehistoric times. If Etheldreda founded a church on the basis of her flowering staff, what connection is there with a pagan site? Unless, of course, she hit on one by pure chance – or was it a current from the leyline that caused the staff to grow? The debate could run and run.

Meanwhile, it seems wise to find an alternative. I planted a ruler on one of Lincolnshire's oldest and best-established ancient sites and it blossomed into a leyline ...

Stow-in-Lindsey church.

THE ASH HILL LONG BARROW LINE (50)

The Ash Hill barrow is some ten miles north-west of Louth in the Lincolnshire Wolds. It has been dated between 3500 and 2500 BC, is wedge shaped and about 130 feet long and seven feet high. It had ditches along the sides, but only an expert can detect them. It aligns with Hoe Hill barrow, just under a mile away, and I extended the line in each direction.

South-eastwards the line goes to St Martin's Church at Welton le Wold. In the thirteenth century it came under Ormesby Priory, but since then it has been thoroughly restored and enlarged by the Victorians and not much survives of the old building. In fact the most

historic item I could find was a venerable-looking banner depicting St Martin in his Roman army officer days.

The Hoe Hill long barrow is wedge shaped like its contemporary on Ash Hill, but considerably larger, at about 180 feet long and eleven feet high. It is protected by a small wood and is quite well preserved.

After passing through the two barrows the line continues past Thorganby and Croxby, still in the rolling landscape of the Wolds – such a contrast to the flat emptiness of the Fens with which Lincolnshire, like Norfolk, is so often associated. The next marker is St Nicholas's Church at Cuxwold, with its stubby tower

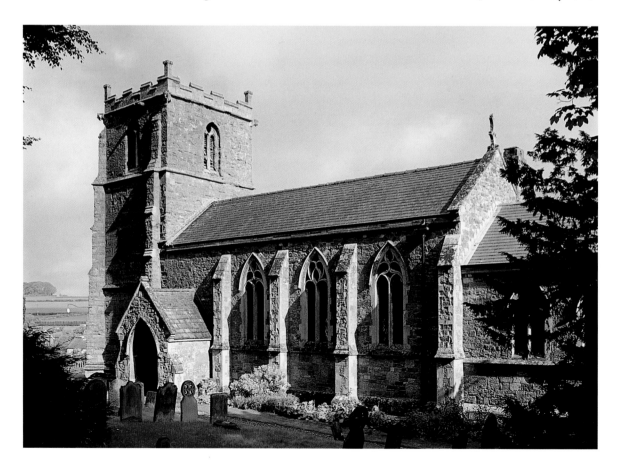

Two churches along the line. Above: *The stubby-towered St Nicholas at Cuxwold.* Left: *The Victorian-restored St Martin's at Welton le Wold.*

and small nave. It was open and obviously old, but instead of any church leaflet, the reading matter was largely confined to the epitaphs on the Thorold memorials. The Thorolds are a leading Lincolnshire family who for many years have been patrons of this living and at least one other, St Mary's at Marston. In fact Marston has a 'Squarson Thorold', fulfilling the almost extinct Victorian role of both squire and parson.

I am not sure if St Nicholas's or St Mary's has more of their memorials, but Nicholas may just have the edge. The most impressive one is a massive tablet on the west wall facing down the nave, which is flanked by more Thorold tablets on both sides. In the days when a Thorold was parson here too, the congregation

was completely surrounded by the Thorold family. Appropriately, the line ends at the family seat, Cuxwold Hall. There are no obvious links either at the church or at the hall with any prehistoric activity, but if anyone is going to be on a leyline in Cuxwold, it has to be the Thorolds.

The Ley Hunter's Companion has no leylines in Lincolnshire, but in Leicestershire it has one called the Bradgate Ley, because it starts in Bradgate Park, north of Leicester. It passes through open country to the village of Anstey, a name that apparently means 'narrow path' and so must be significant. But after that the ley is mostly swallowed up in Leicester, and rather than pursue what is basically a city leyline, I took a second look at Alfred Watkins' *Ley Hunter's Manual.* I discovered one under 'Warwickshire' continuing to the villages of North Kilworth and Sibbertoft. It seemed worth a try.

THE CROSS-IN-HAND LINE (51)

The leyline was contributed to the *Manual* by a Commander A.G.A. Street, who starts it at what he calls Newlands Mill. I could see no mill on the map, but I assume it is connected with Newland Hall Farm, which is just outside Coventry. It continues for fifteen miles, passing through a moat *en route*, until it reaches the Leicestershire border and crosses the A5 trunk road at an unusual junction called the Cross-in-Hand. It is unusual, not only because of its name, but because the roundabout at the junction is a tree-covered mound that looks very similar to many of the ancient barrows that have featured on other leylines.

I did not brave the traffic to get onto the roundabout for a closer look, and I doubt there was much more to see anyway, but even if its appearance, as I suspect, is just a coincidence, for a ley-hunter it is rather a happy one. I wonder what it looked like seventy years ago when Commander Street selected it as a marker.

The next one is St Andrew's Church at North Kilworth. Any church dedicated to St Andrew is encouraging, because of the suggested link with a

Celtic god who had a similar name, and on the tower I spotted what looked like an unexpected bonus. Instead of the customary gargoyles, there was a very large stone owl, perched on the battlement. Could this have some pre-Christian significance, I pondered? And when I saw on the notice board that the emblem of the church Sunday Club was 'Archimedes the Owl', I was tempted to echo his cry of 'Eureka!'

Alas, I had not found it. The owl was on the tower for a very mundane reason – to scare away the pigeons. It was small consolation that it was manifestly failing to do so; there were pigeons all over the tower. Indeed, I gather he has since been removed. I am afraid Archimedes the Owl was just another coincidence. I had to look further.

The church was built in the twelfth century, and there is no information about an earlier building, but it was an interesting site to choose. It is almost outside the village on a back road that continues across a cattle-grid into open country. It has also had the unusual distinction of moving in and out of three different dioceses – not by some form of leyline propulsion, I am afraid, but by the alteration of boundaries. It belonged to Leicester before the Norman Conquest, then to Lincoln, then to Peterborough, and finally back full circle to Leicester.

Consequently, the coats of arms of all three dioceses feature on a stone tablet listing the rectors. One unexpected name is William Laud, Charles I's Archbishop of Canterbury, who fell foul of the Parliamentarians and was beheaded.

The next marker on the line, St Helen's Church at Sibbertoft, cannot claim anything to match it, and indeed I found little to link it with anything unusual. Then the line passes 'near Clipston Station', but the station has long since vanished, and the railway is now a cycle path. As some consolation, Commander Street's line crosses it at what used to be a level crossing, and

Above: *North Kilworth church with its handsome tower and spire.* Left: *The tree-covered mound is the Cross-in-Hand roundabout on the A5.* Below right: *Boughton House, once a monastic building, now a stately home.*

continues straight up a track cutting across the next field. 'Then off the map', says the Commander, but I had another map, and I found a rather more interesting final marker than a disused level crossing, albeit across the county border.

Boughton House is the Northamptonshire home of the Duke of Buccleuch and Queensberry, but it was originally a monastic building, so the site may have an earlier significance. The monks would hardly recognize it today. From the front it looks like a French chateau, but it is a lot more than that. To be precise, it has seven courtyards, twelve entrances, fifty-two chimney-stacks, 365 windows and 1¼ acres of stone roofing. Fortunately, I did not have to work that out myself, it is in the brochure. As a ley marker, Boughton House has the great merit of being open to the public, with a lot to see in the house and the 350-acre park, and a lot to buy in the plant centre and the gift shop and tea shop. And then there is the adventure playground ...

Time to leave for the next county; I am beginning to sound like a brochure myself. Nottinghamshire fails to get a mention by Alfred Watkins, but *The Ley Hunter's Companion* has a leyline that goes through its only prehistoric site, according to *The Guide to Prehistoric England.* Oxton Camp is an Iron Age hillfort with an earlier Bronze Age barrow. Like many places in this part of Nottinghamshire, the hill on which it stands is named after Robin Hood, and the barrow is called Robin Hood's Pot. I am sure he would be impressed.

The leyline starts at a ruined chapel and includes four churches, though with its usual meticulous accuracy the *Companion* admits it misses Walesby church by three yards – it goes through a 'huge ancient tree' instead. It is not caught out by the fact that Boughton church has been on its present site only since the nineteenth century; the line also goes through the site of the original church in the graveyard. And again it notes that the line passes through the moat at Bilsthorpe church, rather than the church itself.

I could not attempt to match such precision, but I thought it might be interesting to line up Oxton Camp with the rather more spectacular Southwell Minster, not too far away.

THE SOUTHWELL MINSTER LINE (52)

The line starts at an earthwork about a mile west of Newark, and it ends some twenty miles away at a motte and bailey in a corner of Annesley Plantation, beyond Oxton Camp. Between the earthwork and the Minster the line passes through the Church of St Michael and All Angels at Averham, in its delightful setting beside the River Trent. According to the map it has the additional attraction to the ley-hunter of a moat, but I could only see a water-filled ditch. It runs alongside the 200-yard footpath which is the only access to the church.

This access, I gather, has been something of a problem for funerals and weddings. Until quite recently the church was reached via the vicarage, but that has now been sold. After an undertaker refused to take a coffin along the muddy path, the chairman of the parish council arranged to have it covered with tarmac. It so happened that he died soon afterwards, and thus he was the first to be carried along the path. I am glad to report he is commemorated by a plaque alongside it.

This has little to do with leylines, of course, but the church itself may have a much closer link. According to Pevsner, the herringbone masonry is early Norman, but I am told there is much debate about its date, and many have claimed it to be Saxon. Early earthworks in the fields nearby indicate there was a substantial settlement here by the Trent, and the Rev. Professor Adrian Armstrong, the non-stipendary minister in charge of St Michael's, tells me there is good reason to say that this is one of the earliest churches in the county. In which case, I would add, it could well date back to the days when the early Christians built their churches on pagan sites.

The other feature in St Michael's that struck me — and indeed one can hardly miss it — is the canopied alabaster tomb to Sir William Sutton, an early seventeenth-century squire. A lengthy rhyming epitaph records his marriage of 'thrice nine years' (it scans better than 'twenty-seven'), and ends:

> *Their generous offspring (parents' joy of heart)*
> *Eight of each sex, of each an equal part*
> *Ushered to Heaven their father, and the other*
> *Remained behind him to attend their mother.*

It was composed, presumably, by the generous offspring.

Southwell Minster is easily spotted from up to twenty miles away because of its three Norman towers, described by one respected gazetteer, with a happy disregard for the finer points of grammar, as 'almost unique'. Work began on the present building in 1108, but its earlier history seems to be rather vague — 'mainly based on legend', as the same gazetteer says.

This could make some of its sculptures and decorations all the more significant to the ley-hunter. Over the door leading to the belfry, for instance, is one of the oldest Anglo-Saxon sculptures in the Midlands, representing St Michael the dragon-slayer with a very scaly

colleagues. Incidentally, the master mason who was presumably responsible for this and the other splendid carvings is himself featured in the chapter house.

It all made a tremendous impression on James I. 'By my blude,' he exclaimed, no doubt in a strong Scottish accent, 'this kirk shall jostle with York or Durham or any other kirk in Christendom.'

It's a pretty good ley marker, too.

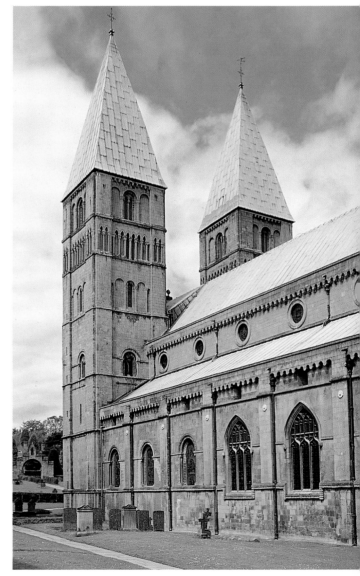

Above: *Carved faces and leaves are plentiful in Southwell Minster* (right). Left: *Averham church by the River Trent.*

dragon. The door of the magnificent chapter house is carved with many varieties of leaves, and there is a lot more foliage inside. It may well just be connected with the proximity of Sherwood Forest, but trees did play a large part in pre-Christian worship.

My favourite carving, I have to admit, has nothing to do with leaves. The Minster was originally a collegiate church, and its secular clergy lived outside the monastery with their families, while the monks lived inside. There must have been a certain atmosphere between the two groups, because in the corridor between the channel and the chapter house there is a carving of a monk having his ears briskly pulled by one of his secular

DERBYSHIRE AND STAFFORDSHIRE

IN this part of the North Midlands all leylines seem to lead to Arbor Low. 'Arbor' is generally associated with trees, but it can mean a rotating shaft in a machine or power tool, and this Neolithic site is shaped like a wheel-hub, with leylines emanating from it in all directions. It consists of a circular bank, 250 feet across, with a wide ditch inside and a raised area in the centre. There are about forty stones lying around this central area, and from the air they look like enormous screws waiting to be inserted into the hub.

Alfred Watkins has an Arbor Low leyline in his *Manual*, and *The Ley Hunter's Companion* has another. Somewhere, I thought, there must be a leyline in Derbyshire that misses Arbor Low, and I turned to Lean Low, another Bronze Age barrow. I lined it up with Stanton Moor, which has a barrow cemetery with some seventy stone cairns and an assortment of standing stones covering about 150 acres, so there is plenty of scope for ruler-wiggling. I drew a line through Stanton-in-Peak, Middleton church, Lean Low and over the Staffordshire border to Sheen church, with a tumulus near Sheen as a bonus.

Alas, Stanton church was built in 1839 and the first vicar appointed in 1875. Middleton church looks a little older but not old enough. Sheen church is a better bet, particularly as the village's name originates from 'shining', which Alfred would seize upon as evidence of a prehistoric beacon. In fact, it derived from a fire marking the burial site of the slain after a battle between two tribes, so Alfred's theory would have been close. There was a chapel at Sheen in 1185, which could have been built on a pagan site, but even I had to discount the other two churches, and the remaining barrows and tumuli hardy added up to a convincing alignment. Reluctantly, I returned to Arbor Low and went for the line in the *Manual*, which looked – and turned out to be – more varied.

The rocky hillside above St Michael's Church, Birchover.

THE ARBOR LOW LINE (53)

The line was contributed to the *Manual* by Edgar Drury. I could find no trace of his first marker, The Wishing Stone, but his next one, Oaker's Hill, was much easier. There is a village called Oaker Side, and it certainly has a hill. It inspired Wordsworth to write a poem about two brothers who climbed the hill and planted two trees on the summit before parting to follow their separate ways. One tree flourished, the other died, and indeed Mr Drury refers to it as 'a one-tree hill'. The hill I saw at Oaker had quite a lot more, but they could have grown since the days of William Wordsworth and Edgar Drury.

There are grass-covered mounds on the hillside, which might be mistaken for ancient earthworks, but I gather they were actually made by colonies of meadow ants. It so happens that the ants emerge in the early morning to cluster round the south-east sides of their mounds, directly in line with the first rays of the sun.

Since the hill is on a leyline, could this be the equivalent in the insect world of prehistoric man's worship of the sun? I rather suspect they just liked to get warm.

Mr Drury's next marker is Wensley Church, but he may have got his churches confused, because if the line is to go through later markers, it cannot go through Wensley. It does, however, go through the church in neighbouring South Darley, and this used to be the parish of Wensley and Snitterton, so it is probably the one he means.

It seems on the face of it to be an excellent marker, because there is a cluster of beak-nosed faces around the door, which are often associated with earlier forms of worship. Alas, they turn out to be another trap for the unwary ley-hunter. The church was only built in 1840 as a chapel of ease, and there is no indication of an earlier one on the site. The faces may well have been copied, like other features of the building, from a

church at Troyes in Normandy. Mr Drury's next marker was also unrewarding. St Michael's, Birchover, dates only from the 1700s, no earlier history is known.

Just up the road, however, is the evocatively named Druid's Inn. Any mention of a druid can be important, but it may have been named after a group of rocks that have no particular connection with druids, just as Robin Hood's Leap, between two standing stones twenty yards apart, has nothing to do with Robin Hood. Even so, Mr Drury includes Robin Hood's Leap on his leyline, and as sustenance is always welcome I am happy to include the Druid's Inn as well.

Mr Drury is on firmer ground with his next marker, the Hermit's Cave, which is still marked on the map. I could find no reference to the origin of its name, but for Alfred Watkins the name alone would be enough. It is derived, of course, from Hermes, the god of the highways!

The line ends at Arbor Low, but as one or two of the markers seem a little shaky, I tried extending it into Staffordshire, in search of one or two more. It passes through the delightfully named Custard Field Farm and then crosses the River Dove and the county border to reach perhaps the most convincing marker apart from Arbor Low itself, St Bartholomew's Church at Longnor. Tradition has it that St Bertram, The First Evangelist to the Moorlands, built a church at Longnor in memory of his wife and child in the early part of the eighth century. The dedication to St Bartholomew may originally have been to Bertelmus, the other version of Bertram. In this very pagan area, he may well have chosen a pagan sacred site for his church.

Less romantic historians say the church is more likely to have been founded some 400 years later, but it must still treasure its connection with the saint, because a statue of St Bertram has been presented to the church and dedicated as recently as 1996. It means there is a span of some 850 years between Longnor's two treasures, its simple Norman font and its modern statue.

I continued the line, but without much success. It just misses the evocative Flash Bottom, in an area where three counties meet – popular among roving

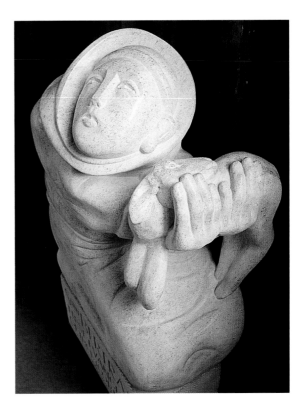

Above: *A modern statue of St Bertram in Longnor church.*
Left: *The circle of fallen stones at Arbor Low.*

rogues like counterfeiters, because the police could not pursue them out of their own county. It is said that this added a slang term to the language; anyone with a lot of money to dispose of became known as a 'Flash Harry'.

Flash may also have some tenuous link with Alfred's beacons, and indeed the line ends on a prominent hillside at Wildstone Rock, which sounds promising, but all the hills in this area are scattered with rocks, and I could not pinpoint the crucial one. It seemed more rewarding to return to St Bertram. He had a great influence in this part of Staffordshire, and his shrine at Ilam church, containing his ancient tomb cover, is still a place of pilgrimage. St Bertram's Well at Ilam does get a mention in the *Companion* leyline through Arbor Low, but I thought it might merit a line of its own. This is the result.

THE ST BERTRAM LINE (54)

On its way from Arbor Low to the well, the *Companion* line passes through what it calls 'the significantly named hamlet of Coldeaton'. Alfred liked to link 'Cold' place names with his leyline beacons, which may seem somewhat contradictory. Beacons are generally hot, not cold. But the link, I gather, is 'coel' or 'cole', which has been defined as a wizard or diviner, and the Cole-men, according to Alfred, were the guiding spirits behind leylines and marked them with beacons. No doubt they enjoyed their work, which is why Old King Cole – or Coel – was such a merry old soul. (In fairness to Alfred, that is my deduction, not his.)

Anyway, my St Bertram Line starts at Coldwall Bridge, which is doubly significant because it not only includes the word 'Cold' but it also stands on what was very prob-ably a prehistoric crossing place on the River Dove.

From here the line heads north-eastwards to St Bertram's Well. According to legend, Bertram was a Mercian prince who eloped with a beautiful Irish princess. Later on their travels the now pregnant princess went into labour and took shelter in a cave, while Bertram went for help. When he returned he found that she and her newborn baby had been killed by wolves. From then on he devoted his life to medita-tion, prayer and evangelism, and founded a number of churches in the area, including Longnor. He died in AD 714.

The well is lined with rocks and fed by a spring. The *Companion* says that a tree above it, known as St Bertram's Ash, was greatly venerated. 'It is in fact a maple,' notes the *Companion*, very fairly, before adding: 'St Bertram's Well is ancient and a profoundly beauti-ful, sacred place. The earth spirit is close at hand.'

From the well my line continues to Long Low, two Neolithic burial mounds linked by a high bank, an

Above: *Coldwall Bridge*. Left: The *view from Long Low*.

arrangement apparently unique in England, though it has not been explained. A wall has been built along the top of the bank and over one of the mounds, which helps it to show up on the skyline. According to *The Guide to Prehistoric England,* a stone burial pit in one mound was found to contain the bones of thirteen people, and in the other there were traces of cremation. Long Low must have been a very special sacred place around 2000 BC; it can still be quite eerie today.

From here a straight road leads towards Wetton and St Margaret's Church, which stands on a hillside with a high tower that dominates the village. It is an imposing site, but the very helpful vicar was unable to provide any information about its early history, or about another of his churches, St Lawrence's at Warslow, which is the final marker on the line.

A church leaflet says the original St Lawrence's was built in 1530 and nothing is known about the site before then. It was replaced by the present building in 1820. It may seem odd, therefore, that the church has a font dating from the early fourteenth century, a couple of hundred years before the first church was built. It came there by an unusual route.

In the nineteenth century the nearby church of Youlgreave acquired a rather splendid font with a built-in holy water stoup and a salamander, the symbol of baptism, carved on the side. The vicar of Youlgreave, a Mr Pidcock, decided the existing font was therefore redundant, and in due course it found its way to Warslow church, where it just so happened that the vicar was Mr Pidcock's son. But in the meantime it had also spent some time in the open – not in the vicar's garden this time, but in the yard of a local pub.

Today the old stone bowl rests on a roughly hewn boulder, repaired and restored to its original use. St Bertram, I am sure, would approve.

SHROPSHIRE AND CHESHIRE

ONSIDERING that it adjoins his local stamping ground in Herefordshire, Shropshire gets surprisingly little attention from Alfred Watkins. In *The Old Straight Track* his main preoccupation in Shropshire is with names like Bellstone Yard in Shrewsbury and Belmore Farm elsewhere in the county. Names involving bells, he reckons, often devolve from the Babylonian god Bel or Baal, introduced into Britain as a sun god. They can also be linked to the Beltane Fires, which used to be lit in various parts of the country to mark festivals. Fires link up with beacons, beacons link up with leylines – so for Alfred, 'bell' has a much greater significance than just going ding-dong merrily on high. And for ley-hunters in search of a marker there is always the chance of being saved by the bell. However, the only Shropshire leyline in his *Ley Hunter's Manual* is provided by a contributor, a Mrs John Clare, who says the first marker on it, a notch on Lord's Hill, Longmynd, is visible from her window and her house is almost on the line, so it would seem she must know her way around. Certainly her line passes through some interesting places and some varied countryside before it ends at the picturesque ruins of Buildwas Abbey. But like some of the other leylines in Alfred's books it seems to make some unexpected wiggles along what is supposed to be a straight line.

I have therefore endeavoured to straighten them out, which means losing one or two of her markers, but in doing so I have come across a very unusual new one, and it has such an interesting tale to tell that I have given its name to the line.

The fake grotto of Hawkstone Park.

170

THE CHRIST'S OAK LINE (55)

The first problem on Mrs Clare's leyline is Lord's Hill. It seems too far south on my map to fit into the rest of the ley. Instead, my line starts at Leigh Manor, a name that would immediately endear itself to Alfred Watkins. Leigh, lea, ley – they all tie in with his leyline theories. As a bonus, just outside the entrance to the Manor, standing discreetly in the shadow of a telegraph pole, I found the Lord's Stone, which, according to local legend, was used as a footstool for the Devil's Chair, on the far side of the valley. It so happens that Lord's Hill is on that side of the valley too, and

somehow the Hill, the Chair and the Stone all seem to be linked. With her local knowledge I am sure Mrs Clare would have been able to explain why the stone is where the hill ought to be.

My revised line crosses Hope valley at a point called Waterwheel, where a stream runs close to the road. The wheel itself has long since gone, but a little community has grown up around the original house. It seems reasonable to suppose that people congregated at this crossing place long before the waterwheel – or even the wheel– was invented.

From there the line climbs the hillside to the little village of Snailbeach – and here again is a name for Alfred to conjure with. The church booklet says the name is 'something of an enigma'. It dates back to the Saxons, and 'beach' could be a corruption of 'batch', meaning a narrow valley with a stream running through it. It does not attempt to explain the 'snail', but any ley-hunter could speedily do so – or indeed anyone who read the opening of this book.

Alfred Watkins, you may recall, christened his prehistoric surveyors 'dod-men', and in some parts of England this is the local name for a snail – 'which carries on its head', says Alfred, 'the dod-man's implements, the two sighting staves'. One might therefore deduce that Snailbeach was where one of Alfred's early surveyors crossed the valley.

It only needed Snailbeach church to be built on a pagan sacred site to clinch the theory. Unfortunately, St Luke's was built in 1872 as a chapel of ease on the edge of Minsterley parish. The pulpit does have a much earlier date on it, which might raise one's hopes, but it came from a church elsewhere.

Mrs Clare does not mention the village in her leyline – perhaps advisedly – and her next markers are the mount at Castle Pulverbatch and the church at Church Pulverbatch, on the far side of the ridge. This gives me another problem, because I can find no way

Above: *The circular churchyard at Church Pulverbatch.*
Left: *Just another rock – or the footstool for the Devil's Chair?*

on my map of lining up both the mound and the church with Buildwas Abbey and the other markers. Only the church seems to be on the line, and fortunately, it has a more promising pedigree than St Luke's. It stands on a hillside facing back along the line to two hills on the ridge that separates it from Snailbeach. They are each about 1000 feet high, with quite a deep dip in between. Could this be the 'notch', I wonder, which Mrs Clare referred to on Longmynd. It is another question that I am sure she could answer.

The present church was largely rebuilt in the 1850s, but the first known priest was 'John the Chaplain', recorded before 1193, and significantly the church is dedicated to St Edith. The church leaflet

points out that there were four Saxon abbesses of that name, and it is possible that the earliest church at Pulverbatch dated back to those days. It was largely destroyed by the Welsh before 1414, and there was a 100-year gap before it was reconsecrated, then twice rebuilt, so any early traces have long since gone.

But more importantly from a ley-hunter's viewpoint, St Edith's stands not only on a hillside but also within a circular churchyard. It has been argued that this is an indication the original site was protected in pagan times because it had some sacred role.

Mrs Clare's next marker is 'upper moat', which I could not identify, then 'ford on Cound Brook'. My line does indeed reach Cound Brook at a point where there may have been a ford. It also continues through a 'crossroads at Pitchford', her next marker, although these days the two side roads are just tracks.

The splendid arcades of Buildwas Abbey, by a key crossing point of the River Severn.

Then she names Cressage church, which is indeed very close to my line – but is not, alas, a good marker. There has certainly been a church in Cressage since early medieval times, but not on the site of the present one, which was built in 1841.

That was the bad news. The good news came as a result of further enquiries in the village and the assistance of Michael Osborn, who wrote the very helpful church booklet. He supplied me with a detailed map showing where the original church used to be. More importantly, it also showed the site of 'Christ's Oak', from which the village took its Anglo-Saxon name of Critesac or Cristesache. In the booklet Mr Osborn speculates: 'Why did an oak tree in an area which was in ancient times predominantly a forest of oaks get the name "Christ's Oak"? Was it perhaps a particularly fine specimen which was held in reverence in pagan times? When the Anglo-Saxon dwellers were converted to Christianity by St Augustine's missionaries, did they

keep an allegiance to this tree but rename it for their new deity?' Mr Osborn is not a ley-hunter, but Alfred Watkins himself could not have put it better.

After 1000 years there is nothing left of Christ's Oak, though confusingly there are the remains of another oak tree just outside the village called 'The Queen's Oak' or 'The Lady Oak', and the present church has a table made from its wood. But while the Lady Oak and the site of the original church of St Samson are just off the leyline, the site of Christ's Oak, which by tradition is where the war memorial now stands, is bang on it. Such are the delightful surprises of ley-hunting.

The refreshing speculation in the church guide-book does not end there. Mr Osborn quotes the Venerable Bede's reference to St Augustine presiding over an unsucessful conference with Celtic bishops at 'Augustine's Oak' on the banks of the River Severn, generally identified as Aust in Gloucestershire, then at a second one for which no location is given.

'It is tempting to think,' says the guidebook, again in ley-hunting style, 'that this second conference took place again on the banks of the Severn, under or near an oak tree which was already named or thereafter was called Christ's Oak.'

As it happened, this conference was unsuccessful too, but if, indeed, it took place at Christ's Oak, what better confirmation could there be that it is a top-grade ley marker?

Incidentally, Mr Osborn told me he tried ruling a line from St Edith's at Church Pulverbatch to Buildwas Abbey and he too found that it passed through the War Memorial site. It also passed through his house, which he had been trying to sell for four months.

'I don't think a horde of little green men from an UFO would be interested,' he commented, 'but I wonder if I got the agent to mention the leyline in the sale particulars whether this would bring in a horde of eager purchasers?'

I assured him that the presence of a leyline could only bring good luck. It might even bring a UFO into his back garden, one of these fine blue moonlit nights.

And so to Mrs Clare's final marker. She may have been wrong about Cressage church, but her mention of it uncovered a wealth of fascinating speculation, and in the case of Buildwas Abbey there is no doubt about its site or its history. Although it is now overshadowed by the Wenlock power station, and the toll bridge over the Severn which provided some of its income has been replaced by a modern one, it is easy to visualize how the abbey occupied a key position on one of the river's main crossing places. Although it was founded only in 1135 there may well have been an SSPI – a Site of Special Pagan Interest – there before.

According to the information from English Heritage, which now looks after it, the history of the abbey was 'comparatively uneventful'. Then it goes on to recall how one abbot was murdered by a renegade monk, another was carried off and imprisoned by marauders from Powys, and its lands were laid waste by the followers of Owen Glendower. There were other occasions also when it suffered from 'the levity of the Welsh'. After such an 'uneventful' 400 years, the dissolution of Buildwas Abbey by Henry VIII should have come as quite a relief.

Turning to Cheshire, Alfred Watkins' *Manual* contains what seems to me a rather over-ambitious line some fifty miles long, starting at Hawkstone in Shropshire before passing through the length of Cheshire and ending at a Roman camp in Manchester. It quotes markers such as Churche's Mansion in Nantwich, which was built in Elizabethan times. The contributor of the leyline, a Lieutenant-Colonel Powell, may have been influenced by the salamander that crawls up the front wall of the mansion, and indeed this was an early emblem of Christian baptism, but here it was an early emblem of fire insurance. Richard Churche, who built it, added the salamander because, according to legend, it could not be destroyed by fire. Six years later most of Nantwich was burned down, but Churche's mansion survived. Lt.-Col. Powell might argue it was thanks to the leyline, but Mr Churche, I am sure, would thank the salamander.

He may also have been deceived by the remarkable range of apparent ley markers in Hawkstone Park, but most of them are 'historical follies' installed by its eighteenth-century owner. The Colonel's marker at Hawkstone is a 'shoulder of hill with earthworks and mounds', but there are many hills and rocky bluffs to choose from and as many artificial features as there are natural ones. This is, in fact, a happy hunting ground for the folly-hunter rather than for the ley-hunter, and like the booklet that has been produced about it by its shrewd commercial operators, called *The Mystery of Hawkstone Park*, it is difficult to know how much of it to take seriously.

However, it might be argued that the same applies to some of the books that have been written about ley-lines, so let us call Hawkstone's bluff, as it were, and see if it can justify a leyline of its own.

THE RED CASTLE LINE (56)

When Sir Rowland Hill started 'adapting' the park there was just one genuine ruin there, dating back to the thirteenth century. It is known as the Red Castle, presumably because of its red sandstone walls, and if any site in Hawkstone can be regarded as a ley marker, it is most likely to be the castle, on the optimistic assumption that its commanding position on the hillside was once a special pagan site.

Then Sir Rowland added the Labyrinth, the Grotto, the 100-foot Obelisk and the Hermitage, which was manned by a resident hermit. Other delights that Sir Rowland and later his son, Sir Richard, provided for their own amusement and the entertainment of their guests included a 'Scene in Switzerland', a vineyard designed to look like a fortress,and even a menagerie.

According to *The Mystery of Hawkstone Park*, most of the features still to be seen in the park had something to do with the search for the Holy Grail, the early days of freemasonry and Poussin's painting *The Arcadian Shepherds*. I shall not attempt to explain how they are connected, but to give you an idea, the story starts with the Grail being handed down through generations of the Grail family, then a seventeenth-century poem is quoted in which the Knights of the White Castle guard the Grail until it is stolen and hidden in the Red Castle.

I am not sure if Alfred Watkins would accept this as a basis for making the Red Castle a ley marker, but because of its genuine medieval origins and what might have preceded it, I looked for a Red Castle leyline. By linking it with the village church at Prees, which has a known history going back to early times, I found a line that continues through a motte and bailey and a couple more possible markers before ending at the ancient church of St Chad at Bruera. It seemed worth a go.

The Romans had a fortified camp at Prees in AD 45,

Above: *The view towards Red Castle.* Right: *The massive buttresses of Buera church, with its slightly crooked bell-cote.*

when they were building their road to Chester, but before then it was a British settlement called Prys-Wyth, 'Hills of Brushwood', and the earliest church could well have been built on their original sacred site. A priest was recorded here in the Domesday Book, and the first stone church was built as a collegiate church of Black Canons in about 1100.

When it was restored in 1600 the Sandford family, who had been lords of the manor since the Conquest, donated thirty oak trees for the splendid cartwheel-and-beam roof that bears their coat of arms. For the next 260 years this was concealed above a fake ceiling, but full marks for once to the Victorians, who uncovered it as part of their restoration.

The Sandfords have their own chapel, but most of the memorials in the chancel are to the Hills, the relatives and family of Sir Rowland Hill of Hawkstone — and another link between Prees and the Red Castle in Hawkstone Park.

The next marker is named on the map as Pan Castle, a motte and bailey outside Whitchurch. The entrance gate was chained and padlocked, with a large notice saying 'No Thoroughfare'. I got the distinct impression that Pan Castle was not accessible to the public.

The next point on the line, however, looked more promising. It is marked on the map as 'Cross o' the Hill', on the road from Malpas to the curiously named No Man's Heath. 'Cross o' the Hill' suggests the site of an ancient preaching cross. The locals knew the name, but no one could tell me its origin and there was no trace of the cross.

Incidentally, my Red Castle Line is now running almost parallel to a leyline in *The Ley Hunter's Companion* from Malpas church, about a mile from the elusive Cross o' the Hill, to Chester Cathedral. I visited the church and the Vaults Inn nearby, which the *Companion* says is haunted by a ghost called George, but nobody knew about the Cross – nor indeed had they seen George.

After passing through Lea Newbold Farm – that 'lea' again – I ended the Red Castle Line at St Chad's Church, Bruera, where there also happens to be a moat. There is known to have been a church on this site for nearly 1000 years, and when the Normans built the present one they used some of the original Saxon stonework.

From the road the first feature to strike you is the massive buttressing on the west wall. It was added in the fifteenth century to stop the wall collapsing, and indeed all the walls are out of plumb and have had to be shored up too. Interestingly, the church leaflet observes that they may have been built that way on purpose. 'It has been suggested that the misalignment was intentional,' it says, 'and followed the traditional nave shape of an upturned boat.'

However, no explanation is offered for the misalignment of the wooden bell-cote that was added about the same time as the west buttress. Ley-hunters may wonder if it was erected to line up with the ley, rather than the nave roof, on which it stands.

St Chad's other interesting feature for the ley-hunter is the decoration of the Norman columns of the chancel arch. There are what the leaflet calls 'eagle's beaks', which look very similar to the beak-heads found in other old churches on leylines, and also some grotesque heads, which the leaflet says have been identified by a noted antiquarian as the Norse gods Woden, Thor and Freya.

So at the end of a leyline that started in the bizarre surroundings of Hawkstone Park, we may not have solved the mystery of the Holy Grail, but we have at least found a trio of Norse gods in an ancient church that has tilting walls and a crooked bell-cote, facing a dried-up moat.

I would not ask for more.

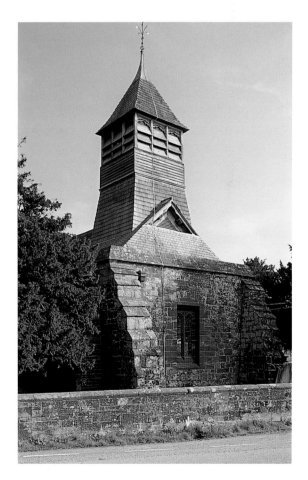

HUMBERSIDE, YORKSHIRE AND CLEVELAND

HE monolith in Rudston churchyard, twenty-five feet high and perhaps the same depth below ground, is said to be the biggest standing stone in Britain, and it is an obvious focal point for any leyline in Humberside. First of all, though, I did attempt to find an alternative, based on a row of Bronze Age barrows at Towthorpe, because *The Guide to Prehistoric Britain*, which never mentions leylines, does suggest that the barrows may be on the line of a prehistoric track.

They run alongside a green lane, which now marks the boundary with Yorkshire, and I found I could line them up with a tumulus and an earthwork, and then end at Thwing church. All Saints' has a Norman zigzag arch over the door, with an unusual tympanum depicting a long-bodied donkey bearing a cross. On one of the roof bosses I also spotted a man's head with either a very long, drooping moustache or a forked beard, but I found it difficult to link leylines with either an elongated donkey or a fork-bearded face.

I returned therefore to Rudston. *The Ley Hunter's Companion* has a ley through the monolith that starts at Willerby church in Yorkshire and passes through a tumulus and two barrows, but it can find nothing to say about the church. So I found my own line through the monolith which includes an earthwork and a long barrow, as well as three interesting churches.

The evocative ruins of Whitby Abbey, a spectacular starting point for a leyline.

THE RUDSTON MONOLITH LINE (57)

The line starts at St Andrew's Church, Boynton, midway between Rudston and Bridlington. It shares the dedication with a number of other local churches, and the booklet says this may be because it was founded by St Wilfred on one of his missionary journeys in the seventh century. I am sure Alfred Watkins would say it had more to do with the Celtic god Grannus, because of the similar name, but either way it seems a church has been there since Saxon times. Like many others, the original one was probably destroyed by William the Conqueror during his 'harrying of the North'. The earliest relic is a small Celtic cross, perhaps thirteenth century, set into a buttress of the tower.

The remarkable Strickland family have been linked with Boynton for four centuries, and their turkey emblem features on the lectern instead of the customary eagle. Bernard Matthews, head of the 'bootiful' turkey empire, might feel envious, but in fact he owes a debt to the Stricklands, because it was William 'The Navigator' Strickland who followed Cabot to the New World and returned with the first turkeys ever seen in Europe. He built Boynton Hall in the 1550s, and the family lived there continuously until the twentieth century. Then the new ninth baronet, Sir Walter Strickland, created an unexpected diversion after attending his father's funeral. It is said he lined up the servants along the drive, and instead of chatting to them he leapfrogged over their backs. He then left the Hall, became convinced that the Foreign Secretary had ordered his assassination, took Czech citizenship, and eventually died in Java.

It is perhaps not surprising, therefore, that the Strickland memorials have one or two eccentricities too. For instance the memorial to the first baronet is garlanded with flowers, while the corresponding one to Lady Elizabeth, the second baronet's wife, is decorated with trophies of arms. One might have thought they would be the other way round.

Above: *The extra, unexplained dragon on the Cottam font in Langtoft church.* Right: *The 4000-year-old Rudston monolith.*

And so to All Saints' Church, Rudston, and the familiar monolith in the churchyard. It was erected about 2000 BC, the same period as the Towthorpe barrows, and its presence is one of the few actual proofs that early Christians took over pagan sacred sites. The first missionaries came to this gathering point to preach, and they were so successful that the village took its name from the Christian rood, or cross, and from the pagan stone.

It seems rather a pity that the church itself is so overshadowed – figuratively as well as literally – by the monolith, because its own treasures are often ignored. It has, for instance, a magnificent decorated Norman font, which has been in continuous use for 900 years. And the organ has its own modest place in church history: it was the first one outside London to be fitted with electrically operated bellows. Across the road from All Saints' is the modern counterpart of the monolith. A dramatic, white-painted cross just about the same height, has been erected as the village's war memorial.

From here the line passes through a long barrow beside a lane near Little Broach Dale and reaches St Peter's Church, Langtoft. It cannot boast a prehistoric monolith, but it does have three fonts. One is a grand affair, carved with saints and bishops, while the next one is quite small and low with an iron grille over it, making it look like a well-head. The most interesting is the 'Cottam font', splendidly carved with Adam and Eve on each side of the Tree of Life, St Lawrence on his gridiron, St Margaret bursting out of the dragon – and an unexpected extra dragon between the two saints.

A helpful notice explains the carvings but makes no mention of the spare dragon. The font came from Cottam church, a couple of miles off the line, and one wonders if this unexplained dragon had anything to do with it being brought to St Peter's to be brought in. On the other hand, of course, the mason may have just included it to fill up the gap.

The line continues across country, briefly joins an earthwork near Sledmere and crosses the county

A modern equivalent of the monolith, perhaps: Rudston's lofty war memorial cross.

boundary into Yorkshire. It ends at St Mary's Church, Wharram le Street, built in 1050 on a hillside but now partly concealed by houses. The outline of the original Saxon doorway can be seen on the west wall of the tower, indicating its pre-Norman origins, with the usual possibility of occupying an earlier pagan site. It seems a sound enough marker to end the Rudston Line.

It does not quite match the pedigree, however, of St Mary's Church, Lastingham, on the edge of the North Yorkshire moors. Its history is well documented, back to its foundation by St Cedd in the seventh century, and I have visited it many times and marvelled at the ancient Norman crypt in which the saint's remains are buried. But when I looked at it from a ley-hunter's viewpoint, a tiny doubt crept in.

For a church to be a ley marker, as I understand it, there has to be at least a sporting chance that it is on a pagan sacred site, but from what the Venerable Bede says about Lastingham, that seems a little unlikely. Bede explains how Bishop Cedd was invited by King Oswald's son, Ethelwald, to accept a grant of land and found a monastery, and he continues: 'The prelate therefore assenting to his wishes chose for himself a place to build a monastery among lofty and remote mountains, in which there appeared to have been more lurking places of robbers and dens of wild beasts than habitations of men.' Bede goes on to record that Cedd studied by prayers and fasting, 'to purge the site he had received for his monastery from its previous defilement of evil deeds'. This hardly seems to follow the procedure recommended to early Christians of adopting a pagan sacred site so that the locals kept on coming, since the site seems anything but sacred, and there were no locals to attract. Or were the 'evil deeds' some unpleasant form of pagan worship indulged in by lurking robbers, and he took over the site and kept purging it until the robbers cried: 'Enough, Cedd!'?

Whatever the answer – and only Cedd can say – *The Ley Hunter's Companion* has a Lastingham leyline, based on St Mary's Church. Looking at it again through a ley-hunter's eyes, I noticed the rams' horns on some of the columns, and I read about the eighth-century dragon's head on the abbot's throne, though it is not kept in the church. Both have a nice leyline flavour.

As additional evidence, the *Companion* notes 'several carved serpents that writhe subtly around parts of the church'. Some people, it says, claim to detect the serpentine earth force, or 'ley power', as a physical sensation when in the crypt. I felt a sensation too, but it was more the sort that is mentioned in one of the church guides: 'Brothers we are treading where the saints have trod.' Apart from St Mary's, the *Companion's* markers are an assortment of barrows, earthworks and tumuli. The neighbouring moorland has a surfeit of them, and it is not too difficult to find some in line. Perhaps this is why Paul Devereux discards the leyline in his later *New Ley Hunter's Guide* – or did he have doubts about the origin of the site too? Anyway, I found a line to the next village of Appleton-le-Moors proved rather more productive.

THE APPLETON LINE (58)

Christ Church, Appleton-le-Moors, was built in the 1860s, but the village dates back to before the Domesday Book, and there was a chapel dedicated to St Mary Magdalene in the thirteenth century. As at Boynton, the original church may have been lost during the 'harrying of the North' just after the Conquest.

Rather more interesting is the carving on one of the stone cottages in the village street, just along from the church. The cottage is called 'Three Faces', and that is just what the carving shows, with an inscription underneath, which neither I nor the author of a local guidebook could decipher. The faces have staring eyes but very different expressions. One is thin and tight lipped, another is chubby cheeked but miserable, the third is long haired, open mouthed and demonic. One theory is they represent a lawyer, a doctor and a parson, who are, according to tradition, always in attendance at a deathbed. But I would hesitate to say which is which, or indeed who they are. Could they date back much earlier, to the original chapel of St Mary Magdalene?

The line follows the lane down into Lastingham, through two roadside crosses, which are named, very logically, High Cross and Low Cross. This part of North Yorkshire has almost as many roadside crosses as tumuli and cairns, and they were erected in various periods and for various purposes. Some merely marked parish boundaries, others were preaching crosses or the remains of stone circles or memorials or just outcrops of rock that were shaped into 'standing stones' by the weather. But some of them, those which particularly interest the ley-hunter, marked prehistoric tracks.

The better preserved the cross, the easier it is to identify, but High Cross and Low Cross are not in very good shape. The popular theory is that they were boundary markers, but until 1868 Appleton was part

Appleton's present church is Victorian, but there was a chapel in the thirteenth century.

of the parish of Lastingham, so which boundary did they mark? I prefer to think they were put there to mark the line of the ancient track from Appleton to Lastingham.

In Lastingham itself, depending on the thickness of one's pencil, the line can take in part of St Mary's

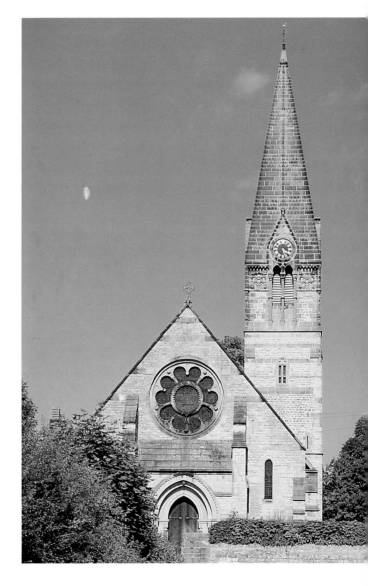

churchyard on its way down to St Cedd's Well. Holy wells are considered just as good ley markers as ancient churches, and presumably this one has been there as long as the church. Indeed, it may have been the reason that St Cedd chose the site for his monastery. The beck that runs beside it would be an additional attraction.

The well is older than it looks. As one vicar wrote some eighty-odd years ago: 'It is covered by a modern structure erected of stones brought from Rosedale Abbey, and likely to deceive the unwary.' Even then the Latin inscription was difficult to read, but it stated that St Cedd, founder of Lastingham Abbey, died in 664 and is buried in the church, next to the altar.

From Lastingham the line heads off across the moors, where it has a wide selection of barrows, crosses and standing stones to choose from. Fainthearted ley-hunters might rule out some of those that commem-

Above: *The stump of one of the roadside crosses on the line to Lastingham.* Above right: *St Cedd's Well, dating from 664 and probably before.* Below right: *A ram's horn capital in the ancient crypt of Lastingham church.*

orate some specific person or event, such as the Elgee Stone, a flat-topped boulder on Rosedale Moor, which is named after the local writer and naturalist Frank Elgee. On it is the date his widow unveiled it, which was in the 1950s, but more optimistic seekers after ley markers might argue that the boulder itself must be many centuries older than that, and who can say that it did not originally mark a prehistoric track?

Once you start on that line of argument, the moors become a ley-hunter's paradise. Not far from the Elgee Stone, for example, there are three others, known as Fat Betty, Old Ralph and Young Ralph. Fat Betty is, indeed, fat, a bulky, white boulder with a small circular 'head' on top. Old Ralph is short and stocky; Young Ralph is a cross, nine feet high. Fat Betty and Old Ralph, so they say, are reminders of a Cistercian nun from Rosedale who was being escorted by a devoted servant to meet a nun from Baysdale called Margery at a halfway point on the moors. Margery failed to appear. Ralph went to look for her, a mist came down, and nobody could find anybody. Then suddenly the mist lifted, and they found they were all within a few yards of each other. The stones celebrate their safe deliverance – and yes, there is a Margery Stone, too.

Young Ralph is said to mark the spot where a starving traveller collapsed and died. A kindly farmer called Ralph erected a cross with a hollow in the top, in which more prosperous passers-by could leave a donation for those less fortunate. The cross has been

damaged more than once by coin-seekers, but it is restored each time, and the custom has continued.

Whatever stories are attached to Fat Betty, the two Ralphs and their motionless friends, I am sure that ardent ley-hunters will still argue that they have a much earlier history or that they replace an earlier marker. But to be on the safe side, I am ending the Appleton Line not at a cross or a standing stone but at an indisputable tumulus on the moors. It is called the Three Howes and is near Bank Top, on the summit of the road across the moors to Rosedale Abbey. It also happens to be on the way to the next leyline.

I have long known about the remarkable history of Whitby Abbey, but it was only when I started looking for leylines that I heard about Freebrough Hill. These two are about as big a contrast as you can get in possible ley markers, but they both have their own qualifications, and a line between them produced some more markers.

THE WHITBY ABBEY LINE (59)

In the year that St Cedd died at Lastingham, the Synod of Whitby made the historic decision at the abbey to commit the English Church to the Roman instead of the Celtic rite, and that is its first claim to fame. But there was probably a Roman signal station there before the abbey, and Alfred Watkins names the site on its dramatic headland as a typical example of a coastal ley marker.

The abbey was destroyed by the Danes and went out of existence for a couple of hundred years until the Benedictines arrived and started afresh. That monastery was dissolved with all the others by Henry VIII, and the monastic buildings have virtually disappeared, but the church was left as a landmark for

mariners. Its exposed position caused it steadily to deteriorate, and the locals speeded things up by stealing all the lead off the roof. Finally, it was shelled by the German fleet during the First World War, but the imposing east façade and parts of the other walls still stand – albeit looking rather battered.

There are many legends attached to the abbey and to its founder, St Hilda. Her best known activity, apart from hosting the synod, was to rid Eskdale of snakes by driving them over the cliff and decapitating them with a shrewdly aimed whip as they fell. In due course, their remains became fossilized into the ammonites that are still found on the rocks below.

It was also at Whitby Abbey in the seventh century that a cowherd called Caedmon had a vision of an angel, who asked him to sing of the creation of the world, and he became renowned as England's earliest Christian songwriter.

A cross commemorating the poetical cowherd stands in the churchyard of St Mary's Church nearby, which is the next marker on the line. It still has its Norman tower, but the interior was filled with galleries and pews in Georgian times, and little remains of its earlier days. It is approached by a climb of 199 steps, but for once I could find no local legend to explain this intriguing figure.

The line heads westwards out of Whitby, and a few miles away it plunges into Mulgrave Woods, where there are three Mulgrave Castles: an ancient motte and bailey, a medieval ruin and a Georgian mansion. The line goes through the first two. The wood also contains a Hermitage and a Wizard's Glen, but like some of the features at Hawkstone Park in Shropshire, they may not entirely justify their description.

The two earlier castles have enough tales to tell anyway. The ancient mound is sometimes called Wade's or Wada's Castle, and many believe it dates from pre-Norman times when Wade – or Wada – was

Above: *Whitby Abbey was destroyed by the Danes, rebuilt, dissolved by Henry VIII, even shelled by the Germans, but the ruins survive.* Left: *A contrast to the nearby abbey, Whitby church has Georgian galleries and pews.*

a hero or a villain, a warrior or a giant, depending perhaps on how he spelt his name. A local ballad accuses him of treason and falsehood. 'Between Guisborough and Whitby, sooth to say, For his treason he was laid by the highway.' And indeed there are at least two different roadside stones in that area which are known as Wade's Stone and reputed to mark his grave. Another version says he was a noble Saxon who slew a Northumbrian king called Ethelred, 'an inhuman monster', and who died in his bed at Mulgrave Castle.

Much more entertaining are the legends of Wade – or Wada – the Giant, and his equally imposing wife, Bell. It is said that he built the castle at Mulgrave

while she built another one at Pickering, and as they had only one hammer they used to toss it to each other whenever they needed it. They must still hold the world hammer-throwing record; the castles were seventeen miles apart.

We are also told that they built the stone causeway between Kettleness and Pickering. Most historians would prefer to give the credit to the Romans, but I like to picture Bell plodding along with her apron full of massive stones, while Wade took each one out and laid it in place on the causeway. The operation was not without its hiccups: Bell's apron-strings snapped under the strain, depositing a heap of stones now known as the Bride-Stones, and during one violent tiff Wade scooped up an enormous clod of earth and hurled it at her. The clod missed her and became the round-topped hill of Blakey Topping, while the crater it left behind is now called the Hole of Horcum.

The mysterious Freebrough Hill, rich in legend.

Like Wade and Wada, I wonder if Horcum has an alternative spelling. Could it perhaps be Hokum?

The second Mulgrave Castle was the stronghold of Peter de Mauley, who apparently endeared himself to King John acquiring the earldom of Mulgrave in the process by blinding and then killing John's rival to the throne, Prince Arthur of Brittany. In Stuart times the then earl had a similar close relationship with the king, but in his case it had the opposite effect. During the Civil War Cromwell's men reduced his castle to ruins. It was after the Restoration that the earl's great-grandson built the third Mulgrave Castle.

From the excitements of Mulgrave Woods the line crosses the border into Cleveland and ends at Freebrough Hill, which is about a mile from the ambiguously named Hole of Horcum. Geologists say that both of them are natural phenomena: the Hole was caused by spring water wearing away the rocks, and the isolated conical hill is the result of resistant sandstone on top of clay. There are, however, just as many legends about the hill as about the hole, as I learned from Graham Aldous, who lives in nearby Moorsholm.

Freebrough is said to be derived from Fria's Burgh, named after the wife of the Norse god Odin. Presumably it could have been created by either one of them, or it could have been a joint operation, like Wade's Causeway. Then again it is reputed to be the last resting place of King Arthur and his knights, although it seems a long haul from Glastonbury Tor. More importantly, it has been associated locally with leylines.

'Certainly it has a mystical feel about it,' says Graham, and others must have thought so too, because he recalls waking a few years ago to see half-a-dozen vertical 'Tibetan-style' banners fluttering near the summit, covered in runic symbols. Their origin was never established, but New Age travellers were around at the time, and perhaps they erected the banners as their version of a leyline beacon, to mark the end of the Whitby Abbey Line.

The Ley Hunter's Companion ignores Freebrough Hill and instead concentrates on the ruins of Guisborough Priory. I thought it might be interesting to line up the Priory with the Hill – and it was.

THE FREEBROUGH HILL LINE (60)

The line goes from Freebrough Hill through a number of tumuli on the moors before reaching Guisborough. Admittedly, there are so many possible markers in this area that they are difficult to avoid, but in Guisborough there are just the priory and St Nicholas's Church – and the line goes through both.

The priory was founded by Robert de Brus in the twelfth century, but it suffered the usual fate of such places and, like Whitby Abbey, there is little left of it except for the east end, which is in the grounds of Gisborough Hall (Gisborough is presumably Guisborough in disguise – or disgise). However, there is more evidence of the de Brus family in St Nicholas's – a cenotaph on which are carved ten knights. They represent both the English and the Scottish branches of the family – Brus also has an alternative spelling, the more familiar Bruce. The church itself is fifteenth-century, but there was one at Guisborough in the Domesday Book, and as the *Companion* considers that St Nicholas' qualifies as a marker, and so do I.

The line ends north-west of the town at a hill-fort that, to judge by *The Guide to Prehistoric England*, is the only prehistoric site in Cleveland – this makes it quite a coup! Eston Nab is an Iron Age fort, built on a promontory above a steep cliff. It is protected on the other side by a rampart fourteen feet high, a clay bank backed by a stone wall fourteen feet thick and a formidable obstacle. The defences enclose an area of over two acres, making it a large target for a leyline – and an impressive final marker for this group of counties.

The twelfth-century Guisborough Priory.

DURHAM AND NORTHUMBRIA

OUNTY Durham holds the curious distinction of being totally unrepresented in either of Alfred Watkins' ley-hunting books or in the later *Ley Hunter's Companion*. I would have thought that Durham Cathedral, with its St Cuthbert connection, and Durham Castle, former home of the Prince-Bishops, might have attracted a little attention, but I found I was starting from scratch.

I began with St Andrew's Church at Winston by the River Tees, because I had heard that its thirteenth-century font features two Celtic-looking dragons biting each other. One dragon can excite a ley-hunter because of its link with ley forces and currents; two of them on one font are irresistible.

I was already familiar with St Mary's Church at Middleton-in-Teesdale, some twelve miles upriver. Although the present church is Victorian there is a thirteenth-century window from the earlier one in the churchyard, and I have always enjoyed the story of how the three bells in the old bell tower could be rung by one agile bell-ringer, using two hands and a foot. So I tried a line between the two churches. On paper it looks promising. It narrowly misses a round Bronze Age barrow, known as Swinkley Knoll, but does pass through a ruined church in the grounds of Eggleston Hall and the church at Little Newsham. Alas, the rector of Middleton, an old friend who is used to my strange enquiries, advised me that the Eggleston ruins had been a private chapel built by the previous family at the hall, with no earlier connections, and the church at Little Newsham had been there for only about 150 years, with nothing significant about its site.

I began to see why Alfred Watkins and his successors had drawn a blank. With only four markers on the line anyway, and two of them so shaky, I reluctantly abandoned the idea. I had better luck, however, with a church that another friend from those parts commended to me. Just its name is sufficient for a ley-hunter; it is known simply as the Saxon church. But I found there was a lot more to it than that – and there were markers to go with it.

St Andrew's Church, Bywell.

The Saxon Church Line (61)

Admittedly the first two markers on this line on the way to Escomb's Saxon church are not what I would automatically choose, though they qualify by Alfred's standards. They are two crossroads on the road from Billingham to Bishop Auckland. By a happy chance, the Rushyford roundabout is a raised mound with a scattering of trees on it, a familiar combination to the ley-hunter, but I have to admit that the trees are very young – and the roundabout is obviously not a barrow. The Coundon roundabout is much the same, but with even younger trees.

My only excuse for using them is to find a leyline through Escomb church, and no matter how undistinguished they may be, they have the great merit of being on a direct line with the Saxon church and the markers beyond it.

'After Durham Cathedral this is the most impressive ecclesiastical building in the county,' enthuses John Betjeman's *Guide to English Parish Churches*, and indeed it is a remarkable church. Most experts agree that it must have been built before the end of the seventh century, and, apart from one or two windows and the addition of the porch, it has remained virtually untouched since the Saxons built it. But that is just the start.

'There is about the church a sense of mystery,' says the church booklet, setting the right tone for what follows. 'There are questions that have no ready answers, and a sense of some deep experience that remains forever just out of reach.'

One fascinating mystery for the ley-hunter is why it was built there in the first place. It looks even more incongruous today, standing in its little churchyard on what has become a traffic island, surrounded by modern houses. But even in Saxon times, why should they have chosen to carry heavy stonework from the ruins of the Roman fort at Binchester, two miles upstream? Happily the booklet has a theory – one that would warm the heart of Alfred Watkins.

'We do not know the event, person or deity originally honoured by the selection of this site,' it says, 'but the use of stones and the efforts made in the construction suggest that this was a religious centre of some importance.' It points out that a stream used to run past the churchyard and there were springs nearby 'which may have provided a focus for Roman worship and settlement'. Also, the River Wear used to flow much nearer the church, 'and the village has always been a recognized crossing point connecting two ancient trackways'.

The site, in fact, has just about all the credentials required of a ley marker. And we haven't even started on the church itself.

First, the outside. There is a sundial on the south wall, which is believed to be the oldest in Britain still in its original place, and it has a serpent above the dial. Serpents are as significant to the ley-hunter as dragons are, and the booklet has spotted the connection. 'The design of the serpent has close similarities to representations of the Teutonic creator God who formed part of the pre-Christian religion of the Angles who settled in Northumbria and Yorkshire.'

On the north wall, above the door, there is another gem for the ley-hunter, a stone with a rosette carved on it, 'which may well have formed part of a Roman altar, later incorporated into the church'. And before going inside, the booklet points out the roughly circular shape of the churchyard. 'This strongly hints at a Celtic origin for the church, and a tradition that may well go back even earlier to the Romano-British period and beyond.'

After all that the interior might be an anticlimax – but not at all. There is the outline of the original consecration cross in the wall behind the pulpit, and behind the altar is a stone cross, probably dating from the ninth century – 'but the date may possibly be much earlier,' the booklet hastily adds. 'Some have

The Saxon church at Escomb: 'There is about the church a sense of mystery ...'

conjectured that it formed part of the original preaching cross that would have pre-dated the church.'

So we have a Roman religious centre, holy springs, a river crossing point, ancient trackways, a circular churchyard, a serpentine sundial, a Roman altar, an early preaching cross – short of actually seeing one of Alfred Watkins' prehistoric 'dod-men' lighting a beacon on top of the bell-cote, no ley- hunter could ask for more. Escomb Saxon church must be the ultimate in leyline markers – and its incomparable booklet could almost be renamed 'The Saxon Church Ley-hunter's Guide'.

Having made up for the shortcomings of the crossroads that featured earlier, I am back to the more average kind of marker with Witton Castle. Unlike the

Saxon church, it has had to adapt itself to changing times. As one distinguished travel writer puts it: 'the castle is run as a kind of holiday camp, with bars in the dungeons, dining rooms in the keep and recreation rooms elsewhere. The park is full of caravans, the courtyard full of cars, the gardens full of campers – so the spirit of the place is lost. It is, however, some compensation that the place survives and is used.'

Nevertheless, Witton has an impressive pedigree. It was built by Sir Ralph de Eure in the early fourteenth century, and parts of the original building still survive – the keep, the outside walls and the angle towers. But in 1689 it was partially dismantled, and after it had been rebuilt a fire caused extensive damage and it had to be rebuilt again. But the Victorians provided some pseudo-medieval additions, and it still looks very grand – once you get past the caravans.

Above: *Witton Castle.* Right: *The commanding view across the Wear valley from Hamsterley church.*

Sir Ralph de Eure no doubt had a good reason for selecting this attractive site. He may have foreseen the day when the Eures gave place to the Euro and the castle became an international holiday centre. I have no evidence, however, of any earlier significance. The final marker, happily, can be traced a little further back.

St James's Church, Hamsterley, was founded in the twelfth century as a chapel of ease. It stands well outside Hamsterley itself, and the church booklet comments promisingly that the reason for its isolation 'has always been a mystery'. Unlike that memorable booklet at Escomb, it does not speculate further, but the church occupies a commanding position overlooking the Wear valley, a wonderful vantage point for any prehistoric surveyor.

In the 1880s the church 'suffered greatly from restoration', but some curious features survive from much earlier times; these have not been entirely explained. For example, while three of the four corbels supporting the chancel roof are coats of arms, the fourth is a griffin 'of unknown origin'. On the chancel wall is a fourteenth-century limestone slab decorated with 'an animal of some sort, possibly a lion couchant' – and possibly not. And a stone eagle stands outside the porch, again for no apparent reason.

The strangest items, however, are two memorial stones jutting out of the wall of the south transept. One is decorated with an elaborate cross, the other has an effigy of a woman lying with her head on a cushion and her hands together in prayer. The booklet suggests they were inserted in the wall after it was built in order to lie 'within the wall', but it seems a curious definition of 'within', when half of them are 'without'. The booklet agrees that they are the most remarkable features of the church – and they provide effective end markers in their own right to the Saxon Church Line.

While I had some difficulty in conjuring up a leyline in Co. Durham, there seems to be no shortage of them in Northumbria. *The Ley Hunter's Companion*, usually content with one or two leys in a county, actually has three – but rather strangely, all of them are rejected by Paul Devereux in his subsequent book. He gives no explanation, but I am quite glad he disapproves of them, because I am not too keen on them either, though probably for a different reason.

All three depend almost entirely on tumuli or earthworks or enclosures or former settlements – the sort of site that archaeologists may find gripping but for the layman ley-hunter that are inclined to pall. In one case the only actual building among the markers is Belford church, and in another there is Hadrian's Wall – a pretty extensive target for a leyline anyway!

The third, the most interesting, goes to Bamburgh Castle and then jumps to a ruined tower on Inner Farne Island, which is accessible only by boat. The other markers are prehistoric camp sites and a flat stone about a foot high, which even the *Companion* is a little dubious about. 'We cannot be the final judges as to whether or not it is a markstone,' it says, 'but it certainly seems as if it could be one.' Judging by the omission of the leyline in the later book, it certainly seems as if it wasn't.

Alfred Watkins on the other hand quotes a much more varied line in *The Ley Hunter's Manual*. It takes in three castles, a church, a ford and a hall. When I checked it, not all of them worked out, but there was enough of it left to be worth a try.

THE PRUDHOE CASTLE LINE (62)

The line was contributed to the *Manual* by a Mr C. Shepherd Munn, who started it at Ravensworth Castle. There is a site marked 'Towers' near Ravensworth Park, which it could be, but it is in a heavily built-up area.

His next marker is described as a 'ford at Winlaton Hill', and indeed there are bridges across the River Derwent that may once have been fords, but they are near Winlaton Mill, not Hill. Maybe the mill became transcribed into a hill between leaving Mr Shepherd Munn and appearing in print. It has been known...

Anyway, I hoped for the best over these markers and moved on to the much more dramatic – and more easily located – Prudhoe Castle, which stands on a wooded spur overlooking the Tyne. Prudhoe – or Proud Hill – commands one of the key crossing points of the river, and its mound indicates that a fort was there in much earlier times. An earthwork defence was built by the Norman d'Umbravilles in about 1150, a stone curtain wall and keep were added later that century, and the fortifications had been strengthened again by the time the Percys took it over in 1381.

It had an eventful history during the troubles with the Scots, and it was twice attacked unsuccessfully by King William of Scotland. But after the union of England and Scotland its main purpose was lost, and it fell on hard times. It suffered a final ignominy when Cromwell knocked it about a bit in the Civil War. These days it is run by English Heritage.

Above: *The line crosses the Tyne at an ancient river crossing where a bridge now links Prudhoe with Ovingham.* Left: *Prudhoe Castle stands on 'Proud Hill', where a hill-fort could well have stood before.*

The chapel above the twelfth-century gatehouse contains one of the oldest oriel windows in England, but the ley-hunter may be more interested in the legend that a tunnel connects Prudhoe with another castle at Bywell. It must have been quite an engineering feat, because Bywell Castle is four or five miles upriver on the opposite bank, but Alfred Watkins liked to link tunnel stories with leylines, and it so happens that Bywell lies on the next of my lines. Perhaps the tunnel linked the two leys as well as the two castles.

The line I am following now, however, crosses the Tyne from Prudhoe to Ovingham, immediately opposite. Mr Shepherd Munn says the river is fordable here, and indeed a local guide confirms that there used to be a

ford, in the days when Prudhoe and Ovingham were in the same parish and the d'Umbravilles owned both. But the Tyne was in flood while I was there, and I did not fancy trying it. Fortunately, there is a narrow single-carriageway bridge, which now provides a drier alternative.

St Mary's church at Ovingham, the next marker, could date back to the seventh century, and the oval churchyard indicates it could have been a pagan burial site long before that. It has a remarkable relic of those pre-Christian days, a 'tetracephalon', which stands on a window ledge in the south aisle. It is a square stone with a human head carved on each of its four sides. Apparently it was one of the less endearing practices of the pagan Celts to cut off their prisoners' heads and put them in their temples to keep away evil spirits. The Romans may have suggested they try something less barbarous, so they carved stone heads and put them in the temples instead. Presumably this one has four heads to make sure the evil spirits did not creep up from behind.

Ovingham got its name from Offa, who is assumed to be the Saxon chief who took over when the Romans left; indeed, St Mary's is known as Offa's church. The village lay on the main east–west route from Newcastle to Carlisle, as well as on the river crossing to the south, and no doubt St Cuthbert, St Wilfred and other seventh-century saints passed this way. It must have been a good incentive for building a church.

Understandably, there is not much left of the original building, but the church has a carved fragment of a stone cross dating from a couple of centuries later, after the Vikings arrived. They were led by Halfdan of the Wide Embrace; his embrace, one gathers, was not a very comfortable one. But many Vikings settled in the area, and the fragment shows a scene from a Norse saga, which was adapted for Christian use.

When the tower was built in about AD 990 the locals were still wary of invaders, and put the doors

Above: *The terrace of St Aidan's Chapel, Stagshaw, overlooks a former Roman vineyard.* Left: *A carving in Ovingham church illustrating a Norse saga.* Right: *Aydon Castle.*

high up in case of attack. They are among many other reminders of those early days, all admirably explained in the guidebook. At a more practical level, a notice in St Mary's gives the location of the nearest public conveniences, a thoughtful touch, which I do not often encounter in churches. The convenience is actually in Prudhoe, on the far side of the river, so I hope you spot the notice in good time.

Mr Shepherd Munn's next recognizable marker is Aydon Castle. It is actually a fortified manor house, built at the end of the thirteenth century by a wealthy merchant, but like Prudhoe Castle it stands in a commanding position, so the same theory about an earlier use may apply. The Scots managed to burn it down, but it was restored and used as a farmhouse. The Great Hall still survives, reached by an outside staircase, and it is considered 'one of the most attractive and best preserved fortified manor houses in Britain'. English Heritage think so, anyway.

As one or two of Mr Shepherd Munn's markers are difficult to establish, I tried extending his line further west, and I was gratified to find it passed through a chapel at Stagshaw. St Aidan's Chapel stands high above the Tyne, with Hexham on the opposite bank, far below. In fact, it is sited in yet another commanding position, and when I learned that the hillside beneath it had been a Roman vineyard, there seemed a good chance that St Aidan's stood on the site of a Roman building, preferably a temple.

Alas, there is no evidence to confirm it. The Stagshaw estate was bought in 1868 by John Straker, great-great-grandfather of Mrs Burnell, the present owner. He fell out with the local vicar and decided to build his own family chapel, and St Aidan's was dedicated in 1885. Although there was a great deal of Roman activity in the area and researchers frequently request access to other parts of the estate, Mrs Burnell tells me that nobody has ever shown any interest in the chapel.

Nevertheless I am reluctant to discard my theory. It seems as valid as some of those used by Alfred Watkins

to justify ley markers, and anyway those other researchers were probably not looking for leylines. It still seems odd, in an area where churches and chapels are comparatively sparse, that St Aidan's falls so neatly onto the Prudhoe Castle Line. Is it just another of those coincidences that seem to crop up around leylines? I know what Alfred Watkins would say.

Finally, I checked on a pair of churches commended to me by the same local friend who told me about the incomparable Saxon church at Escomb. The village of Bywell – the one said to be connected by tunnel with Prudhoe Castle – has two Saxon churches within 100 yards of each other, plus a castle, a hall and a market cross – and very little else. With this large assortment of markers to choose from in one small area I felt that there really ought to be scope for a leyline – and there is. It runs north-westwards from Bywell, mostly along the Tyne Valley.

THE BYWELL LINE (63)

The mere fact that Bywell acquired two churches in Saxon times indicates that it was rather a special place. Certainly the Romans thought so and built a bridge here across the Tyne. St Wilfred may have thought so too, because tradition has it that he founded one of the churches. And so agreed the White Canons of Blanchland and the Black Canons of Durham, who became associated with what have always been known as the 'white' and 'black' churches of Bywell.

Some say the churches were founded by two sisters who owned adjoining manors and fell out with each other, so they built rival churches right on the boundary between their properties. But this story is told about other churches in close proximity, notably in

Norfolk, where churches sometimes even share the same churchyard. Yet another theory is that they were built so close in order that the clergy could be company for each other. Whatever the reason, St Andrew's and St Peter's are so close that, with the addition of the market cross on the lane between them, they could be regarded as one conveniently large ley marker to start the Bywell Line.

In medieval times Bywell had 500 inhabitants; now there is just a handful. These days St Andrew's, the 'white' church, is looked after by the Churches Conservation Trust, while the 'black' church of St Peter's functions as the parish church. Originally it is thought that one church was attached to a monastery and the other was for the villagers, but no one seems certain which was which. When I visited them the interior of St Andrew's was draped with dustsheets and St Peter's was in the process of getting a new roof. I trust both are back in good shape again.

Of the two, perhaps St Andrew's has most for the ley-hunter. In the chancel there is the shaft of a pre-Conquest preaching cross, which originally stood in the area of the tower. The tower itself, also built before the Conquest and claimed to be one of the finest of its kind, contains a lot of Roman stonework.

St Peter's, dating from the eighth century, has had a tougher time. It was destroyed by the Vikings, and in 1771, when the Tyne burst its banks, coffins were washed out of the graveyard. Bywell Castle had eight feet of water, so the squire's horses were taken into St Peter's for safety; it is said they held on to the backs of the pews with their teeth as the water swilled around them. One horse is said to have climbed onto the altar to get above the flood. The combination of water, horses and teeth must have been pretty devastating.

Both the castle and the hall are still privately owned. The fifteenth-century castle tower is just off the line; the Hall is just on it. The present building dates from 1760, but there was an earlier house on the same site. The gardens are sometimes open to the public, but unfortunately not while I was there, so I could not look for any earlier traces.

Above: 'Warden Man', in the porch of Warden church, is thought to be a Roman altar. Left: The market cross at Bywell is now conveniently sited between the two churches.

From Bywell the line crosses to the south side of the Tyne and runs parallel with it, across a stream that enters it from Dilston. The stream is known locally as 'Devil's Water', which is believed to be an adaptation

of the Celtic 'Black Water'. I am sure Alfred Watkins would find either description significant. The line crosses it near the ruins of a castle that was never completed. It was being built for the Earl of Derwentwater when he decided to take a hand in the Jacobite Rebellion of 1715. The rebellion was put down, the earl was executed, and the builders packed up and went home. If he had chosen a site on the leyline instead of just near it, would the project have fared any better? Probably not.

The line then returns across the Tyne as it curves round Hexham and reaches the confusingly named St John Lee Church. I assumed this must be dedicated to a little known saint called John Lee, and I hoped the 'Lee' – an alternative form of ley – might be significant. Actually St John Lee is the name of the hamlet in which the church stands, and it is dedicated to St

Above: *The Oakwood Stone, preserved in St John Lee Church, has the cup-and-ring design associated with prehistoric burials.*
Right: *The ancient cross at Warden may commemorate King Oswald's victory over the pagan Cadwallon.*

John of Beverley. He is reputed to have lived there in the late seventh century, in a place known as Eagle's Nest, which has been identified as the site of the church. But he spent much of his time in a clearing in the woods, a 'lee', enjoying the life of a hermit, and when a community developed it took its name from his non-leyline lee.

There is, however, a connection between St John of Beverley's church and earlier times. Just inside it is the Oakwood Stone, which has a cup-and-ring design connected with Bronze Age burials. It was found in a clump of beech trees on the road to Oakwood and was probably the capstone of a grave on a sacred site. The line runs along this road for part of its length before reaching the church.

Also in St John's, near the Oakwood Stone, is a Roman altar of unknown origin, another link with pre-Christian times. But the present building largely dates from the last century; Scottish raiders reduced the original church to ruins.

From St John Lee, St John of Beverley headed back east to his native Yorkshire, became Bishop of York and finally established a monastery at Beverley. The Bywell Line, on the other hand, continues westward to Warden church and its nearby motte. This is a typical mound with a cluster of trees on top, but I could not find it mentioned in the church guidebook. The guidebook has plenty about the history of the church, however, and claims that St John of Beverley was based at Warden. It quotes the Venerable Bede's reference to John of Beverley having an oratory dedicated to St Michael and All Angels – 'as our church is,' it notes – near the Tyne about one-and-a-half-miles from Hexham, the same distance as Warden. It admits that St John Lee also claims this distinction, 'and neither is proven'. As both churches are on the line, perhaps John shuttled back and forth along it between the two.

Whether it was he who founded Warden church, or more probably St Wilfred, it certainly dates from at least the eighth century and still contains reminders of that period. The Norman arch connecting the nave with the tower incorporates a Roman stone with a chequerboard pattern on it. Near the porch is part of an ancient cross, believed to mark the Christian King Oswald's victory over the pagan Cadwallon at the Battle of Heavenfield, three miles away. And in the porch itself is perhaps the most unusual relic, 'The Warden Man'.

It is a stone carved with a human figure, and one expert has identified it as a Roman altar which was re-used in Christian worship. Admittedly, another expert has dated it rather later, but taking all these indications together, and with an Iron Age hill-fort not far away on Warden Hill, there seems every likelihood that there was a pagan sacred site at Warden before the church

was built. From Bywell to Warden the line is eleven miles long, and it could well end here, but if it were extended for another eight miles it would reach Hadrian's Wall. This, one might say, is no big deal; any line in that general direction is bound to hit it somewhere. But *The Ley Hunter's Companion* has a leyline that ends at the Wall, and it seems an effective barrier to end this section too.

LANCASHIRE
AND CUMBRIA

BLEASDALE is not a name that may be immediately familiar to anyone who lives south of Manchester, but in archaeological terms it is Lancashire's answer to Stonehenge. The Bleasdale Circle is a Bronze Age woodhenge that dates back to the same prehistoric era as the famous circle stones of Stonehenge. Indeed, there was a henge like the circle only a couple of miles from the stones, though there is little to see of it today.

Woodhenges are a lot rarer than stone circles, for the obvious reason: wood just doesn't last as long. It is only when the circle of oak posts has been buried under, say, a peat bog, like the one recently uncovered by the tides at Holme in Norfolk, that remnants still survive, and once they are exposed to the air they soon disintegrate.

At Bleasdale they have found an interesting compromise. When the remnants of the posts were dug out and taken to Preston Museum for preservation, someone had the bright idea of putting concrete pillars into the holes instead, to show where the oak circle used to be. They should provide an interesting puzzle for future archaeologists in a few centuries' time if they are still there and the records of the original circle are lost.

The Bleasdale Circle, dated about 1900 BC, is the only Bronze Age site recorded in Lancashire. It therefore seems to be an obvious focal point for a leyline, but it gets no mention in Alfred Watkins' books or in *The Ley Hunter's Companion*. Indeed, there is no mention of Lancashire at all. So I put a rule on the site to see if I could find one to fill the gap.

The tower of twelfth-century Shap Abbey was added
only a few years before the abbey was dissolved.

THE BLEASDALE CIRCLE LINE (64)

Bleasdale lies on the edge of what used to be Bowland Forest, now mostly moorland and fells. There is nothing north of the village for a dozen miles, and to the east it is fairly empty too, until you reach the Hodder valley. To the west you hit the M6 motorway and the expanding environs of Garstang, and if you go too far south you are in Preston. It is not the easiest marker on which to plot a leyline.

Eventually I found one, which starts at Beacon Hill – its name would have caught Alfred's eye straight away. It is about 1000 feet high, some ten miles east of Bleasdale Circle, near Grindleton, and not too difficult to spot. I could find no hint of an actual beacon, but I am sure that would not have discouraged Alfred.

The line then heads for the summit of Waddington Fell, some 300 feet higher than Beacon Hill, and made even more prominent by the radio mast at the top – a modern equivalent of those prehistoric beacons. Its dominating position would have made a likely marker for one of Alfred's early surveyors, but any traces have long since been obliterated by much more recent activity. The area around the mast has been extensively disfigured by quarry workings, and there are discouraging 'Danger – Keep Out' notices on the perimeter fence. Even so, it is worth the drive from Waddington to the summit, and with your back to the quarry admire the splendid view of the line's route from Beacon Hill and Grindleton Fell.

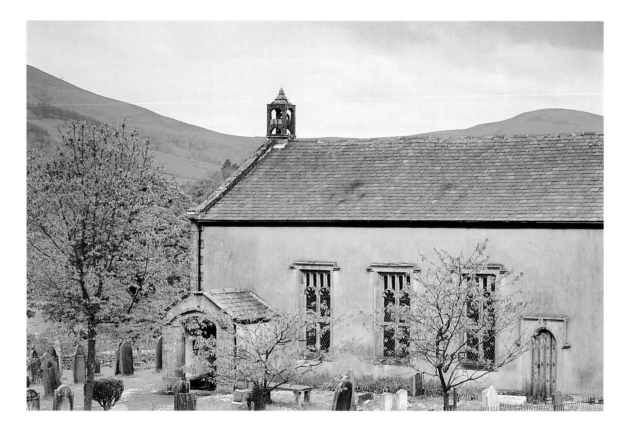

Above: *Whitewell church lies in the Hodder valley, which has been inhabited since the Bronze Age.* Left: *The red and white roses are a reminder that Whitewall used to be on the border of Lancashire and Yorkshire.*

From here the line heads across country to Whitewell church in the Hodder valley, which rightly claims to have some of the finest scenery in Lancashire. Until 1974 only one side of the valley was in the county; the river marked the old boundary between the County Palatine of Lancashire and the West Riding of Yorkshire. As a reminder of the parish's divided loyalties in the past – which may well still exist – there is a stained-glass window in the church with the red and white roses of Yorkshire and Lancashire.

The valley has been inhabited since the Bronze Age, and a cave known as Fairy Holes contained fragments of pottery and other relics from about 1000 BC.

There was even a stone 'pounder', which was used by the cave dwellers for smashing up bones to get at the marrow. Then the Romans turned up and built roads through the valley, installing a garrison nearby.

With all this early activity there seems little doubt that there were pre-Christian sacred sites in or around Whitewell. Any name with 'white' in it was significant to Alfred Watkins, because he linked it with the 'whitman' who carried the white salt along the prehistoric tracks. Coupled with a 'well', it would certainly qualify as a marker. Sceptics might argue that in this case the whiteness in Whitewell referred to the limestone from which the valley was formed and which is very evident all around, but for the sake of the leyline I shall stick with Alfred.

St Michael's Church, Whitewell, dates from the fourteenth century, when a Royal Forester called Walter Urswyck came to live in Whitewell Manor and

built a small chapel for his family and his fellow foresters. Although St Michael is linked by ley-hunters with former pagan sites, the chapel was not dedicated until after the Reformation. It became the parish church in 1878, by which time it had been enlarged to about eight times its original size. Little trace of its origins survives. But as the manor house is now a comfortable hostelry, and the surroundings are so attractive, I am content to rely on the 'white' in Whitewell to justify it as at least worthy of inspection as a marker.

From Whitewell the line goes across country again to the Bleasdale Circle, with not a road and hardly any habitations all the way, just fells and open moorland. Even using the maze of little lanes along the river valley to the south, Bleasdale village is tricky to reach, and although the circle Lancashire's most famous prehistoric site, the public are not exactly encouraged to visit

Above: *The 'concretehenge' at Bleasdale where the original wooden posts have been replaced by concrete blocks.* Right: *Along the route from Whitewell to Bleasdale.*

it. The only access is by a road with a large 'Private – No Entry' sign, but as this is also the only route to the village school and the church the locals obviously ignore it. I drove past it too. A few hundred yards beyond the school the road reaches the church and becomes just a rough track. There is a modest fingerpost inscribed 'Bleasdale Circle' pointing up the track – the first indication of its existence.

Ten minutes' walk up the track, near a lonely farmhouse, another fingerpost inscribed 'Concessionary Footpath' points across a field at a grove of trees, and here at last are the concrete pillars marking the position of the original wooden posts. They encircled a mound about thirty-six feet across, and inside the mound archaeologists have discovered two urns filled with cremated human bones and charcoal. In one of them there was an incense cup among the remains.

Originally there was a much larger palisade around the circle, about 150 feet across, consisting of alternate large and small posts, but there is nothing left of it now – not even substitute concrete pillars. *The Guide to Prehistoric Britain* does not hazard a guess as to the reason for this outer ring, but possibly the inner posts supported a roof to form a kind of prehistoric mausoleum, and the palisade was to protect this sacred place from roving tribes, from wild animals foraging in the area or just from evil spirits. It seems a lot of trouble to go to, in such a remote place.

The line continues westward past Calder Vale to the ruins of Greenhaugh Castle, just outside Garstang. It was built in 1490 by the Earl of Derbyshire to defend his estates, but, like Mr Urswyck of Whitewell, the earl has left no hint that I could find of why he selected that particular site. During the Civil War it was besieged by Cromwell's men, and he later ordered it to be dismantled. Only the tower still stands; it is on private land but is visible from the road.

The castle is sixteen miles from where the line started at Beacon Hill, and ought to mark the end of it, but I continued it for a mile or so – and I found another of those coincidences that crop up so often on leylines. Garstang town church was built comparatively recently to serve the town's expanding population, and Nateby Baptist Chapel is a comparative newcomer too, so it is difficult to see how they can qualify as markers – but both these places of worship are on the line.

Fascinated, I extended the line a little further and found myself – perhaps too appropriately – on Trashy Hill. Can it be telling me something, I pondered.

FALSE TRAILS

Remembering Paul Devereux's later leaning towards ghost paths and corpse trails, I headed for a church in Eskdale that I had discovered on a previous visit to the Lake District, St Catherine's Church at Boot.

I first went to Eskdale in the same spirit of adventure as David Livingstone went to Africa – but instead of seeking the source of the Nile I was seeking the source of the Ravenglass & Eskdale Railway. Boot Station, at the top of the dale, was the loading point for iron ore from the Nab Ghyll mines, just above the village. Then the mining company collapsed, the railway closed, and when Bassett-Lowke took over the old track-bed to test his miniature locomotives, the final climb to Boot proved too much for them and he used a different route to Dalgarth. That is where the present tourist railway goes, while Boot is left with its derelict station and its memories.

But while I was there I heard of another unusual route into Boot, long before the railway was built. In the fifteenth century the little chapel of St Olaf's at Wasdale Head, five miles away on the far side of Burnmoor, could not provide consecrated ground for burials, and funeral parties had to bring the coffin on a donkey across the moor and over the saddle of the hill to Boot church. If indeed leylines can be based on corpse trails, this might be a dramatic example. And better still, I could call it the Boot and Saddle Trail.

At first there seemed a sporting chance. St Olaf's, one of the smallest churches in England, has a long pedigree as a chapel of ease. St Catherine's is probably one of the four dale churches founded in the twelfth century by the prior of St Bees, though the present building is mostly Victorian. Both could well occupy earlier sacred sites. If the corpse trail followed a straight line between the two, I only needed two or three more markers.

But on closer inspection, the theory collapsed. To start with, a straight line from St Olaf's would mean an extremely hazardous scramble up the steep scree slopes that overlook Wastwater, followed by a splash through one end of Burnmoor Tarn. There are cairns and cairn circles up on the moor, but none of them is on the line.

Just in case I had missed something, I did extend the line in each direction. Beyond St Catherine's it just climbs up into the fells again, but beyond St Olaf's I had a moment's excitement when it went through an unfamiliar symbol on the map with the evocative name 'Black Sail'. It turns out to be a youth hostel converted from a shepherd's bothy, which hardly seems to fit in with a corpse trail. But I clutched at a straw. The hostel is at one end of Black Sail Pass, St Olaf's is at the other. 'Black' was always significant to Alfred Watkins. So could a body meet a bothy coming through the pass? Ah well.

I turned for consolation to *The Ley Hunter's Companion*, and found a leyline that starts from a Plague Stone in the unlikely surroundings of an old people's home on the outskirts of Penrith. It goes to Askham church via a Neolithic sacred site called the Mayburgh Henge. But Paul Devereux later discards it in *The New Ley Hunter's Guide* after discovering that the Plague Stone was not in its original position. He does not say how the old people's home acquired it nor indeed why they should want it.

Another leyline in the *Companion* involving the Goggleby Stone near Shap looked more promising, but Devereux later discarded this one too, on the grounds that the Goggleby was part of a ruined avenue of stones. However, this is actually pointed out in the *Companion* and did not seem to be a problem. Indeed, the Goggleby is a very handsome stone with a very distinctive name, and for want of a better idea I put a ruler on it myself.

The first efforts were not too successful. I found a line that runs from Orton church through the

The Goggleby Stone, part of a prehistoric avenue to a stone circle which was partly destroyed when the railway came.

Goggleby Stone to Pooley Bridge church, hitting two or three cairns on Askham Fell on the way. All Saints' at Orton may be on a pre-Christian site, though its known history begins in the thirteenth century, but St Paul's at Pooley Bridge was founded only in 1867, on land donated by a local family.

However, the vicar of St Paul's also told me about the mother church at Barton, and this has an impeccable pedigree for a ley marker. It is sited on a mound with a circular churchyard, indicating a prehistoric origin, and it is dedicated to St Michael, which the church guide confirms as being a 'traditional dedication when Christianity supplanted pagan gods'.

So I tried a line from St Michael's to the Goggleby, but it was well wide of all those cairns on Askham Fell, it missed a stone circle on Knipe Moor, and it even avoided what looks like a medieval moat near Helton. In short, it didn't work.

I made one more attempt. The helpful vicar told me about the other two churches in his charge, St Martin's and St Peter's at Martindale. St Martin's, which is known as 'the old church' to distinguish it from the more recent St Peter's up the road, stands on an ancient site with a yew tree in the churchyard. Experts have dated this yew at nearly 2000 years old,. indicating a site sacred before the arrival of Christianity in the area. Other features, too, which make St Martin's a likely ley marker. So I tried yet another line to the Goggleby Stone – and this time it worked.

THE MARTINDALE 'OLD CHURCH' LINE (65)

Starting from the other end of the line – because Martindale is such a pleasant place in which to finish – the first marker is beyond the Goggleby, a tumulus on top of a 1000-foot hill at Bank Moor. The line could, in fact, be extended further to Whitewell and Whitestones, names that Alfred Watkins would link with leylines, just like Whitewell in Lancashire, but the sixteen miles from the Bank Moor tumulus to Martindale makes a neater line.

The ruined avenue in which the Goggleby Stone stands led to a stone circle, which mostly disappeared when the railway was built. One or two of the other stones in the avenue are still there, but for some reason the Goggleby seems to be the only one with a name. This obviously not impress Paul Devereux, but for me it sufficiently singles it out as a marker. Certainly, when it fell over several years ago it was thought significant enough to be re-erected (on the same site, unlike the Penrith Plague Stone). That must have been quite an effort; it is a massive chunk of rock rising seven feet above the ground, with a lot more of it out of sight underneath.

Soon after the Goggleby the line crosses the bridge leading to the ruins of Shap Abbey, founded in the

Above: *View from Loadpot Hill.* Left: *Shap Abbey.*

twelfth century in an area noted for its prehistoric remains. It could well stand on an earlier pagan site. The main feature of the ruins is the tower, which had a very brief useful life; it was completed just before the Reformation, then the Abbey was dissolved. From here the line takes a dramatic cross-country route. It crosses Swindale Beck and climbs past Thornthwaite Hall and the northern end of Haweswater Reservoir to the 2000-foot upper slopes of the curiously named Loadpot Hill. With memories still fresh of Trashy Hill, I hoped it did not derive from 'Load-o'-Rot'.

On the way it crosses the Roman road along the top of the ridge, which has the more obvious name of High Street. This was originally a prehistoric route known as Bretestrete, and in the Middle Ages it became, among other things, a corpse trail for mourners taking their dead to Barton for burial. The combination of pre-historic track, Roman road and corpse trail makes it a candidate as a leyline in its own right, but unfortunately for the ley-hunter its route was governed more by the terrain than by surveyors with sighting staves. It does have some straight stretches – probably thanks to the Romans – but mostly it just follows the curve of the ridge, above what used to be the tree line. Below that was a forest of oak trees, then undrained marshes.

Nonetheless, High Street has provided Martindale's 'old church' with a remarkable relic, a standing stone that is believed to have been a wayside shrine on the Roman road. When it was first brought down to the hamlet it was used for sharpening tools, since it was much tougher than the local stone; it still has the grooves in the sides. Then, says the church guide, some cleric saw its possibilities for use in church, first as a holy water stoup, and then as a font. In 1688 a visiting parson noted this unusual adaptation: 'A standing stone is used as a font, upon which they place a basin of water when they christen their children.'

Apart from this useful acquisition, the little dale chapel has a fascinating story behind it. There is no doubt that not only the chapel but the dale itself takes its name from St Martin, the Roman soldier who was converted and became a bishop. He is best known perhaps for using his sword to split his cloak in two, so that he could give half of it to a ragged beggar. One of his enthusiastic followers was St Ninian, a fourth-century Briton, and he in his turn was a great influence on St Patrick, who although associated mainly with Ireland also spent much time in the Lake District. It is possible that nearby Patterdale is named after him.

Though we may never be able to prove it,' says the

Above: *St Martin's Church*. Left: *The scarred font of St Martin's believed to have been a Roman roadside shrine.* Right: *The end of the line at St Martin's.*

Martindale guidebook, written by a former vicar, 'we like to think that St Martin's name and fame came here with St Patrick and under the influence of St Ninian in the fifth century.'

The guidebook dismisses the idea that a ruined enclosure nearby was the original chapel of St Martin, and goes on to point out the age of the present church site, the ancient yew tree and the close proximity of Christy Bridge, which derives its name from being near a church. Without actually saying so, it does indicate that this is where the original chapel stood, and in that case it could well have taken over a pagan sacred site.

It is difficult to think of any other reason for building it in such a remote spot. It is almost as great an adventure to reach it by road as to attempt the cross-country hike from the Roman road along the Goggleby line. The little lane from Pooley Bridge, at the other end of Ullswater, runs alongside the lake, at first in a deceptively innocuous fashion — then suddenly has a convulsion. It writhes up a series of near-vertical hairpin bends to climb the fell overlooking the lake, just one car's-width all the way. After taking a breath beside Martindale's 'new church', with a couple of cottages nearby, it descends almost as precipitously to the 'old church' of St Martin's, nestling on its own in the dale below. Then it crosses Christy Bridge over a little stream before petering out altogether.

The present modest building only dates from the sixteenth century, but the remnants of the earlier one can still be seen beside it. St Martin's was extensively 'restored' by the Victorians, though not it seems very effectively, because it was in such a bad state in the 1880s that the new church of St Peter's was built to replace it as the parish church. On the day St Peter's was consecrated in 1882 a storm ripped off the roof of the 'old church' as a final humiliation. Happily, the damage was made good, and St Martin's survived, to be used

first as a mortuary chapel, and these days for occasional services, including one in Cumbrian dialect.

But it is not so much the building as the history behind it, coupled with its former Roman shrine and that ancient yew, which make it special. Its history will appeal to the ley-hunter, the Roman relic and the yew tree will appeal to the curious, and the setting must delight everyone who sees it. The 'old church' seems a very appropriate place, finally, to draw the line.

At the end of it all, having followed those 'old straight tracks' all over England – sometimes successfully, sometimes a little sceptically, but always with the chance of another unlikely discovery ahead – I still cannot come to a definite conclusion about the validity of Alfred Watkins' leyline: whether such a thing really does exist, and if so, how it originated and what was its purpose. I am still asking: 'What *is* it all about, Alfie?' Perhaps we shall never really know.

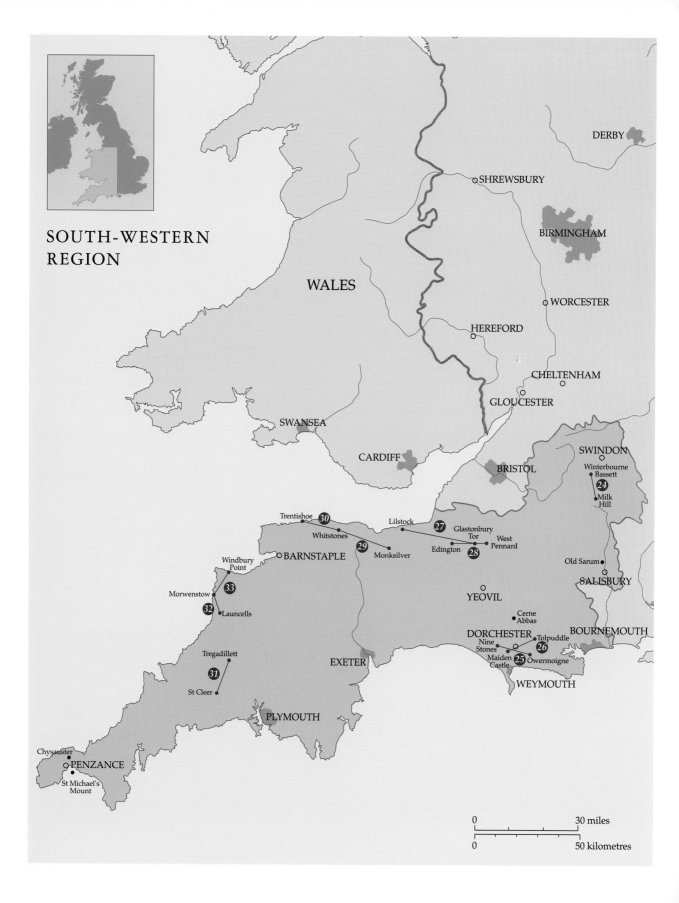

SOUTH-WESTERN
REGION

DERBY

SHREWSBURY

BIRMINGHAM

WALES

WORCESTER

HEREFORD

CHELTENHAM

GLOUCESTER

SWANSEA

SWINDON

CARDIFF

Winterbourne
Bassett
24
Milk
Hill

BRISTOL

Trentishoe **30**   Lilstock   **27**
Whitstones   Glastonbury
         29   Tor   West
BARNSTAPLE   Monksilver   Edington Pennard
                                    28

Old Sarum

SALISBURY

Windbury
Point
33
Morwenstow
32
Launcells

YEOVIL

Cerne
Abbas

DORCHESTER   Tolpuddle
Nine   **26**
Stones

BOURNEMOUTH

Tregadillett
31
St Cleer

EXETER

Maiden
Castle **25**
Owermoigne

WEYMOUTH

PLYMOUTH

Chysauster
PENZANCE
St Michael's
Mount

0   30 miles

0   50 kilometres

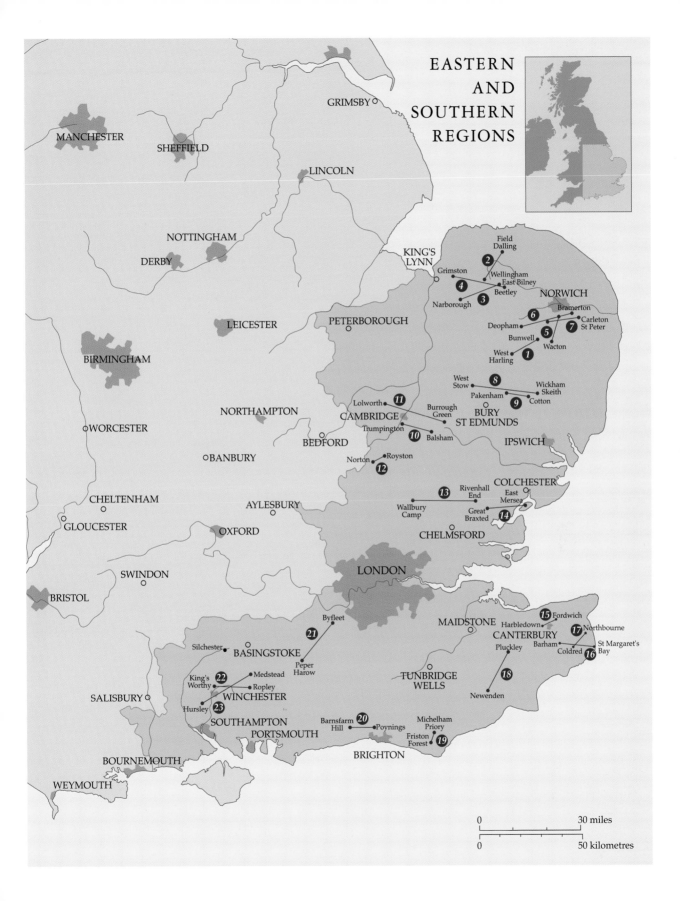

EASTERN
AND
SOUTHERN
REGIONS

MANCHESTER
SHEFFIELD
GRIMSBY
LINCOLN
NOTTINGHAM
DERBY
KING'S LYNN
Field Dalling
2
Grimston
Wellingham
East Bilney
4
Beetley
3
Narborough
NORWICH
Bramerton
6
Carleton St Peter
Deopham
5
7
Bunwell
Wacton
1
West Harling
LEICESTER
PETERBOROUGH
West Stow
8
Wickham Skeith
Pakenham
Cotton
9
BIRMINGHAM
BURY ST EDMUNDS
IPSWICH
NORTHAMPTON
Lolworth
11
Burrough Green
CAMBRIDGE
WORCESTER
Trumpington
10
Balsham
BEDFORD
BANBURY
Norton
Royston
12
COLCHESTER
CHELTENHAM
AYLESBURY
Rivenhall End
13
East Mersea
GLOUCESTER
Wallbury Camp
Great Braxted
14
OXFORD
CHELMSFORD
SWINDON
LONDON
BRISTOL
Byfleet
Fordwich
15
MAIDSTONE
Harbledown
Northbourne
17
21
CANTERBURY
Barham
St Margaret's Bay
Silchester
BASINGSTOKE
Pluckley
Coldred
16
Peper Harow
TUNBRIDGE WELLS
18
King's Worthy
Medstead
22
Ropley
Newenden
SALISBURY
WINCHESTER
Hursley
23
SOUTHAMPTON
PORTSMOUTH
Barnsfarm Hill
20
Poynings
Michelham Priory
Friston Forest
19
BOURNEMOUTH
BRIGHTON
WEYMOUTH

0   30 miles

0   50 kilometres

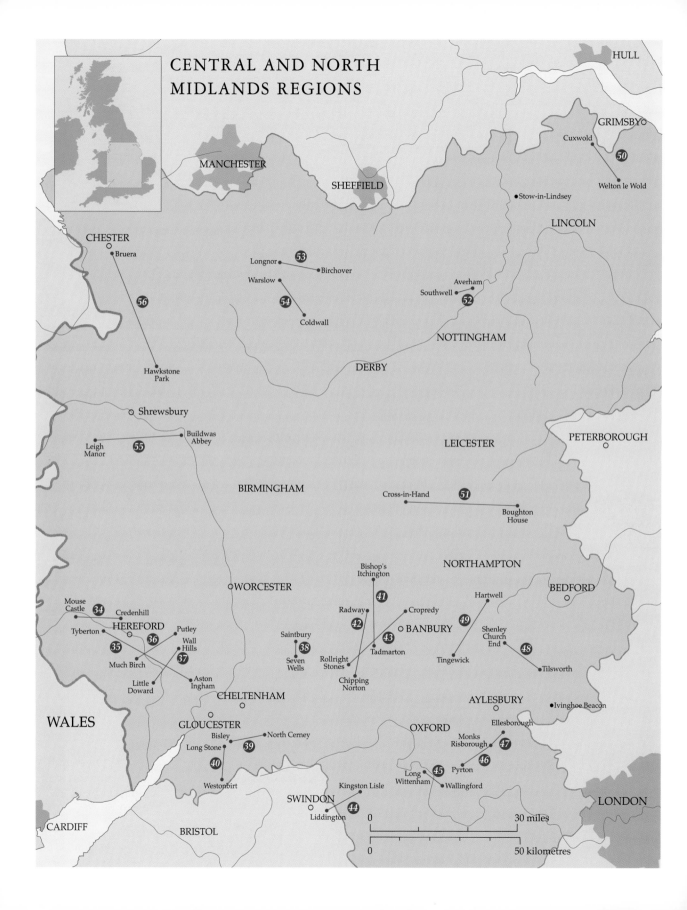

CENTRAL AND NORTH MIDLANDS REGIONS

HULL

GRIMSBY

Cuxwold

⑤⓪

Welton le Wold

MANCHESTER

SHEFFIELD

•Stow-in-Lindsey

LINCOLN

CHESTER ○

•Bruera

Longnor• ⑤③ •Birchover

Warslow•

⑤④

Coldwall

Averham•

Southwell• ⑤②

NOTTINGHAM

DERBY

⑤⑥

Hawkstone
Park

Shrewsbury ○

Leigh
Manor •   ⑤⑤   • Buildwas
Abbey

LEICESTER

PETERBOROUGH ○

BIRMINGHAM

Cross-in-Hand• ⑤① •Boughton
House

WORCESTER ○

Bishop's
Itchington•

NORTHAMPTON

Hartwell•

BEDFORD ○

Mouse
Castle • ③④ • Credenhill

Tyberton•

HEREFORD ○

③⑤

③⑥

Much Birch•

Putley•

Wall
Hills•

③⑦

• Aston
Ingham

Little
Doward •

Saintbury•

③⑧

Seven
Wells•

Rollright
Stones•

Chipping
Norton•

Radway•

④②

④①

④③

Tadmarton•

Cropredy•

○ BANBURY

④⑨

Tingewick•

Shenley
Church
End•

④⑧

• Tilsworth

Ivinghoe Beacon•

CHELTENHAM ○

AYLESBURY ○

WALES

GLOUCESTER ○

Bisley•

Long Stone•

③⑨ • North Cerney

④⓪

Westonbirt•

OXFORD ○

Ellesborough•

Monks
Risborough•

④⑥

④⑦

Pyrton•

Kingston Lisle•

Long
Wittenham•

④⑤

•Wallingford

SWINDON ○

④④

Liddington•

LONDON

CARDIFF

BRISTOL

0   30 miles

0   50 kilometres

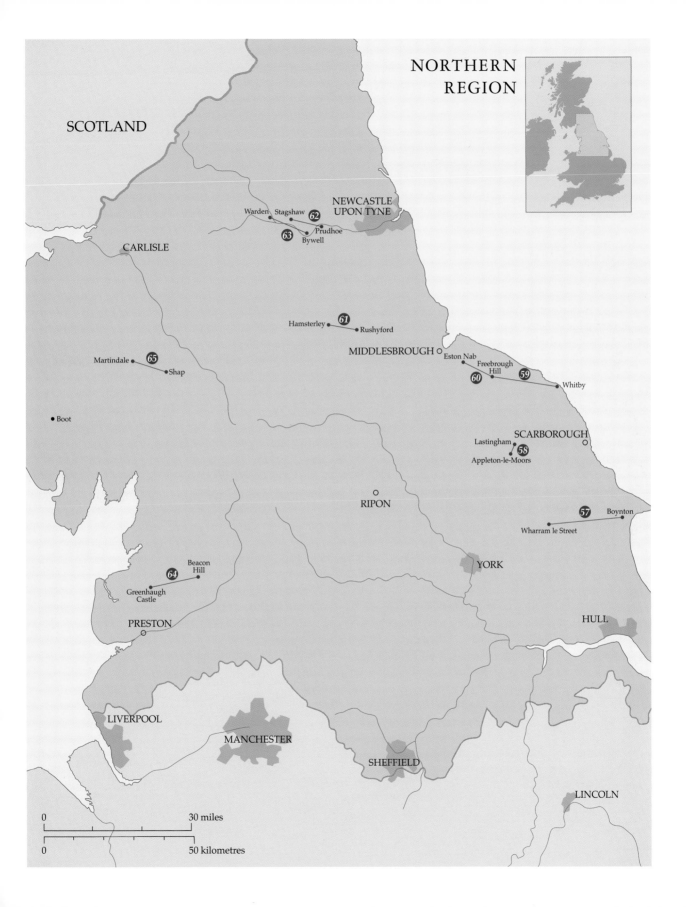

NORTHERN
REGION

SCOTLAND

CARLISLE

NEWCASTLE
UPON TYNE

Warden Stagshaw *62*
63 Prudhoe
Bywell

Hamsterley *61*
Rushyford

MIDDLESBROUGH

Martindale *65*
Shap

Eston Nab Freebrough
Hill *59*
60 Whitby

Boot

SCARBOROUGH

Lastingham *58*
Appleton-le-Moors

RIPON

Boynton
57
Wharram le Street

YORK

Beacon
Hill
64
Greenhaugh
Castle

HULL

PRESTON

LIVERPOOL

MANCHESTER

SHEFFIELD

LINCOLN

0   30 miles

0   50 kilometres

Further Reading

Bord, Janet and Colin, *The Secret Country*, Paladin Grafton, London, 1976

Bord, Janet and Colin, *Ancient Mysteries of Britain*, Grafton, London, 1986

Brewer's Dictionary of Phrase and Fable (15th ed.), Cassell, London, 1988

Devereux, Paul, *The New Ley Hunter's Guide*, Gothic Image, Glastonbury, 1994

Devereux, Paul, and Thomson, Ian, *The Ley Hunter's Companion*, Thames & Hudson, London, 1979

Folklore, *Myths and Legends of Britain*, Reader's Digest, London, 1973

Hadfield, John (ed.), *The New Shell Guide to England*, Michael Joseph, London, 1975

Thomas, Nicholas, *The Guide to Prehistoric England*, Batsford, London, 1976

Walker, Charles, *Mysterious Britain*, Regency House, London, 1989

Watkins, Alfred, *The Old Straight Track* (first published 1925), Abacus, 1974

Watkins, Alfred, *The Ley Hunter's Manual* (first published 1927), Turnstone Press, Wellingborough, 1983

Williamson, Tom, and Bellamy, Liz, *Ley Lines in Question*, World's Work, London, 1983

Eastern Region

Dutton, W.A., *Norfolk*, Methuen, London, 1901

Dymond, David, *The Norfolk Landscape*, Hodder & Stoughton, London, 1985

James, M.R., *Suffolk & Norfolk*, Dent & Sons, London, 1930

Jebb, Miles, *Suffolk*, Pimlico, London, 1995

Mee, Arthur, *The King's England – Norfolk*, Hodder & Stoughton, London, 1951

Puddy, Eric, *Litcham*, Coleby, Dereham, 1957

Seymour, John, *East Anglia*, Collins, London, 1970

Toulson, Shirley, *East Anglia – Walking the Leylines*, Wildwood House, London, 1979

Tully, Clive, *Visitors' Guide to East Anglia*, Moorland, 1985

Southern Region

Barton, John, *Landmark Visitors' Guide: Hampshire and the Isle of Wight,* Landmark Publishing, 1998

Cleland, Jim, *Visitors' Guide to Sussex*, Moorland, 1990

South-western Region

Burl, Aubrey, *Prehistoric Avebury*, Yale University Press, New Haven, 1979

Burton, S.H., *Exmoor*, Robert Hale, London, 1984

Dunning, Robert, *History of Somerset*, Philimore, Chichester, 1983

Freethy, Ron and Marlene, *Discovering Exmoor and North Devon*, John Donald, Edinburgh, 1992

Hunt, Robert, *Cornish Folklore*, Tor Mark Press, Penryn

Lauder, Rosemary, *Picture of Devon*, Robert Hale, London, 1989

Lawrence, Berta, *Exmoor Villages*, Exmoor Press, 1984

Little, Bryan, *Portrait of Somerset*, Robert Hale, London, 1966

Tregellas-Pope, Rita, *Landmark Visitors' Guide: Cornwall and the Isle of Scilly*, Landmark Publishing, 2000

Wightman, Ralph, *Portrait of Dorset*, Robert Hale, London, 1966

Williams, Michael, *Strange Happenings in Cornwall*, St Teath, 1981

Central Region

Catling, Christopher, and Meary, Alison, *Shell Guide to Gloucestershire and Worcester*, Michael Joseph, 1990

Cull, Elizabeth, *Portrait of the Chilterns*, Robert Hale, London, 1982

Disbury, David, *On and Around White Horse Hill*, published privately

Greasby, Rosemary, *Farming in Brightwell-cum-Sotwell*, Village History Group, 1998

Hall, Michael, *Stratford-upon-Avon and the Cotswolds*, Pevensey Press, Newton Abbot, 1993

Sale Richard, *Landmark Visitors' Guide: Cotswolds and Shakespeare Country*, Landmark Publishing, 1997

Withers, Charles, *Discovering the Cotswolds*, John Donald, Edinburgh, 1990

North Midlands Region

The Mystery of Hawkstone Park, Hawkstone Park Leisure, 1996

North Region

Falconer, Alan, *Rambler's Rising*, Robert Hale, London, 1975

Freethy, Ron and Marlene, *Discovering Northumberland*, John Donald, Edinburgh, 1992

Mead, Harry, *Inside the North Yorkshire Moors*, David & Charles, Newton Abbot, 1978

Spencer, Brian, *Shell Guide to Northeast England*, Michael Joseph, London, 1988

Thorold, Henry, *Shell Guide to Co. Durham*, Faber & Faber, London, 1980

INDEX

Page references in *italics* are to captions

ACKNOWLEDGEMENTS

I am particularly grateful to that unseen army of writers and researchers, often unnamed and invariably unpaid, who produce the guides for our parish churches. They range from lavishly illustrated 'glossies' to simple information sheets, from learned discourses on ecclesiastical architecture to entertaining memories of scheming squires and eccentric parsons, but all of them are invaluable to inquisitive visitors like myself. And so often, if only unintentionally, they have provided me with just the material I was looking for.

It is always a great delight to find churches open to visitors, and my thanks and congratulations to parishes that still manage to provide this valuable facility. May their visitors never prove to be unwelcome! Where churches have been locked I have subsequently received very helpful responses to my requests for information from clergy, churchwardens and other church helpers. My grateful thanks to you, too.

Finally, my thanks to all the friends and contacts who have become honorary ley-hunters, providing me with information, advice and the occasional warning – and in the case of Alan Mitchell, allowing me the full use of his comprehensive collection of Ordnance Survey maps. He must still be trying to rub out all those pencil lines.

To you all: May the Force go with you!

JOHN TIMPSON

First published in the United Kingdom in 2000 by Cassell & Co

Text copyright © John Timpson 2000
Photographs copyright © Derry Brabbs 2000
Design and layout copyright © Cassell & Co 2000

Distributed in the United States of America by Sterling Publishing Co., Inc.
387 Park Avenue South, New York, NY 10016-8810

A CIP catalogue record for this book is available from the British Library

ISBN 0-304-35402-3

Designed by Peter Butler
Printed and bound in Italy by Printer Trento S.r.l.

Cassell & Co
Wellington House
125 Strand
London
WC2R 0BB